Mr. Lincoln's
Brown Water Navy

Mr. Lincoln's Brown Water Navy

The Mississippi Squadron

Gary D. Joiner

ROWMAN & LITTLEFIELD PUBLISHERS, INC.
Lanham • Boulder • New York • Toronto • Plymouth, UK

ROWMAN & LITTLEFIELD PUBLISHERS, INC.

Published in the United States of America
by Rowman & Littlefield Publishers, Inc.
A wholly owned subsidiary of The Rowman & Littlefield Publishing Group, Inc.
4501 Forbes Boulevard, Suite 200, Lanham, Maryland 20706
www.rowmanlittlefield.com

Estover Road
Plymouth PL6 7PY
United Kingdom

British Library Cataloguing in Publication Information Available

Library of Congress Cataloging-in-Publication Data

Joiner, Gary D.
Mr. Lincoln's brown water navy : the Mississippi Squadron / Gary D. Joiner.
p. cm. — (American crisis series)
Includes bibliographical references.
ISBN-13: 978-0-7425-5097-1 (cloth : alk. paper)
ISBN-10: 0-7425-5097-4 (cloth : alk. paper)
ISBN-13: 978-0-7425-5098-8 (pbk. : alk. paper)
ISBN-10: 0-7425-5098-2 (pbk. : alk. paper)
1. United States. Navy. Mississippi Squadron. 2. United States—History—Civil War, 1861–1865—Naval operations. 3. United States—History—Civil War, 1861–1865—Blockades. 4. United States. Navy—History—Civil War, 1861–1865. I. Title. II. Title: Mister Lincoln's brown water navy.
E591.J58 2007
973.7'58—dc22

2007008665

Printed in the United States of America

∞™ The paper used in this publication meets the minimum requirements of American National Standard for Information Sciences—Permanence of Paper for Printed Library Materials, ANSI/NISO Z39.48-1992.

In memory of my parents,
Frank Dillard Joiner and Rudy Rachel Henderson Joiner,
who taught me everything
I needed to know to find my own way,

and

In memory of Allan Colle Richard, Jr.,
an engineer who loved history more than anything except his family.
Farewell, author, researcher, traveling companion,
and much-missed dear friend.

The signs look better. The Father of Waters again goes unvexed to the sea.

—Abraham Lincoln in a letter to James C. Conkling
Washington, August 26, 1863

Contents

List of Maps

Preface

The Union inland navy that became the Mississippi Squadron is one of the least studied aspects of the Civil War. Without it, however, the war in the West may not have been won, and the war in the East might have lasted much longer and perhaps ended differently. The men who formed and commanded this large fighting force have, with few exceptions, not been as thoroughly studied as their army counterparts.

The sailors of the elegant blue ocean naval sloops, who called the ugly ironclads "stink pots" and "turtles," looked down on the gunboats used in the western waters. They did not consider the crews of these gunboats real sailors. These specialized craft operated in the narrow confines of the western rivers in places that could not otherwise receive fire support. They protected army forces and convoyed much-needed supplies to far-flung Federal forces. They patrolled thousands of miles of rivers and fought battles that were every bit as harrowing as land engagements yet inside iron monsters that created stifling heat with little ventilation. This book is about the intrepid men who fought under these conditions and the highly improvised boats in which they fought. The tactics their commanders developed were the basis for many later naval operations. Of equal importance were lessons learned about what not to do. The flag officers and admirals of the Mississippi Squadron wrote the rules for modern riverine warfare.

All authors, especially historians, compose their works with the assistance of others. Other historians, archivists, friends, and a network of others who openly share their knowledge often render assistance. I want to thank those who have assisted in my efforts, either directly or indirectly, in this volume. For those I fail to mention, please forgive me.

I particularly want to thank Terry Winschel, National Park Service historian at Vicksburg National Military Park; Elizabeth Joyner, director of the USS *Cairo* Museum at Vicksburg National Military Park; Stacey Allen, National Park Service historian at Shiloh National Military Park; and Dr. Timothy Smith, formerly historian at Shiloh National Military Park. These National Park Service historians are among the best in the world. This book would not be possible without their unflagging willingness to help a colleague. Their friendship means more than they will ever know.

I have been privileged to know and work with some of the best historians, researchers, and writers working on the history of the Mississippi Valley and the region to its west. Each has helped with this project, making it stronger in every way. I consider them my friends as well as colleagues: Ed Bearss, Chief Historian Emeritus of the National Park Service; Arthur Bergeron, archivist at the U.S. Army Military History Institute at Carlisle Barracks, Pennsylvania; Jeffrey Prushankin, professor of history at The Pennsylvania State University, Abington; Steven Woodworth, professor of history at Texas Christian University in Fort Worth, Texas; and Steve Mayeux of Avoyelles Parish, Louisiana.

Two outstanding historians of the Civil War who helped hone this work during the academic process under which it was crafted are Dr. Alan Farmer and Dr. Robert Poole of St. Martin's College, Lancaster, England. Their guidance was thoughtful and indispensable.

Archivists are the historian's best ally. They collect and organize primary source material that is vital for study. I have been fortunate to work with some of the best, particularly DeAnne Blanton at the National Archives and Records Administration in Washington, D.C.; Sherry Pugh at Jackson Barracks in New Orleans, Louisiana; and Laura McLemore at Louisiana State University in Shreveport, Louisiana. This book would not have been possible without them. I also want to thank the archivists at Hill Memorial Library at Louisiana State University in Baton Rouge; the Howard Tilton Library at Tulane University in New Orleans; Wilson Library at the University of North Carolina, Chapel Hill; the U.S. Army Military History Institute at Carlisle Barracks, Pennsylvania; the U.S. Naval Historical Center at the Washington Navy Yard in Washington, D.C.; the Hamilton County Library in Cincinnati, Ohio; and the Cayuga County Museum in Auburn, New York.

Lastly, although great care has been taken to eliminate them, any errors in the research and writing are solely the author's.

MATERIAL PREVIOUSLY PUBLISHED

Some preliminary researches were published in Gary D. Joiner and Charles E. Vetter, "The Union Naval Expedition on the Red River,

March 12–May 22, 1864," *Civil War Regiments* 4, no. 2 (1994): 26–67. Portions of chapter 8 were produced in Gary D. Joiner, *One Damn Blunder from Beginning to End: The Red River Campaign of 1864* (Wilmington, Del.: Scholarly Resources, 2003), and Gary D. Joiner, *Through the Howling Wilderness: The Red River Campaign of 1864 and Union Failure in the West* (Knoxville: University of Tennessee Press, 2006).

1

✛

Blue Water and the Anaconda

Any study of the Civil War on the western waters, particularly of the Mississippi Squadron and its predecessor in name, the Western Gunboat Flotilla, must begin with the state of the U.S. Navy before the bombardment of Fort Sumter in April 1861. Most historians and armchair theorists have accepted the position that the navy was at least a generation behind in technology. Another commonly held belief has been that the service was all but obsolete, unable to defend itself against a modern well-equipped foreign foe, much less an internal threat. Although grievous flaws within the system existed, the navy was, as a whole, progressive and moving toward modernity.

The Navy Department realized the need for improving the training of midshipmen during the late 1840s. A site at the antiquated Fort Severn at Annapolis, Maryland, was chosen for instruction, and the U.S. Naval Academy was formally established in 1850. Through a fairly rapid series of conceptual changes, the methods of training future naval officers solidified. Initially, the curriculum was a five-year schedule with academic training at the facility in the first and last years only. The intervening years were spent at sea. This order of study quickly changed, moving its midshipmen through a four-year course structure preparing them for command careers. During the eleven years before the Civil War, the navy graduated a new generation of officers with a uniform, high-quality education.

Following the War of 1812, the United States wanted to advance its position as a player in international affairs. It desired to be a leader in trade, exploration, and discovery. The Federal government also needed to fly the American flag in every ocean to advance and protect these interests from pirates, particularly in the early days. The momentum for action increased with each succeeding decade, and the navy was the obvious instrument to carry out the various missions.

The immediate result was the formation of designated areas of patrol, called stations or squadrons. All naval vessels were assigned to one of six stations, most of them based overseas. The Mediterranean Squadron, organized in 1815, was based in Minorca. It was originally charged with quelling the Barbary pirates of North Africa and later was instrumental in protecting American interests as the Ottoman Empire rapidly declined in the face of European pressure. The West Indies Squadron, created in 1822, was tasked with destroying rampant piracy in the Caribbean Sea. It also supported U.S. Army operations in the Seminole War in Florida and along the Gulf Coast during the 1830s and early 1840s. The Pacific Squadron, also organized in 1822, was created to help establish and protect the burgeoning trade with the South Sea island chains and to preserve American interests from the colonial European powers expanding in that region. The Brazilian Squadron was formed in 1826 to protect American flagged vessels in the South Atlantic Ocean. The East Indies Squadron was formed in 1835 to establish a presence in Southeast Asia. Almost as an afterthought, the Home Squadron was formed in 1841, when it was noted that all long-range U.S. flagged vessels were stationed overseas. Its small number of ships was based in ports on the Atlantic, Pacific, and Gulf coasts. It was the only squadron in domestic waters. The final force, the African Squadron, was an evolutionary command, beginning with the effort to resettle black slaves in Africa and to support the establishment of the nation of Liberia. The squadron was instrumental in the suppression of the slave trade.[1]

In order to prove to European powers that the United States was just as interested in science and exploration as they were, Congress and the Navy Department undertook several efforts beginning in the 1830s. The navy established the Hydrographic Office and the Naval Observatory and mounted expeditions to map foreign coastlines, define water depths, explore island chains, and retrieve samples of exotic flora and fauna. The two most famous expeditions were carried out in the Pacific. In 1838, a four-year expedition began under Lieutenant (later Admiral) Charles Wilkes. The U.S. Exploring Expedition consisted of six naval vessels with 500 officers, crew, scientists, and artists. The expedition achieved unprecedented success, created maps and charts of over 200 islands in the Pacific, and mapped much of the Antarctic coastline. The specimens gathered and the information digested from this first great American overseas expedition created the core of the collections of the U.S. Botanic Garden, the National Herbarium, the Naval Observatory, and the National Museum of Natural History.[2] The accomplishments of this spectacular mission were eclipsed when Commodore Matthew Perry forcefully opened diplomatic relations with Japan during a voyage from 1852 to 1854.

During the late 1830s and early 1840s, the navy, following the lead of larger European fleets, realized that it needed to evolve from sail to steam power. Congress contracted with the brilliant marine engineer John Ericsson in 1842 to design an engine, propeller, and a 12-inch bore gun for a vessel to be known as the *Princeton*. A second competing gun design was also built and installed in the vessel. The sea trials of the vessel proved that it was very fast. The navy sent the *Princeton* to Washington, D.C., for review in 1844. During a firing demonstration, the second gun exploded, killing the secretaries of state and the navy.[3] This dramatically slowed the efforts to modernize the fleet, but it did not halt research and development. About the same time that Ericsson began his work on the *Princeton*'s machinery, Congress ordered the design and construction of an ironclad warship. Although work continued until 1856, the vessel was never completed. Congress, the War Department, and the Navy Department followed the development of French and British warship design, again realizing that they must play catch-up. The result was the authorization to build steam sloops and frigates. Between 1854 and 1859, thirty of these vessels were either built or acquired, with six being sloops with screw propellers. The most famous of these during the Civil War was the *Hartford*, Admiral David G. Farragut's flagship, and the *Merrimack*, destined to be the substructure for the Confederacy's first ironclad, the CSS *Virginia*.[4] During the authorization proceedings, southern senators required that the draft of the new vessels be deeper than the navigable depth of major southern harbors and most rivers.[5] This would have a major impact on operations in the Mississippi Valley in 1862 and 1863.

The new steamers needed new long-range armaments. These guns would be the work of Lieutenant (later Rear Admiral) John Adolphus Dahlgren. From 1845 until the beginning of the war, he led all ordnance design and construction at the Washington Navy Yard and held the position of chief of the Bureau of Ordnance.[6] Dahlgren was innovative and controversial. He also was a confidant of the president and had close ties with several other cabinet members, senators, and congressmen. During the late 1840s and 1850s, he created ever-larger smoothbore guns, each with a distinctive soda or milk bottle silhouette. The Dahlgren guns could fire round shot and shells. The navy adopted 9-inch, 10-inch, and 11-inch bore weapons of Dahlgren's designs. He designed even larger guns with bores of up to thirteen inches. The navy also used breech-loader rifled cannon, which were faster loading and more accurate, but Dahlgren left his indelible print on naval ordnance. By the beginning of the war, naval guns ranged from fifty-year-old antiques to modern high-powered pieces.

At the outbreak of hostilities, the navy was far from the fleet needed to prosecute the war. The naval list of vessels in 1861 showed ninety ships. Twenty-one were shown as unserviceable. Of the remainder, thirty-nine were in commission and ready for duty. Of these, twelve were attached to the Home Squadron, six to the East Indies Squadron, three to the Mediterranean Squadron, three to the Brazilian Squadron, eight to the African Coast Squadron, and seven to the Pacific Squadron.[7] With the exception of auxiliary craft, none was capable of riverine duty.

The navy—and for that matter the army—had placed heavy emphasis on war plans to fight a European foe. Since the War of 1812, the United States dispersed its various squadrons in far-flung regions to keep trade routes free from pirates or from possible interdiction policies, such as the impressments of seamen by foreign navies. The British, with their expanding empire, offered, by far, the greatest threat. Coastal fortifications, the so-called Third Tier System, all had their major armaments facing seaward in anticipation of an attack from a fleet. These "star" fortresses were typically based on a loose pentagonal design, although many had broad, curved main battery fascias of either hemispherical or ellipsoidal construction. Some, such as Fort Pulaski in Georgia, featured outer walls of at least seven and one-half feet of solid brick. Fort Sumter, in the Charleston, South Carolina, harbor, boasted outer walls five feet thick and fifty feet high.[8] Among the other coastal fortifications were forts Pickett, Jefferson, and Taylor in Florida and forts St. Philip and Jackson on the Mississippi River below New Orleans, Louisiana. All protected coastal cities, harbors, or rivers with major commercial interests. At the beginning of the Civil War, no naval guns firing solid shot could penetrate the walls of these forts.

Since such confidence was placed in the strength of their walls, no commitment was made to adequately staff them. Almost all the forts were manned with skeleton crews commanded by noncommissioned officers. Most gun tubes were not mated to caissons or barbettes. Conventional wisdom held that if an international crisis arose, forces would be mobilized, garrison troops would be sent to each fort, and the installations would be ready to withstand an attack from sailing fleets within a relatively short span of time. The plans remained relatively unchanged from the 1820s until the Civil War.

Even with the severe lack of fighting hulls, the greatest problem facing the U.S. Navy was the structure of the officer corps. No rank higher than captain existed. There was no forced retirement system, and the entrenched political support lobby within Congress served to protect senior officers. Any of these problems alone could hamper the service, but all working in conjunction thwarted the navy's modernization. Annapolis turned out many bright new graduates in the years before the Civil War, but a limited number of officer slots blocked advancement. Many of the best new officers left for greener fields or bluer oceans. With no rank higher than the equivalent army rank of colonel, squadron commanders were designated flag officers, and each was allowed to fly a pennant or a personal flag to show his presence. Thus, the commander's vessel was the flagship. With only six squadrons, there were only six at-sea flag officer posts. The navy allowed the informal term "commodore" to be used for its flag officers, but this was never made an official rank. This caused confusion until the rank of flag officer was made the equivalent of a major general in the army and the rank of admiral was created for David Glascow Farragut. This lack of a general officer equivalency created problems with the U.S. Army when seniority matters arose.

The lack of a mandatory retirement system was the most troublesome of these issues at the outbreak of the war. Senior officers did not retire; in fact, death was the only way an officer was removed from active service. Old age or infirmity was disregarded out of respect for long years of service. The thought at the time was that, if needed, these men could come back into the service as senior advisers, sharing their long-term institutional memory. The British used this system long before the United States won its freedom, and the new country had adopted the system wholeheartedly. Eighty-five years after the signing of the Declaration of Independence, large numbers of officers were still alive, and these doddering old seadogs blocked the promotion ladder for active-duty officers. At the beginning of the Civil War, the oldest man on the navy list was a seventy-five-year-old captain who had been promoted thirty years earlier.[9] Congress tried to address this situation in 1855, instituting a mandatory retirement system for naval officers. A retirement board was authorized. This body recognized 201 officers unfit for duty because of age or health problems. When the list of these men was published, a huge public outcry bombarded the legislators.[10] Almost all enforcement authority was removed from the law. After this attempt, an unofficial list was created that kept the elderly commanders off the rosters for sea duty but not off the rolls; thus, it still blocked younger officers from gaining senior rank. By 1861, the result was a very top-heavy roster of senior officers, a large base of junior officers with little chance for advancement, and a relatively small cadre of middle-management ranks who hoped that death would create a vacancy.

A good example was David Dixon Porter, destined to be the commander of the Mississippi Squadron and rear admiral in the U.S. Navy. Porter was granted an appointment as a midshipman on February 2, 1829, at the age of sixteen. He passed his midshipman rank on July 3, 1835, and did not receive the rank of lieutenant until February 27, 1841. He remained in that rank for twenty years, until after the firing on Fort Sumter.[11] He was made commander on April 22, 1861.

Three men, more than any others at the beginning of the war, shaped the navy into the war-winning service it became and crafted the theory that won the war for the Union. Two were civilians and one an army general. The first was a politician, the second a former naval staff planner, and the third a lionized hero of the War of 1812 and the Mexican War. Gideon Welles, Gustavus V. Fox, and Winfield Scott were an odd group. Welles and Fox did not agree with the ancient Scott on almost anything; however, before the end of the war, when Scott was long retired from active service, his theory on how to end the war was proven correct.

Welles was an anachronism. He was a consummate politician who shunned the limelight. An attorney, he refused to allow the easy virtue that often corrupted the bar in New England at the time to interfere with what he believed to be right. He was not gregarious or ostentatious, yet he had a flowing white beard and was never seen in public without a conspicuous brown wig. Philosophically, he was a proponent of states' rights but became an early supporter of the Republican Party. He backed Salmon P. Chase against William H. Seward in the 1860 Republican convention in Chicago, only moving his support to Abraham Lincoln on the third ballot. He was incorruptible, a man of the highest morals, and an organizational genius.[12]

Secretary of the Navy Gideon Welles. Library of Congress image LC-B813-1375A.

Welles came to national prominence when most men his age were looking forward to retirement and relaxation. Soon after Lincoln was elected, he appointed Welles, age fifty-nine, as secretary of the navy. He would serve in that capacity under two presidents, from 1861 to 1869. This was not a plum assignment, and most politicians shunned it. While not a dead-end office, it was certainly not one for a rising star in politics.

Lincoln could not have chosen a better man for the job. Welles's organization skills made him the ideal head of this crucial service arm. Lincoln held great respect for both the navy and its new head, allowing Welles to handle his department with only occasional interference. Welles did not particularly like the press and did his best to keep information from leaking out. Some naval officers, glowing in the limelight of their new positions in Washington, scoffed at Welles's attempts at secrecy, calling him the "Rip van Winkle of the Navy Department."[13] The press responded with vicious attacks of their own, but the secretary ignored them and went about the business of creating a new navy.

The new secretary's initial problems dealt not only with reorganization and modernization of the fleet but also with monumental egos like those of David Dixon Porter and John Dahlgren. Porter was socially prominent and displayed no hesitation in taking his case to the cabinet or president if he believed his ideas were not taken seriously. Welles allowed Dahlgren to run the Ordnance Bureau at the Washington Navy Yard as he saw fit and kept a somewhat distant relationship with the future overly ambitious admiral.

Gustavus Vasa Fox was a naval officer and a graduate of West Point who had resigned to enter into private business by managing the Bay State Woolen Company's mill in Lawrence, Massachusetts. Fox had a streak of audacity that inspired confidence. After South Carolina sent an ultimatum that Fort Sumter must be turned over to that state, Lincoln's highest circle of advisers were split on whether to give up the fort or reinforce it. Fox hatched a plan to supply the garrison. His chief supporter was his brother-in-law, the always-belligerent Montgomery Blair.[14]

Fox intended to use high-speed armed tugs with shallow drafts or iron-hulled whaleboats to run the gauntlet of the Charleston batteries and bring supplies and reinforcements to the island fort. A supporting flotilla of gunboats would accompany the vessels and offer assistance if needed. It was a very simple and straightforward method of replenishing the garrison, which otherwise would be starved into submission in a few weeks. Then subterfuge entered into the scenario. David D. Porter also wanted to command a mission to occupy Fort Pickens at Pensacola, Florida. The secretary of state, William Seward, obscured plans and orders until, soon, no one had a clear idea of what was to be done.[15]

Assistant Secretary of the Navy Gustavas Vasa Fox. U.S. Naval Historical Center image NH 61175.

Several issues were at risk. If a belligerent U.S. government attacked a state in secession, it might drive the other slaveholding states out of the Union. Virginia had not yet left, and Florida had not committed. Maryland's leaving would cause the national capital to be completely surrounded by a new country, forcing the government to move to New York or Philadelphia. Lincoln still hoped for a negotiated solution. Rather than risk a potentially escalating confrontation, Fox's plan was revamped.

Instead of a well-armed flotilla, a single vessel was sent. The unassuming *Star of the West*, a 1,172-ton coastal side-wheeler, was dispatched from New York harbor with supplies and 200 men from the U.S. 9th Infantry Regiment under First Lieutenant Charles R. Woods.[16] The *Star of the West* steamed into the entrance of the broad harbor, and almost immediately, long-range fire came very close to the small, slow-moving paddle wheeler. Discretion became the better part of valor, and the *Star* turned around, dooming the small garrison at Fort Sumter to either surrender or hold out during a prolonged siege.[17] South Carolina forces, commanded by Louisiana-born General P. G. T. Beauregard, fired on the fort on April 12, and it surrendered the following day.

The plan failed, but Fox's bold idea to supply Fort Sumter earned him the president's admiration. Fox was made the assistant secretary of the navy, serving as Welles's second in command. Like the secretary, he had a penchant for organization and administration. Fox became the day-to-day detail "czar," and Welles focused on the broad issues that required his attention. There have been very few, if any, better teams in American history than these two hardworking men.

The third man to have a long-lasting effect on the navy and its operations was General-in-Chief Winfield Scott. Scott was one of the most honored and controversial figures in American military history. Born on June 13, 1786, near Petersburg, Virginia, he was a graduate of William and Mary College and studied law at Petersburg. President Thomas Jefferson appointed him to the army in 1808. Scott achieved fame in the War of 1812, fighting on the Canadian frontier, and was promoted to the rank of brigadier general of regulars. He was promoted to the post of general in chief in 1841. Twenty years later, at the age of seventy-four, he still held that position. Scott led American forces in the Mexican War, gaining national fame at the head of the American army as it landed at Vera Cruz and in the drive for Mexico City. He was brevetted lieutenant general in 1847. Scott was the Whig nominee for president in 1852, losing to Franklin Pierce.[18]

Famous for his nickname, "Old Fuss and Feathers," Scott was the senior officer in the U.S. Army at the outbreak of the Civil War. When asked whether he would go with the Confederacy, as did Robert E. Lee, he boldly declared, "I have served my country, under the flag of the Union, for more than fifty years, and so long as God permits me to live, I will defend that flag with my sword, even if my native state assails it."[19]

In 1861, Scott suffered from dropsy and gout and could not sit on a horse. He was still sharp and outspoken and held a commanding presence. He alone believed that a civil war would be long and hard-fought and that the most strategic part of either nation lay in the Mississippi Valley, not in the intervening 100 miles between Washington and Richmond. He saw with remarkable clarity what the Union must do to win a conflict with the southern states. His idea, all but scrapped by most Washington planners after the war began, became reality in 1864 and was followed through until the war's end in 1865. His idea of a grand strategy was not possible at the outbreak of the war because the necessary resources to prosecute it did not exist. The only high-ranking officials who listened to him and heeded his advice almost from the beginning were Abraham Lincoln and Gideon Welles.

Scott's concept of the grand strategy was to create a two-step process. First, the U.S. Navy must blockade all ports and commercially active rivers from the northernmost seceded Atlantic coastal state (eventually the Maryland–Virginia line), then extend the blockade south around Florida and along the Gulf Coast to the southern tip of Texas at the Rio Grande. This would prohibit foreign commerce from entering these ports and prevent the South from exporting its one valuable commodity, cotton, to overseas trading partners, particularly England and France. Starving the South from foreign commerce would bring it, economically, to its knees. Although the blockade did not address the importation of goods from Mexico, the effect would be devastating to the Confederacy.

The second part of the plan called for the creation of fortified supply depots as bases of operation on the Ohio River, particularly at Louisville or Paducah, Kentucky. The Mississippi River would be penetrated, and then other great, fortified supply depots would be created at Memphis, Tennessee; Vicksburg, Mississippi; and New Orleans, Louisiana. From there, Union armies would spread out and reduce the war-making capability of the South, splitting it into two parts. With the South's greatest manpower reserves in the East and its cattle, cotton, and food producing areas in the West, neither could long exist without the other. The war could be concluded in three to four years. President Lincoln immediately understood the implications and called for a blockade of southern ports after the fall of Fort Sumter.

Issues arose not from the president but from headstrong members of his cabinet. About the same time Lincoln proclaimed the blockade, Scott met with some of the cabinet officers, among them Simon Cameron, secretary of war; Salmon P. Chase, secretary of the treasury; and William Seward, secretary of state. Scott explained his plan to them, estimating that 80,000 men would be needed to advance down the Mississippi Valley in order to take the required future supply bases. These men and a flotilla of gunboats would protect and patrol the "national highway." At the same time, a naval blockade would seal off southern ports. He told the cabinet members that the Union needed to begin working on the requirements for this plan immediately and that all available resources should be moved into staging areas for the struggle.[20] The three politicians were not enthusiastic; in fact, they seemed not to care for the strategy at all. Soon the concept was leaked to the press, which was screaming for one grand Armageddon-like battle at or near Richmond to end the war. The armchair strategists, full of venom for the idea, dubbed it the "Anaconda Plan."[21]

Welles initially believed that the plan was too defensive, lacked assertive action, and was much too conservative.[22] The 80,000-man army did not exist. The 15,000-man regular army in service at that time was scattered around the periphery of the country, and many of the men either stayed there or headed south. Ninety percent of southern-born army officers left the U.S. Army. Fully 25 percent of naval officers left for the Confederacy at the beginning of the war. In addition, the number of ships Welles needed to blockade the southern coast did not exist on the Navy list of active vessels. Gunboats on rivers did not exist in any form, and the army claimed control over all matters on interior waters. Furthermore, he was overwhelmed with the problems of the blue water navy. His views would change within a few months as military needs in the West took precedence.

NOTES

1. Bern Anderson, *By Sea and by River: The Naval History of the Civil War* (New York: Knopf, 1962), 10; Donald L. Canney, *Lincoln's Navy: The Ships, Men and Organizations, 1861–65* (Annapolis, Md.: Naval Institute Press, 1998), 9–10.

2. The best short history of this expedition and those who participated in it is found at www.amphilsoc.org/library/guides/stanton/3644.htm.

3. Anderson, *By Sea and by River*, 7–8.

4. Paul H. Silverstone, *Civil War Navies: 1855–1883* (Annapolis, Md.: Naval Institute Press, 2001), 15–24.

5. Anderson, *By Sea and by River*, 9.

6. William B. Cogar, *Dictionary of Admirals of the U.S. Navy, Volume I: 1862–1900* (Annapolis, Md.: Naval Institute Press, 1989), 40–41. For a thorough discussion of iron ordnance types before, during, and after the period, see John C. Reilly Jr., *The Iron Guns of Willard Park: Washington Navy Yard* (Washington, D.C.: Naval Historical Center, 1991).

7. U.S. War Department, *Official Records of the Union and Confederate Navies in the War of the Rebellion*, 31 vols. (Washington, D.C.: U.S. Government Printing Office, 1895–1929), 1, xv–xvi (cited throughout this book as ORN).

8. Other sources vary. At least one states that the outer walls varied from eight to twelve feet in thickness and were forty feet high. Since the fort was only 90 percent completed at the beginning of the Civil War and the structure received massive damage, it is easy to see differences quoted. See Jay W. Simson, *Naval Strategies of the Civil War: Confederate Innovations and Federal Opportunism* (Nashville, Tenn.: Cumberland House, 2001), 12, 73.

9. Anderson, *By Sea and by River*, 6.

10. Anderson, *By Sea and by River*, 6.

11. Cogar, *Dictionary of Admirals of the U.S. Navy*, 131–32; Richard S. West Jr., *The Second Admiral: A Life of David Dixon Porter* (New York: Coward-McCann, 1937), 27–80; Chester G. Hearn, *Admiral David Dixon Porter: The Civil War Years* (Annapolis, Md.: Naval Institute Press, 1996), 18–29.

12. By far the best account of Welles's life is found in John Niven, *Gideon Welles: Lincoln's Secretary of the Navy* (Baton Rouge: Louisiana State University Press, 1994).

13. Anderson, *By Sea and by River*, 5.

14. Niven, *Gideon Welles*, 327.

15. Niven, *Gideon Welles*, 326–45,

16. U.S. War Department, *War of the Rebellion: The Official Records of the Union and Confederate Armies*, 128 vols. (Washington, D.C.: U.S. Government Printing Office, 1890–1901), *OR* 1: 9–10, 134–40 (cited throughout this book as *OR*). All references to the *OR* are to series I and part 1 of the specific volume unless otherwise identified. The number following the abbreviation *OR* indicates the volume number.

17. *OR* 1: 9–10, 253.

18. Ezra J. Warner, *Generals in Blue: Lives of the Union Commanders* (Baton Rouge: Louisiana State University Press, 1964), 429–30.

19. Douglas Southall Freeman, *Lee's Lieutenants: A Study in Command* (New York: Scribner, 1942–1944), I 712n.

20. William M. Fowler Jr., *Under Two Flags: The American Navy in the Civil War* (Annapolis, Md.: Naval Institute Press, 2001), 48.

21. Theodore Ropp, "Anaconda Anyone?" *Military Affairs* 27 (summer 1963): 71. Shortly after the Battle of First Manassas, Winfield Scott was unjustly blamed for tactical errors that allowed the Confederates to combine their forces and defeat the Union army. A new rising star, George Binton McClellan, was made commander of the Army of the Potomac, and Scott requested retirement from his country's service on October 31, 1861. He died on May 29, 1866, and was buried at West Point. Warner, *Generals in Blue*, 430.

22. John T. Morse, ed., *The Diary of Gideon Welles* (Boston: Athenaeum, 1911), 1: 68.

2

✝

Mr. Welles, Mr. Eads, and Mr. Pook: Creating the Brown Water Navy

Fortune Favors the Brave. "Drive On" is my motto.

—James Buchanan Eads

The blockade—its design, creation, staffing, and a thousand other details—kept Welles and Fox busy. There was still no concept of how or whether Winfield Scott's idea for pursuing the war in the Mississippi Valley should be attempted in the near future. The two men put their considerable skills to work reorganizing the navy. Welles was engrossed in procuring appropriate vessels in any manner he could and shepherding the design of new craft, particularly the *Monitor*. His remaining time was spent defending himself from hostile members of the press and from members of Congress who did not like the military. Controversies sprang up at every turn. The most serious was the manner in which ships destined for the blockade were purchased from private companies and individuals. The Navy Department came under scrutiny almost as a side note to an investigation of the War Department. The department was so poorly run, organized, and managed that once Congress attacked the waste and graft, its secretary, the inept Simon Cameron, offered his resignation in early 1862. Political cartoonists had a field day with Cameron and Welles, both of whom they thought were too old for their jobs as well as hacks for Lincoln. Welles's two nemeses were Senator John P. Hale, chairman of the Senate Committee on Naval Affairs, and Congressman Charles H. Van Wyck of New York, Hale's counterpart in the House of Representatives.[1] Fortunately for the secretary, when attacks were made in hearings or in the press, a variety of authoritative people came to his aid. Welles had the equivalent of an unpaid but highly effective public relations firm. These men, including *Monitor* mastermind John Ericsson, praised his work, his ethics, and his ability to run the navy.

One of the greatest challenges for the department was that naval procurement officers were apparently being obscenely overcharged for vessels of questionable virtue to be used in the blockading squadrons. Both internal and congressional investigations pointed to irregularities in New York and Boston. Among those examining the improprieties was the senior naval constructor in New York, Samuel R. Pook. Known as a brilliant vessel designer and builder, Pook also possessed a keen eye for acquiring materials at a fair price and knew better than most how much a project should cost and how long it should take. His assessment of the procurement problem proved to Welles that the problem did exist and that an entirely new system of acquisition should be undertaken.[2] More important for future operations, this assistance to Welles earned Pook the confidence of the secretary of the navy and placed Pook in a position to continue to assist.

The problem of what to do about the Mississippi River Valley offered a completely different set of obstacles for Welles and Fox. Oceangoing, blue water vessels were easily defined as being under U.S. Navy jurisdiction. Welles and his commanders cooperated with their army counterparts in the initial combined operation seizing Alexandria, Virginia, and in raids on the Carolina coastline. Tasks were well defined, and both services knew their roles intimately. However, inland waterways ("brown water" rather than "blue water") were different, and the army had its own strategies for affairs west of the Appalachians. The army claimed jurisdiction in all matters in the West. Who would man the gunboats, or "floating batteries," as they called them? Would naval officers be subservient to their army counterparts? What was the chain of command? The primary strategy was to secure a line of defense based on the northern bank of the Ohio River and then prepare to take control of the Mississippi River Valley. Before a coherent policy agreeable to both the army and the navy could be devised, several actions occurred that were destined to drive the course of the naval war in the Mississippi River Valley.

A casual examination of a map of the valley yields the obvious. The point of the confluence of the Ohio and Mississippi rivers forms the arrowhead shape of the southern tip of the state of Illinois. The little town of Cairo (pronounced KAY-ro) is located at this point. Whoever controlled Cairo would command the upper Mississippi River, the Ohio River, and the Missouri River. The Confederates could interdict trade on those rivers, and the North could drive a wedge into southern-held territory. Southern Illinois points like a dagger aimed southward, intimidating northeastern Arkansas and western Tennessee and threatening to cut off the then-neutral border states of Kentucky from Missouri. St. Louis is 145 river miles north of Cairo, and

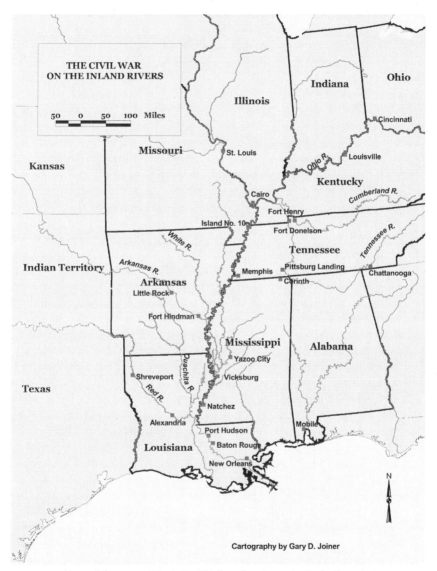

Map of the upper Mississippi Valley showing principal tributaries.

the vital railheads of Paducah and Columbus, Kentucky, lie to the east and south, respectively. At that period of the war, Cairo was the most strategically important real estate on the North American continent, excluding the District of Columbia.

Kentucky and Missouri would affirm Cairo's importance. The Confederates knew that Kentucky was the linchpin to their plans in the West. The

Ohio River was the best natural boundary they could use to their advantage. Winfield Scott realized this from the beginning of his grand design plan. The Confederacy's problem lay in the infrastructure of the state. The Louisville and Nashville Railroad connected the Ohio River with the great transportation hub of Nashville, Tennessee. Just south of Bowling Green, Kentucky, the Memphis and Ohio Railroad intersected the Louisville and Nashville. The Mobile and Ohio Railroad had northern termini in Paducah and Columbus, Kentucky. From there, it headed almost due south through Jackson, Tennessee, and Corinth and Meridian, Mississippi, on its way to the Gulf of Mexico at Mobile, Alabama. Columbus was across the river just south of Cairo.[3] These railroads could bring troops northward quickly and efficiently. They could also be invasion routes heading south. If the South could not keep Kentucky neutral, it must occupy it. An invasion of Kentucky by either side would provide the other with higher moral ground. It would also give the occupying side a tremendous strategic advantage.

The governor of Kentucky, Beriah Magoffin, opposed Abraham Lincoln's call for 75,000 volunteers to rally to the Union. He declared on April 15, 1861, that Kentucky would furnish no troops to be used against her sister southern slaveholding states. The legislature thought otherwise. The state had a large pro-Union contingent and feared a Union invasion on less than favorable terms, but it remained neutral. This neutrality was shattered when Leonidas Polk led Confederate forces across the border in an attempt to secure both Kentucky and the Mississippi River. Polk soon relinquished his command to Albert Sidney Johnston and became one of Johnston's corps commanders. Johnston, thought by many to be the most able general that the South ever produced, established fortifications to counter Union activity at Cairo. He built up forces in Tennessee and Mississippi and constructed fortifications at strategic points at Belmont and New Madrid, Missouri; Columbus, Kentucky; Memphis and Fort Pillow, Tennessee; and Vicksburg, Mississippi. This spurred the second phase of the Anaconda Plan into action.

Missouri was an almost diametric opposite of Kentucky. It was heavily pro-southern, with the only true Union stronghold in and around St. Louis. The city was home to several powerful men who worked together not just to keep the state in the Union but to return the entire Mississippi Valley to Federal control. While the newspapers, the governor, and the legislature talked about secession, these men met in each other's homes and plotted their courses of action. Among them were Edward Bates, who shortly would become Lincoln's attorney general; Francis Preston Blair, the archrival of the governor of Missouri and the son of the editor of the *Washington Globe*; Benjamin G. Brown and James Rollins, both of whom would become U.S. senators; and James Buchanan Eads.

Eads was already a legend, and he would achieve even greater fame and fortune. He created a salvage company that retrieved cargo and wrecks on the Mississippi. He invented a successful diving bell and was the first man to walk on the bed of the great river. Eads expanded on the ideas of Henry Miller Shreve, the engineer who cleared the Great Raft of logs from the Red River, by creating catamaran salvage boats that could lift tremendous weights. His concept included putting all the machinery, including the vessel's engines and boilers, above the main deck to allow for the operation of large craft in very shallow water. He accomplished all this before the age of twenty-three. Eads purchased a fleet of vessels and converted them to snagboats, and in 1857 he proposed to conduct all of the snag removal duties for the U.S. government on a contract basis. He lost the bid through the efforts of Mississippi Senator Jefferson Davis, who did not believe he had the expertise to perform the task. He then talked to insurance companies and formed a coalition or syndicate, performing the work for them and keeping the Federal government out of it. Eads was so successful that, in that same year, he retired at age thirty-seven with half a million dollars in cash.[4] His retirement would not last long. National affairs would draw him back into business and into the forefront of military strategy for the Federal government.

As talk of secession reached a fever pitch in Missouri, Eads met with the group to discuss some of his ideas. In characteristic laconic fashion, Eads told his friends how he believed he could convert existing salvage vessels or create new ones along the same basic design principles and turn them into ironclad gunboats. With these, the Union navy

James Buchanan Eads. Library of Congress image LC-BH832-32531.

could split the South into two parts as the gunboats supported the army in its push southward. It was a method to accomplish what Winfield Scott had suggested and Gideon Welles had not yet contemplated.[5] Soon after Fort Sumter fell, Eads was summoned to Washington by his friend Edward Bates to meet with the president and his cabinet.[6] A contract was let for building seven gunboats, and Eads, who had never built a gunboat, was the low bidder. The deciding factor was his promise to build them in sixty-five days. No one had ever seen anything like what he proposed, but within two weeks, he had shipyards and machine shops working on the project in St. Louis and Carondelet, Missouri; Cairo and Mound City, Illinois; and Cincinnati, Ohio. He personally financed the entire operation.

Eads's nimble mind was entirely consumed with the gunboats. He knew the river better than any man alive, and he focused on the possible uses of Cairo. In a letter to Welles in April 1861, Eads had recommended fortifying Cairo as a major base of operations for the army and navy and had suggested that existing salvage vessels be converted into gunboats for the defense of Cairo and possibly of the mouths of the Tennessee or Cumberland rivers. Eads also described what already existed at Cairo and what it would take to make his idea work:[7]

> The city of Cairo has a broad levee front on the Ohio River, raised about fourteen feet above the natural level of the city and extending for a distance of about three miles immediately along the river. On the Mississippi side extends a levee of the same height and about the same length, but removed from the bank of the river from 100 yards to half a mile distant, to be out of danger from the caving in of the bank. From this levee, across from the Ohio River [to the Kentucky shore], a levee extends of the same height, by which the town is protected from the backwater, the whole forming a delta. These levees would afford admirable defenses upon which to plant batteries at proper points. The great Central Railroad of Illinois, in addition to the Ohio and Mississippi rivers, would afford means of supplying this point with great rapidity with troops, munitions of war, and provisions, and the place would be capable of accommodating a force on land of 50,000 men, if need be. The levees are perfectly safe, and the drainage system established in connection with the steam pumps of the corporation are amply sufficient to remove all seepage water. The health of the place has been greatly improved by this system of drainage. From the bank on the Ohio side that river can be completely commanded. A large bar of sand lies between the Missouri shore and the levee on the Mississippi side of Cairo and throws the channel along the Missouri shore nearly two miles distant from the town. A floating battery upon the river would be needed to fully command the commerce on the Mississippi River.[8]

Additionally, Eads suggested using the fortifications at Cairo and the gunboats as an internal blockade to interdict commerce between the South and potential markets in the Midwest:

The effect of this blockade would be most disastrous to the South, as it would effectually close the main artery through which flows her food. It would establish a tollgate through which alone her dutiable goods could enter, or through which her products could find their way to market. The only outlets or inlets which would remain to her would be the Tennessee and Cumberland rivers and the railroads from Louisville to Nashville and Chattanooga. The Tennessee and Cumberland rivers are navigable only by very small steamers, except in short seasons of high water. Their mouths can be easily commanded by batteries on the Illinois shore or by floating batteries. The railroad is very vulnerable, as one man could blow up a culvert or bridge and render it useless for the time being. If Kentucky were friendly to the Union, these three inlets could be effectually guarded; if she were unfriendly, their northern termini would be completely at our mercy. Once close them and the great Mississippi, and starvation is inevitable in less than six months.[9]

Welles forwarded Eads's letter to the secretary of war in May. The text set off a flurry of activity. On the same day that Cameron received it, he responded to Welles:

The Government here deeming very favorably of the proposition, but unwilling to decide positively upon the matter without the knowledge and approval of the general in command of that department, it is ordered that the subject be referred to General [George Binton] McClellan, who will consult with Mr. Eads and with such naval officer as the Navy Department may send out for that purpose, and then, as he shall find best, take order for the proper preparation of the boats.[10]

Welles knew when to cooperate, even though he did not fully comprehend the situation and did not know how to respond properly in the best interests of the navy. Welles ordered Commander John Rodgers to Cincinnati to meet with General McClellan, who had been promoted to the position of commander of the Western Department. Rodgers's orders were peculiar for a naval officer. He was to report to McClellan with the intent of establishing a naval presence on the Mississippi and/or Ohio rivers to blockade commerce. Additionally, Welles inadvertently created a combined arms force that would last for the next eighteen months and placed Rodgers in the very uncomfortable position of being subordinate to the army:

This interior nonintercourse is under the direction and regulation of the army, and your movements will therefore be governed in a great degree by General McClellan, the officer in command, with whom you will put yourself in immediate communication. Whatever naval armament and crew may be necessary to carry into effect the objects here indicated, you will call for by proper requisition.[11]

Officially, Rodgers's title was supervisor of construction of ironclad gunboats, and he was to be based in Cincinnati, where McClellan's headquarters was located.[12] He held this post from May through September 1861. Rodgers's tenure in this position was stormy, primarily because of the restrictions Welles placed on him and his almost constant disagreements with the secretary. Welles seemed irritated by anything that Rodgers did, and it is clear that the secretary treated everything on inland waters as a nuisance that kept him from solving the problems on the Atlantic seaboard. Logically, Rodgers's orders should have directed him to Eads in Washington so that they could jointly pursue the gunboat venture. Welles's relaying of Secretary Cameron's directive was given as an absolute command rather than a suggestion to drop in on McClellan before proceeding to the center of action on the St. Louis–Cairo axis. In his own mind, Welles was simply complying with the request of Eads through Secretary of War Cameron. He did not see the navy's commitment as extensive. Rodgers did go to Cairo, but he would be peripatetic.

Rodgers, considered by all to be a very capable officer, was dispatched west to act as a liaison with the army. Correspondence clearly indicates that Rodgers was not authorized to spend funds and that the navy was responsible only for his salary. After reading his orders, Rodgers believed that he was there to build a gunboat flotilla to assist the army. He also understood that the vessels were to be navy controlled. Rodgers read his orders literally, particularly the portion that stated, "This interior nonintercourse is under the direction and regulation of the army, and your movements will therefore be governed in a great degree by General McClellan, the officer in command, with whom you will put yourself in immediate communication."[13] General McClellan needed gunboats to assist in any troop movements along the Ohio and Mississippi rivers and wanted Rodgers to find them or build them because Eads's gunboats were still incomplete. Thus, he quickly signed requisitions for anything Rodgers requested.[14] McClellan was very supportive of Rodgers. However, Winfield Scott retired, and McClellan succeeded him. McClellan's replacement was less sympathetic to Rodgers, who frequently encountered Welles's anger. Welles ordered Rodgers to send all reports to his office in order to keep him in the loop. He was particularly hard on Rodgers, whom he considered at that time to be a loose cannon if not a power-hungry rogue officer. Rodgers was neither. His legacy was to present the navy with the core of its brown water muscle.

Capt. John Rodgers, USN. Image from a carte de visite. U.S. Naval Historical Center image NH 88390.

Welles ordered Samuel Pook to go to Cairo and report to Rodgers for "special duty under his direction," after which Pook would return to the Washington Navy Yard and continue his duties there.[15] Pook arrived in Cairo to find that Rodgers had gone to examine an invention for a new type of paddle-wheel propulsion system. With Rodgers absent, Pook met with Eads. Pook was a shadowy figure, which is odd considering his substantial fame and talent as a ship designer or "constructor." There are no known images of him, and no biography has been attempted to date, yet he left his mark indelibly on American military history in that quick visit to Cairo in late May 1861. Although Eads had not yet received his official contract, he met with Pook. Eads told Pook what he had to work with and shared his ideas about how to use salvage boat technology to build shallow-drafted ironclad gunboats. Within a few days of the meeting, Pook had drafted plans for the most famous gunboat fleet in U.S. history, forever to be known as "Pook Turtles." By then, Rodgers had returned. Reporting to him, Pook consulted and commented on Rodgers's efforts before returning to the Washington Navy Yard. While Eads was working to complete his gunboats in sixty-five days, Rodgers faced a different path to achieve the creation of the gunboat fleet.

Rodgers encountered problems beginning with a letter from an attorney, J. K. Moorhead of Pittsburgh, Pennsylvania, to Secretary of War Cameron. The letter contained a complaint that Rodgers was in Cincinnati trying to buy any steamboats he could for the new flotilla. Moorhead was irate and felt this was an encroachment on the army's area of expertise. He indicated that he believed Rodgers had given himself the assignment and that the navy did not know what it was doing, that McClellan was "chagrin[ed]" at the naval officer's presence. He added "an old sea captain, however well he may understand the sea and seagoing vessels, can, of course, know nothing of rivers and river steamboats."[16] Cameron forwarded the letter to Welles at about the time Rodgers sent his first report to Welles on June 7. Rodgers's report stated that he felt there should initially be three gunboats for use on the Mississippi to protect Cairo and that they would need "sixteen cannon, 32-pounders, 57 cwt., 16 gun carriages complete, with gear for them, gunpowder, shot and shells; 50 rounds service charges; 50 rounds practice charges; small arms, swords, and pistols for three vessels; the united crews being 198 souls."[17]

The next day, Rodgers sent another report to Welles, indicating that he had conferred with General McClellan and Samuel Pook and had purchased three steamboats at Cincinnati for naval service. The three vessels were the *A. O. Tyler,*[18] the *Lexington,* and the *Conestoga.* With all necessary changes and additions, the vessels were to cost about $34,000 each and would be ready for service before the end of June. Only wooden laminate was to be used as armor; thus, these three vessels were to be known as timberclads.

John Lenthall, the navy's chief of the Bureau of Construction, Equipment, and Repair, knew that the three timberclads alone would not be strong enough to fight the upcoming battles in the Mississippi Valley. He wrote to General Joseph Totten, the chief engineer of the army, that the army needed paddle-wheel gunboats with light drafts, ideally of five feet, that could carry large numbers of heavy guns.[19] Totten recognized the importance of the idea and immediately forwarded Lenthall's letter to Winfield Scott. Scott concurred because it reinforced the center of his planned strikes down the Mississippi River. Scott forwarded the endorsed proposal but added that there should be sixteen gunboats and that they should be ready for service no later than September 20, 1861.[20]

On June 11, Welles received a letter from the secretary of war in which Cameron said that he had been in communication with Scott and that Scott "understood that a commander in the navy [Rodgers] is already on such duty upon the Ohio and Mississippi. The attention which he [Rodgers] has already given to this subject no doubt had prepared him to act efficiently in this matter [of selecting gunboats.]" Cameron added that the army would "supply rifled 42-pounder cannon in adequate numbers for the sixteen gunboats required by the lieutenant-general [Scott.]"[21]

Welles had not yet read Rodgers's reports, and he exploded, believing Rodgers had acquired sixteen gunboats. After reading the report, Welles sent Rodgers a reply to his letter of June 8. The secretary told the commander that he had not heard from him until then, that he had no authority to buy gunboats, and that all the activity that Rodgers was undertaking was under the authority of the army. He added that members of Congress had been questioning Rodgers's actions and that no other officers could be sent to command the vessels. Welles further stated that river boatmen knew the rivers, whereas Rodgers did not, and that all requisitions must be presented to and paid by the War Department. Welles then sent a message to the War Department indicating that if neither Pook nor Rodgers was needed, they were to return to Washington. Then he telegraphed Rodgers that all movements and purchases of vessels were the responsibility of the War Department and that Rodgers was not authorized to make any requisitions whatsoever except for armament and crew.[22]

On the same day, Welles sent another letter to Cameron, indicating that the navy could not send officers to command the vessels or supervise construction of vessels or machinery. He added that since western boatmen knew the rivers, they would be the best ones to accomplish these tasks. He did offer to assist the army by loaning them Pook as one of the naval constructors. He asserted that the army was responsible for all construction costs, and he enclosed Rodgers's report with the letter. In response to the secretary's diatribe, Rodgers telegraphed Welles on June 12 telling him that General McClellan had approved the bills for the steamboats. He added, "The written approval of a superior officer makes an act of purchase his own."[23] Rodgers received more assistance from the army than he did from his own chain of command, and, considering those with whom he was sparring, he did an outstanding job. For the next several weeks, letters and orders were mailed or telegraphed back and forth, with each party lacking information about the current position of the actions and plans of the others.

The three vessels that Rodgers had acquired provided their share of problems because no one had ever converted river steamers of such size into men of war. Pook designed the changes to the three existing side-wheelers, creating the unmistakable high-walled sides and majestically tall chimneys that became their trademarks. Five-inch oak panels protected the crew and guns since iron plating was not available. Timbers and beams were to be installed to hold the weight of the big naval guns, and steam pipes were to be lowered as much as possible. Pook ordered the engines and boilers to be dropped into the hold. He knew that they would be susceptible to cannon fire there, but felt he had no alternative.[24]

In June, Rodgers obtained the services of three experienced men to assist him with his new vessels: Lieutenant Seth Ledyard Phelps, Lieutenant Roger Stembel, and Master Joshua Bishop. Stembel and Bishop were immediately sent to recruit crews for the boats, and, when the Ohio's water level began to drop quickly, Phelps was sent to Louisville to get the boats moved to Cairo.[25] On arriving, Phelps found the water already too low to

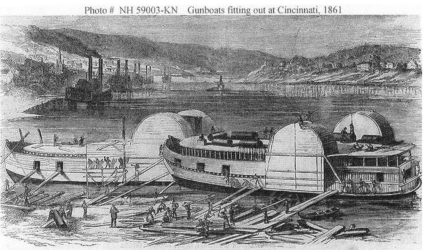

Timberclads undergoing conversion at Cincinnati, Ohio. Harper's Weekly *engraving. U.S. Naval Historical Center image NH 59003.*

bring out the boats. He also discovered that the carpenters working on the boats had fouled the job, and he struggled to rectify the problems. The carpenters had constructed the boats' ladders of soft poplar wood, which would not stand up to use. They had placed a single ladder on the *Lexington* to access the main deck, and another ladder was forward on the forecastle. Because of this, anyone attempting to get to the pilothouse when the boat was under fire was in danger of being killed. Additionally, there was no access to the lookout house aft. The *Conestoga* had no permanent supports on its centerline; therefore, if the temporary supports were removed, the pilothouse and ship's bell would fall into the middle of the vessel. In addition, the vessels lacked enough staterooms for the officers, and because they had not been painted, the boats were vulnerable to the elements.

During the remainder of the summer, the major problems on the timberclads were corrected. The guns were loaded aboard, although they were not uniform in number or type. This problem stemmed from the inability to get the proper requisitions from the army. The *Conestoga* was armed with four 32-pounder smoothbores, and both the *Lexington* and the *Tyler* carried two 32-pounders and four 8-inch smoothbores.[26] The waters in the Ohio River began to finally rise in early August, and Phelps herded the boats into Cairo on August 12.

Rodgers's problems had increased in late July when McClellan was promoted to command the Army of the Potomac and was replaced by Major General John Charles Frémont. Frémont was stubborn to the point of abstraction. He had gained fame as "The Pathfinder," laying out the immigrant trails to California and becoming immensely wealthy when gold was found on his land there. He was son-in-law of Senator Thomas Hart Benton and one of the first four major generals promoted by Abraham Lincoln at the beginning of the war.[27] Frémont interpreted orders the way he saw fit, and, as the senior-ranking army officer west of the Allegheny Mountains, few people dared to dispute him. His glory days were behind him, and the stubbornness that made him great opening the West now made him difficult. The commanding general saw that money had been set aside for Eads and Rodgers, but he took it for his own projects. Initially, he did not want gunboats. He preferred mortar rafts with tugs to pull them. Although very useful later, they were useless for the project as planned. He ordered sixteen 9-inch naval shell guns and thirty 13-inch mortars to be built. Each of the shell guns weighed 9,000 pounds, and the mortars weighed 17,500 pounds.[28]

Rodgers had other problems too. Frémont was involved in an ongoing quarrel about purchasing and payment procedures with Rodgers's brother-in-law, Montgomery Meigs, the quartermaster general of the army. Frémont tried to play by his own rules and did not like anyone in

Washington second-guessing him. Since Meigs was not available, Rodgers was the target of Frémont's wrath. In June, Rodgers placed himself in line for additional problems when he rejected Eads's offer to sell the government the pride of his salvage fleet, a behemoth known as the *Submarine No. 7*. At that time, "submarine" was a term used to signify a snagboat, a vessel that worked to pull up underwater obstacles. In a rare mistake, Rodgers refused to accept the vessel because he thought it was too large. Frémont bought it, gave Eads the contract to convert it on the same basic format as the Pook Turtles, and renamed it *Benton* after his father-in-law. Welles saw a major fight looming between the general and Rodgers, and he realized the navy would not come out on top. On August 20, he ordered Rodgers to give up his command to Captain Andrew Hull Foote, the head of the Brooklyn Navy Yard at the time. Welles did not send a telegram; instead, Foote delivered the news in person. Rodgers was given the choice of staying as Foote's second in command or being reassigned. Rodgers requested a command at sea and left Cairo in September.[29]

Meanwhile, the plans for Eads's ironclads were progressing rapidly. Although John Lenthall's proposal had caused a stir in the Navy Department in June, Welles had forwarded it to Pook, who examined Lenthall's ideas. He believed the concept to be sound, but he made changes that were exclusively his. He designed the vessels more along the recognizable lines of the CSS *Virginia* than of a Union vessel. Pook's alteration of Lenthall's design was not an imitation of the *Virginia* but a wise use of a riverine snagboat's structural features. Rather than using side wheels, he changed the design to a modified stern-wheeler. The wheel was brought inside the vessel, just aft of amidships, to make it less vulnerable if attacked. The forward portion of each boat would be conventional, but the aft would be a catamaran. To accomplish this, the vessels would be twice the width and five feet longer than what was originally proposed. Pook also changed the unarmored signature of the boats, making them partially casemated to save weight. Their weakness would be in the decks, the area aft of the gun ports and below the waterline. They were vulnerable to plunging fire from mortars or elevated gun positions as well as mines, then known as "torpedoes." Combinations of iron plating and railroad iron would be used on the slanted surfaces of the gunboats. His initial design called for each boat to have twenty guns.[30]

The army approved the plans and sent out requests for bids on July 18. The bids were opened on August 5, and Eads was the clear winner. The finished boats were to be delivered sixty-five days later on October 10. The contract called for seven boats instead of sixteen, and the number of guns was reduced from twenty to thirteen. These vessels constituted a separate class, known variously as the "*Cairo*-class" or "City-class" vessels. Rodgers, as the senior naval commander in the West, had intended to name them after famous American officers: Nathaniel Lyon, George B. McClellan, John C. Frémont, John Rodgers (the commodore, his father), Nathaniel P. Banks, Montgomery C. Meigs, and another that he had not named.[31] Captain Andrew Foote feared this would create problems with the men's egos and changed the names to recognize the towns important to the boats' construction. The vessels would be named *Cairo, Carondelet, Cincinnati, Louisville, Mound City, Pittsburg,*[32] and *St. Louis.*

The original plans called for vessels measuring 175 feet in length with fifty-one-foot, two-inch beams; they were to have a 512-ton displacement and a draft of six feet when fully loaded with ordnance. Each had a cabin for the captain, eight more for junior officers, and two messes. The wheel, mounted amidships, would be twenty-two feet in diameter. The engines would be mounted at fifteen-degree angles, with cast-iron cylinders, a bore of twenty-two inches, and piston stroke of six feet.[33] Their casemates consisted of a roughly rectangular configuration. The sides and rear casemates sloped at a fifty-five-degree angle. The forward casemate sloped at forty-five degrees. The pilothouse would also be protected but with thinner armor plates. The side-facing armor only extended to the rear of the aftmost gun ports. The armor consisted of seventy-five-ton charcoal/iron plates, each thirteen inches wide, eleven feet long, and 2.5 inches thick. The pilothouse consisted of 1.25-inch-thick plates, thick enough to stop a minié ball but insufficient to deflect larger ordnance.[34] These seven vessels originally looked almost identical, differentiated only by different colored bands near the tops of their tall chimneys: *Cairo,* gray; *Carondelet,* red; *Cincinnati,* blue; *Louisville,* green; *Mound City,* orange (not officially confirmed); *Pittsburg,* light brown; and *St. Louis,* yellow.[35] The officers at times added additional adornments. In two photographs, the *Mound City* sports a five-pointed star on the bow-facing portion of her chimneys directly below her colored stripe.[36] After a name change to the *Baron De Kalb* later in the war, the *St. Louis* displayed a device similar to the Masonic emblem hanging from the spreader bar between its chimneys.[37]

Eads's original contract called for the seven City-class gunboats, but Frémont's orders called for the conversion of Eads's *Submarine No. 7* into the *Benton.* The vessel was originally a true catamaran separated by a twenty-foot common deck. On completion, the vessel was 202 feet long with a beam of seventy-two feet and a draft of nine feet. The *Benton's* massive paddle wheel was mounted similarly to that on the City-class boats. The gunboat was propelled by twin inclined engines with 20-inch bores with seven-foot stroke.[38] By far the most powerful gunboat afloat, the *Benton* became the flagship of the Western Gunboat Flotilla. William D. Porter, captain of the *Essex,* did not care much for the boat. While watching its trials on the Ohio River, he told Foote that it moved much too slowly. Eads replied, "Yes, but plenty to fight with."[39]

City-class ironclads being built at the Carondelet shipyard prior to October 1861. The vessels shown are the Carondelet, Louisville, Pittsburg, *and* St. Louis. *National Archives and Records Administration image 165-C-703.*

Soon after Frémont signed the contract with Eads to convert the *Benton*, he signed another to convert the *New Era* into one as well. The vessel was to be under the command of William D. Porter, the brother of David Dixon Porter. They renamed it the *Essex*, the vessel commanded by their father in the War of 1812. The boat presented a very unusual appearance. From the bow, the ex-snagboat was similar to the City-class boats. The difference was in the aft, which was rounded. It was 159 feet long with a beam of forty-six feet, six inches, and a draft of six feet. The twin engines had an 18-inch bore and a six-foot stroke. The *Essex* carried from five to eight guns.[40]

The ironclad construction was not centralized in a single shipyard. Nothing existed on inland waters that could handle a project of this magnitude. Eads employed five sawmills, a rolling mill, and two foundries in and near St. Louis to prepare lumber, iron plating, and the machinery for his ironclads. The St. Louis and Iron Mountain Railroad transported this material to more specialized facilities. He leased the largest shipyard in the region, located eleven miles south of St. Louis on the River des Peres at Carondelet. This energetic little hamlet mushroomed almost overnight into a boomtown with foundries, ways, cranes, a marine railway to launch vessels, joineries, paint sheds, and hundreds of houses, boardinghouses, stores, restaurants, saloons, and bawdy houses to keep the workers sheltered, fed, clothed, and

Two City-class ironclads under construction at the Carondelet shipyard prior to October 1861. The view is along the main deck of one gunboat, with the boilers in the foreground and casemate timbers shown on the sides. A sister vessel is shown behind, with some spar deck beams atop the casemate side timbers and upright framing in place for its wheel box. National Archives and Records Administration image 165-C-702.

entertained. Although there were six production sheds in the complex, they could not accommodate all the boat construction.[41] The *St. Louis, Carondelet, Louisville,* and *Pittsburg,* as well as the larger *Benton,* were built there. The *Mound City, Cincinnati,* and *Cairo* were built a few miles up the Ohio River from Cairo at Mound City, Illinois. Thanks to the construction of the river ironclad gunboat fleet, the Mississippi and Ohio rivers from St. Louis to Pittsburgh bustled with commerce. As the vessels were built and launched, they were floated downriver 145 miles to Cairo for the ordnance and training. Once construction was completed at Carondelet, the yard was not used again during the war for massive construction projects. Cairo, and, to a lesser extent, Mound City would handle the repair and outfitting of the flotilla.

Eads did not achieve his sixty-five-day deadline, but in January 1862, less than six months from the date the contract was signed, all of the seven City-class boats were commissioned . They were not commissioned in the order in which they were launched. The vagaries of completing the boats at Cairo and Mound City and of finding and training crews altered the schedule. The *St. Louis,* the first to be completed, was laid down on September 27, 1861; launched on October 12; and commissioned on January 31, 1862.[42] The launching of the *Carondelet* came ten days after the launch-

Naval yard at Mound City, Illinois. Miller's Review of Reviews, *1911.*

ing of the *St. Louis*. The *Benton* was acquired in November 1861 and commissioned on February 24, 1862. Although the exact date was not recorded, the *Essex* was acquired sometime in 1861 and commissioned on October 15, 1861.[43] The *Essex* was the first of the ironclads to be commissioned, but the *St. Louis* was the first to be built from the keel up. Other lighter-armored vessels, known as tinclads, would be quickly added to the fleet, but truly massive firepower lay in this cadre of boats. These twelve gunboats became the backbone of the Union inland navy.

Blue water sailors thought these ungainly monsters ugly, calling them "stinkpots" and "turtles." Indeed, the gunboats lacked the graceful lines of Admiral Farragut's steam sloops. Moreover, the ironclads were cramped, stiflingly hot, poorly ventilated, and cumbersome. The officers slept in tiny staterooms, while the crew slept in hammocks on the decks when possible. Despite these drawbacks, the ironclads and tinclads of the brown water navy drove a stake into the heart of the Confederacy.

NOTES

1. Gideon Welles, "Memorandum," October 20, 1861, Welles Papers, Huntington Library, Malibu, California; John Niven, *Gideon Welles: Lincoln's Secretary of the Navy* (Baton Rouge: Louisiana State University Press, 1994), 373–77.

2. Niven, *Gideon Welles*, 361–62.

3. U.S. War Department, *Atlas to Accompany the Official Records of the Union and Confederate Armies* (Washington, D.C.: U.S. Government Printing Office, 1891–1895), plate 117.

4. John M. Barry, *Rising Tide: The Great Mississippi Flood of 1927 and How It Changed America* (New York: Simon & Schuster, 1997), 22–31.

5. Barry, *Rising Tide*, 29.

6. Edward Bates to James Buchanan Eads, April 16, 1861, Eads Papers, Missouri Historical Society, St. Louis, Missouri.

7. *ORN*, 22: 277.

8. *ORN*, 22: 278.

9. *ORN*, 22: 279.

10. *ORN*, 22: 279.

11. *ORN*, 22: 280.

12. William B. Cogar, *Dictionary of Admirals of the U.S. Navy, Volume I: 1862–1900* (Annapolis, Md.: Naval Institute Press, 1989), 150–51.

13. *ORN*, 22: 280.

14. *ORN*, 22: 284.

15. *ORN*, 22: 280.

16. *ORN*, 22: 281–82.

17. *ORN*, 22: 282.

18. The name *A. O. Tyler* is misleading and the confusion it caused rippled through official reports and later through some historians' analyses. Rodgers thought that the name "Tyler" carried a negative connotation for the U.S. Navy. Former president John Tyler was a secessionist and the commander wanted to change the vessel's name to "Taylor," apparently after former president Zachary Taylor. Rodgers began using "Taylor" on his reports. The name was never officially changed, but it was simply referred to by the single word "Tyler." To confuse matters, beginning in 1862 and lasting throughout the war, David Dixon Porter, perhaps in a show of support for his friend John Rodgers, consistently referred to the vessel as the *Taylor*. He continued this in his postwar publications. David Dixon Porter, *Incidents and Anecdotes* (New York: Appleton, 1885), and *The Naval History of the Civil War* (New York: Appleton, 1886).

19. *OR*, Series 3, 11: 814–15.

20. *ORN*, 22: 284–85.

21. *ORN*, 22: 284.

22. *ORN*, 22: 285–86.

23. *ORN*, 22: 286.

24. *ORN*, 22: 283.

25. Jay Slagle, *Ironclad Captain: Seth Ledyard Phelps and the U.S. Navy, 1841–1864* (Kent, Ohio: Kent State University Press, 1996), 116–17.

26. Paul H. Silverstone, *Warships of the Civil War Navies* (Annapolis, Md.: Naval Institute Press, 1989), 158–60.

27. See Anonymous, *John C. Frémont: Pathfinder of the West* (Boston: John Hancock Mutual Life Insurance Company, 1927).

28. *ORN* 22: 295.

29. Rodgers served a short stint at the Navy Department and was then given command of the USS *Flag* in the South Atlantic Blockading Squadron. Rodgers's career was not appreciably harmed by his short time on the Ohio River. He was promoted to the rank of captain in July 1862, commodore in June 1863, and finally rear admiral in December 1869. *ORN* 22: 307–8; Cogar, *Dictionary of Admirals of the U.S. Navy*, 150–51.

30. William M. Fowler Jr., *Under Two Flags: The American Navy in the Civil War* (Annapolis, Md.: Naval Institute Press, 2001), 134–35.

31. Fowler, *Under Two Flags*, 139.

32. The spelling of vessel was "Pittsburg." Although the spelling of the city name was and is Pittsburgh, the Federal government and other entities periodically dropped the "h." It was not officially added until 1911.

33. Silverstone, *Warships of the Civil War Navies*, 151–53.

34. Silverstone, *Warships of the Civil War Navies*, 151–53; Jack D. Coombe, *Thunder along the Mississippi: The River Battles That Split the Confederacy* (New York: Sarpedon, 1996), 24; H. Allen Gosnell, *Guns on the Western Waters: The Story of the River Gunboats in the Civil War* (Baton Rouge: Louisiana State University Press, 1949), 16–17.

35. Personal conversation with Elizabeth Joyner, USS *Cairo* Museum, Vicksburg National Military Park, August 23, 2006; "Identification Colors for Chimney Bands," credited to Mrs. Edwin C. (Margie) Bearss, from a list by a Mr. Shepard, engineer on the *Carondelet*; Donald L. Canney, *The Old Steam Navy Volume Two: The Ironclads, 1842–1885* (Annapolis, Md.: Naval Institute Press, 1993), 54; a remarkable catalog of items contained in or attached to the City-class vessels is found in Elizabeth Hoxie Joyner, *The USS* Cairo: *History and Artifacts of a Civil War Ironclad* (Jefferson, N.C.: McFarland & Company, 2006).

36. Naval Historical Center Photograph No. 72806; photograph of a portion of the Mississippi Squadron trapped above "The Falls" at Alexandria, Louisiana. Rare Book, Manuscript, and Special Collection Library, Duke University, Durham, N.C.

37. Canney, *Old Steam Navy*, 54.

38. Silverstone, *Warships of the Civil War Navies*, 155.

39. *Battles and Leaders of the Civil War, Being for the Most Part Contributions by Union and Confederate Officers*, 4 vols. (Edison, N.J.: Thomas Yoseloff, 1956), 1: 341–42.

40. Silverstone, *Warships of the Civil War Navies*, 155.

41. NiNi Harris, *History of Carondelet* (St. Louis, Mo.: Southern Commercial Bank, 1991), 25–26.

42. Silverstone, *Warships of the Civil War Navies*, 151.

43. Silverstone, *Warships of the Civil War Navies*, 151–55.

3

✛

Early Actions from Belmont to the Battle of Shiloh

Parson, for God's sake pray! Nothing but God Almighty can save that fort.

—Confederate Colonel Nathan Bedford Forrest

The Commander of Confederate Department No. 2 had an enormous territory under his authority, if not under his control. It comprised the states of Tennessee and Arkansas and that part of the state of Mississippi west of the New Orleans, Jackson, and the Great Northern and Central Railroad. He was also in charge of all military operations in Kansas, Kentucky, Missouri, and the Indian country immediately west of Missouri and Arkansas.

Major General Leonidas Polk, "the Fighting Bishop," graduated from West Point in 1827 and then almost immediately resigned to study theology. He never actually served in the army prior to the Civil War. Polk was appointed the Episcopal missionary bishop to the Southwest. Confederate President Jefferson Davis, a close friend from Polk's West Point days, appointed him as one of four major generals on June 25, 1861. He was given command of the western theater, officially Department No. 2, and created the Army of Mississippi before General Albert Sidney Johnston superseded him on September 10, 1861.[1]

Of all the huge area under his leadership, Kentucky offered the most serious threat and at the same time his greatest promise. If Polk invaded the neutral state, the Confederacy would be seen as the aggressor; however, if he did not and Union forces entered Kentucky, his defensive line would be shattered because of the north–south structure of Kentucky railroads and the courses of the Cumberland and Tennessee rivers. Polk also needed the Ohio River as a northern boundary of the western Confederacy, but at what cost? How many of his scarce resources would be required to hold this line? He and his staff knew that if Federal forces fortified Cairo, Illinois, the Confederacy must prevent the invasion of the Cumberland and Tennessee.

Polk decided on a dual strategy, hoping to confuse his foes. Although short on troops, he invaded Kentucky, but not up to the Ohio as he would have liked. Shortly after Polk began his invasion, Johnston arrived to assume command of Department No. 2 and established his headquarters at Bowling Green. Without sufficient forces to occupy and hold the southern bank of the Ohio River, the Union army countered the Confederate threat and crossed from Indiana, compromised Louisville, and secured the vital shipyard at Jeffersonville, Indiana. For the Rebels, it was simply a matter of too much land to control and too few troops to hold it. The second portion of Polk's plan, which became the core of Johnston's strategy, was to fortify strategic points at Columbus, Kentucky; Belmont and New Madrid, Missouri; Memphis and Fort Pillow, Tennessee; and Vicksburg, Mississippi. Although Federal commanders believed that Johnston's forces were much larger, he had only a tiny fraction of the number of men needed to hold these areas, and many of these soldiers were very young, barely trained, undisciplined, and ill equipped. Johnston wanted most of the forces west of the Mississippi River transferred to Tennessee and Kentucky because he considered these states to be his immediate concerns. Troops were very slow in coming, and their movement only increased with military defeats in Missouri and Arkansas. After Johnston arrived, Polk commanded the First Grand Division, actually a corps, and held Johnston's left flank. This placed the concentration of forces on and near the Mississippi River.

City-class ironclads Baron De Kalb, Cincinnati, *and* Mound City *anchored off Cairo Naval Yard. Library of Congress image LCB816-3123.*

Johnston and Polk wanted to neutralize Cairo, but the Union presence there prevented them from doing so. The next-best course of action was to block any Federal land or naval force from descending the Mississippi from that point. Polk chose to fortify the high bluffs at Columbus, Kentucky, and also the small town of Belmont, Missouri. These towns were located across the 800-yard-wide Mississippi River from one another. If these areas could be held, then Cairo would lose some of its importance. Polk's engineers created complex earthworks at Columbus, and he placed forty-two 32-pounder and 64-pounder cannon there. Under the cover of Lucas Bend in the Mississippi, he positioned two gunboats to protect the earthworks and the 10,000 men garrisoned there.[2] Across the river at Belmont, Polk garrisoned an artillery battery, a squadron of cavalry, and an infantry regiment. During August, he began fortifying Island No. 10, the tenth island south of Cairo, as a separate major obstruction to Union forces rather than a fallback position. By September 2, Union forces were aware that the Confederates had mounted ten heavy guns on the island.[3]

Union Brigadier General Ulysses S. Grant had assumed command of the District of Ironton, Missouri, on August 8. Knowing that the Confederate fortifications at Columbus and Belmont had to be taken before other operations south of Cairo could commence, Grant gathered his forces and secured the assistance of the navy. The *Tyler*, under Commander Henry Walke, and the *Lexington*, under Commander Roger N. Stembel, patrolled the Mississippi River south of Cairo during this time. With Grant's preparations complete, the two timberclads set out to assist the army. During September and October, the gunboats, working either alone or with army forces, conducted multiple reconnaissance missions near Columbus. On November 7, Grant made his move with 3,000 troops, planning to dislodge the Rebels from the Missouri side. His Union troops landed about three miles above Belmont, marched down near the shore, and met a Confederate column of similar size. The Federal troops drove the southerners back into their camps. Grant's transports had landed the men and remained nose-up on shore awaiting their return while the two gunboats moved to about one mile above the bluffs at Columbus. Hoping to draw the Confederate batteries' attention away from Grant, the boats steamed in circles to confuse the Confederate gunners. Together, the vessels had fourteen guns, and they used them effectively, diverting the batteries away from the land forces. The *Tyler* received one hit, and the *Lexington* was unharmed. The Union plan worked until Polk sent reinforcements, tipping the balance of the fighting. Grant herded his men back to the transports with the Confederates in close pursuit. The gunboats moved close to shore and pounded the advancing southerners.[4] Grant was the last man up the gangplank, riding his horse with flair. The attack was not a great success, but it did yield three very important outcomes. First,

Grant saw what gunboat firepower could do in covering troops and discovered that he could trust the navy to help him in combined operations. Additionally, he made long-lasting friends in the Western Gunboat Flotilla. The navy's ability to support land operations and perform reconnaissance missions proved worthy not only on the Mississippi and Ohio rivers but also on other vital waterways, particularly the Cumberland and Tennessee rivers.

After Union Naval Lieutenant Ledyard Phelps brought the three timberclads to Cairo on August 12, he busied himself obtaining and training crews, preparing the boats for fighting, and carrying out missions on the Ohio and Mississippi rivers. Large pockets of southern sympathy still existed on the south bank of the Ohio, and Confederate troops and irregulars raided sporadically. The *Conestoga*, under Phelps's command, and the *Lexington* made runs up the Ohio River past Louisville and also down the Mississippi above Columbus during September.[5] For several months, Phelps was the face of the navy in the region, and he was indispensable to the army throughout the later half of 1861. Phelps took the *Conestoga* up the Cumberland and Tennessee rivers at the behest of Brigadier General Charles Ferguson Smith, who commanded at Paducah, Kentucky. In a glowing report to the adjutant general in Washington on November 8, Smith described all the Confederate defenses that Phelps had discovered:

USS Tyler. *Image misidentified as the U.S.S.* Lexington. *William D. McPherson, photographer. McPherson & Oliver (Studio: New Orleans, Louisiana). Marshall Dunham Photographic Album (Mss. 3241), Louisiana and Lower Mississippi Valley Collections, Louisiana State University Libraries, Baton Rouge, Louisiana.*

SIR: In my report of the 6th instant, in relation to the forces of the enemy, I accidentally overlooked in my notes the works on the Tennessee and Cumberland rivers.

The more important is Fort Henry, 71 miles up the Tennessee, just at the State line. It is a strong earthwork on the water front, but not nearly so strong on the land side. It has three 24 or 32 pounders, one or two 8-inch columbiads, and the remainder of field guns, in all, from 14 to 16; its garrison was, two weeks since, about 1,200. They have been under apprehension of attack from here for the past two weeks.

Some 8 miles above Fort Henry the enemy has been for many weeks endeavoring to convert river steamers into iron-plated gunboats. This fort is an obstacle to our gunboats proceeding to look after such work.

I sent an intelligent person to see what progress had been made on these gunboats, but he was captured. It is my only weak point (this river), made so by the use of gunboats.

The Conestoga, gunboat, admirably commanded by Lieutenant Phelps, of the Navy, is my only security in this quarter. He is constantly moving his vessel up and down the Tennessee and Cumberland. From the latter river he came in this morning, having gone into the State of Tennessee as far as Dover, where the enemy have a work called Fort Gavock, or Fort MacGavock, or something else, usually called Fort Gavock [Fort Donelson]. He could not give me an idea of its armament.[6]

Lieutenant Phelps's discovery of the two Confederate forts on the Cumberland and Tennessee rivers was cause for alarm. General C. F. Smith at Paducah rightly believed his position was vulnerable. The Tennessee River's headwaters were in the mountains of eastern Tennessee. The river flowed southwest to Chattanooga before making a graceful arc down into Alabama and northward near Corinth, Mississippi. From there, it moved through Tennessee and joined the Ohio River just east of Paducah. After rising in the Cumberland Mountains, the Cumberland flowed through parts of Kentucky; descended to Nashville, Tennessee; and flowed north to parallel the Tennessee River before emptying into the Ohio, east of the Tennessee. The average distance between the two streams where they flow parallel is only twelve miles. Confederate forces concentrated their defenses in this area. Given enough time, the fortifications might have been all but impregnable. Time was not on their side, and neither was the Tennessee River.

Fort Henry was located in an abysmal place. In the low area prone to flooding, the waters of the Tennessee flowed over the low parapets and at times filled the bastions at least two feet deep. In the winter, the Tennessee's water often moved swiftly, carrying with it the detritus of its valley: trees, logs, debris from man-made structures, and occasionally ice. Confederate Captain Jesse Taylor later wrote that the decision to place Fort Henry at that location was "made with extraordinary bad judgment."[7]

Additionally, Brigadier General Lloyd Tilghman, who commanded Fort Henry, recognized that if the fort was ever to be abandoned, the troops had only one way out since a single road led inland to Fort Donelson. If that escape route were blocked, the garrison would have few options in the event of attack.

Fort Henry featured ten separate emplacements, five facing the river and five facing landward. Tilghman ordered the trees to the east to be cut with the tops facing eastward to form an abatis, or anti-infantry obstacle. According to Captain Jesse Taylor, the fort also was armed with six 32-pounder smoothbores, two 42-pounders, one 128-pounder Columbiad,

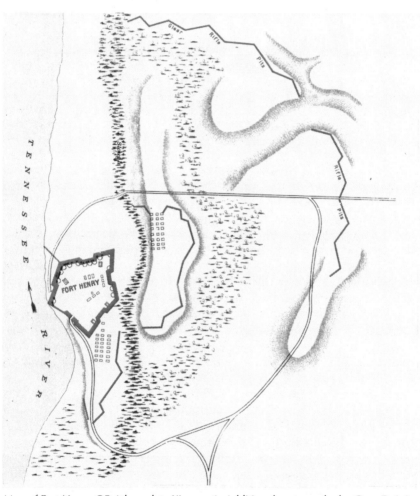

Map of Fort Henry. OR Atlas, plate XI, map 1. Additional cartography by Gary D. Joiner.

five 18-pounder siege guns, and one 6-inch rifle.[8] All these guns, but particularly the Columbiad, could be deadly against a naval force.

Grant read Phelps's reconnaissance reports and General Smith's letters with interest. He knew that if both forts could be destroyed or captured, General Johnston's defensive line in Kentucky would evaporate. The Confederate fort at Columbus would become untenable, opening the Mississippi down to Island No. 10, and Johnston's headquarters at Bowling Green would be rendered useless without support. Taking the two forts would, in effect, destroy the Confederate's upper defense line and endanger the great rail and supply center of Nashville. If Nashville were taken, a strike down the railroad to Mobile would shut that vital port and split the Confederacy.

Less than two weeks after the Battle of Belmont, Major General Henry Wager Halleck had assumed command, reorganized the department, and realigned forces and missions. Grant informed Halleck of his plan and asked for permission to conduct the operation on January 6, 1862.[9] Halleck, like Gideon Welles, could be recalcitrant, moody, and bullheaded. Halleck denied Grant's request, but Grant was not willing to abandon his strategy. He persisted, this time telling Halleck that he would take the fort and "establish and hold a large camp there."[10] Flag Officer Foote, also under Halleck's command and by then on very friendly terms with Grant, sent Halleck a letter offering to support Grant with vessels. Grant then renewed his plea. Halleck gave Grant and Foote permission to proceed on February 1.[11]

Another factor that must be considered regarding Halleck's actions is that he was extraordinarily self-protective. He crafted an order in such a fashion that if a mission succeeded, Halleck could claim all the credit; however, if it failed, the tactical commander would be blamed. Halleck wrote McClellan of the plan, making it his own, adding that the operation should be conducted with 60,000 men. He wrote Grant to be swift in conducting the operation and told Foote that men would be dispatched for his service at Cairo very soon.[12] Grant did not have 60,000 men but only a quarter that number. Halleck knew that if the mission failed, Grant would be blamed for not taking the number of men he ordered and also that it was impossible to assemble 60,000 men quickly.

Foote chose a very powerful mix of vessels, making the operation the first attack by the Pook Turtles. He made the *Essex* his flagship, with Commander William D. Porter commanding, and included the *Carondelet* under Commander Henry Walke, the *St. Louis* under Lieutenant Commander Leonard Paulding, and the *Cincinnati* with Commander Roger N. Stembel commanding. He also incorporated the three timberclads: the *Tyler* under Lieutenant Commander William Gwin, the *Lexington* under Lieutenant Commander James W. Shirk, and the *Conestoga* under Lieutenant Commander Phelps.[13] The small but powerful flotilla left Cairo and rendezvoused with the Army Quartermaster Corps troop transports from Paducah. Together, they steamed into the Tennessee River.

Rain was plentiful that winter, and the Tennessee was at flood stage. While the defenders in Fort Henry were miserable, the flotilla was experiencing its own problems. The river seemed to be giving the Confederacy an advantage. Trees, snags, portions of buildings, and other dangerous objects were either floating on the surface or lying just below it; all were carried swiftly by the torrent. Sailors were stationed at the bows of the vessels with poles to push the debris away from the boats. Progress was very slow, and the column of vessels anchored at night on February 6 in a sheltered turn of the river, away from the current. The next day, the fleet steamed up the river in single file until it reached the designated anchorage at Panther Island, about six miles upstream from Fort Henry.

Grant decided to put his men ashore near Panther Island and to approach along and near the shore on both sides of the river. Grant himself would stay with Foote. As the Union troops moved forward, the flotilla faced a new threat: the first Confederate torpedoes floated down the river. The torpedoes were probably torn from their moorings, but the defenders at the fort may have cast them. The "infernal machines" were cylinders about five feet long, designed with iron grapples to attach to a hull and explode seventy pounds of black powder via a percussion fuse. One of the torpedoes was brought aboard the *Essex* for Foote to inspect. A seaman pried it open, and gas escaped with a high-pitched whistling noise. Believing the contraption was about to explode, everyone in the vicinity ran for the nearest place of safety, if indeed there was one. This was a very close call, but the powder was wet. The bomb was a dud.[14]

Foote planned to have all four of his ironclads approach the fort in line abreast, allowing full use of all the bow batteries. At about 12:30 P.M. on February 7, the gunboats began firing at the fort at a range of 1,700 yards. They slowly approached to about 600 yards, at which point the fort began returning fire very accurately. Fort Henry's 6-inch rifle fired a round that penetrated the *Essex*, ripping through the pantry, the officers' cabins, and some of the boilers and lodging firmly in steerage. This round disabled the ironclad. To make matters worse, the boiler explosions and ancillary damage from the shell killed ten men and wounded twenty-six, including Porter, who was scalded. Fortunately, the fort was upstream, and the *Essex* floated downstream out of range.[15] The *Cincinnati* was also damaged, causing both vessels to need extensive repairs. The *Essex* was out of service for almost two months.[16]

Seeing the gunboats approaching prior to the opening salvos, Tilghman realized that his position was all but hopeless. He sent all but ninety men to Fort Donelson and remained to slow the attack as long as possible. The floodwaters of the Tennessee had slipped over the low bulwarks and flooded the interior with knee-deep water. The ironclads destroyed the 6-inch rifle and two 32-pounders, and after about two hours of exchanging fire, Tilghman surrendered. He had lost five men killed and sixteen wounded or missing, but the damage he, Captain Taylor, and their gunners wrought on the Union vessels speaks volumes of their training and dedication.

The *Carondelet* remained at Fort Henry to support Grant and the army, while Foote took the others to Cairo for repairs and refitting. With the garrison from Fort Henry now reinforcing Fort Donelson, Grant knew he should act quickly. He intended to use the *Carondelet* for support and told Halleck about his plan, wanting to attack the fort the next day, February 8; however, the *Carondelet* could not steam the distance, over seventy miles downstream, and then cross over into the Cumberland and up to the fort in that amount of time. The gunboat could not arrive until February 12, shortly before the remainder of the fleet. Halleck ordered Grant to acquire at least two additional ironclads for support. This put Foote into a precarious position. With dead and wounded crew members from the Fort Henry fight, Foote needed to shift crews among the ironclads to make up full rosters. He had enough for three additional ironclads. Foote selected the *St. Louis* as his flagship and then chose the newly arrived *Pittsburg* and *Louisville*. He also recalled the timberclads *Tyler* and the *Conestoga* from the Tennessee, leaving the *Lexington* to help patrol that river. Grant was adamant that Fort Donelson be taken as soon as practicable. Foote did not believe his gunboats were ready to take on another fort, and from Phelps's reports, this fort presented a greater threat to his flotilla than did Fort Henry.

Fort Donelson was not really a fort but described by one authority as a "bastioned earthwork of irregular trace."[17] The fortification was located on a high bluff rising 120 feet above the east bank of the Cumberland River. Its guns were set to shoot downward so their projectiles could pierce the thinner armor plate and decking of gunboats as they attempted to either pass by or make a direct assault. The fort was well armed with heavy ordnance—one 128-pounder, 10-inch Columbiad; one 128-pounder rifled cannon; two 9-pounder field pieces; and ten 32-pounder smoothbores—although two were obsolete carronades that would be effective only at very close range. These guns were arrayed in two belts, or bands. The slope of the ridge faced downstream from the direction that any naval threat should approach. The Confederate engineers dug two water batteries. The dirt was thrown onto the perimeter, making them secure and difficult to enfilade. The lower of the belts was twenty feet above the mean water line. The engineers placed eight of the 32-pounders and the

10-inch Columbiad in that battery. The second battery was dug into the slope, fifty feet above the water. The engineers placed the 128-pounder rifle and the two 32-pounder carronades on this level. At the summit in what was called the "fort" were the bombproof (where troops not manning the cannon could withstand a bombardment) and the arsenal as well as powder, shells, and fuses. This area was connected to the batteries below via what was termed a "covered way," actually a deep trench, covered over with a roof.[18] The fort encompassed an area of approximately sixty acres, with its earthen walls conforming to the contours of the land and the banks of the river. The only entrance was at the southeast corner. The walls varied from eight feet to twenty feet high, depending on the terrain. The Confederates had created a firing platform built of driven stakes and woven brushes near the top of the interior wall. Gun platforms were built adjacent to the interior walls at various points so that cannon could be moved around to answer specific threats.[19] By late January 1862, the fort had 904 rounds of 32-pound rounds, 165 rounds of 12-pound shells, 100 rounds of 10-inch, 250 rounds of 12-pound howitzer, and 190 pounds of 6-pounders.[20] The presence of the smaller-caliber rounds indicates that there were additional field pieces not listed on the census of ordnance. The fortification also included exterior lines of rifle pits and about 400 log cabins or barracks. The fort had been completed on February 5, just before the assault was to take place.[21]

Unlike Fort Henry, Fort Donelson had a plethora of command staff. After Brigadier General Lloyd Tilghman was captured at Fort Henry, General Albert Sidney Johnston ordered Brigadier General Bushrod Rust Johnson to take command of Fort Donelson.[22] Brigadier General Gideon Pillow superseded Johnson in date of rank. Albert S. Johnston then ordered Pillow to take his command to Fort Donelson on February 7. Brigadier Generals John B. Floyd and Simon Bolivar Buckner were ordered to take their commands to the fort as well. Pillow was not the best choice for command of the four, but his orders were firm. This did not last. Floyd's commission to brigadier was older, dating from May 23, 1861, whereas Pillow had earned his on July 9. One Union officer later described this group thusly: "General Floyd, the most worthless officer in the Confederate camp, had command of their forces. Next in rank was their next most worthless officer, Gen. Pillow. Buckner and Bushrod Johnson were next, both educated and practiced military men."[23]

Grant ordered his force to begin the twelve-mile trek between the forts on February 11. Union Major General John McClernand led his First Division out that afternoon, making five miles before sunset.[24] Commander Henry Walke steamed the *Carondelet* down the Tennessee, into the Ohio, and up the Cumberland, arriving below Fort Donelson about 11:20 on the morning of February 12. While Grant's 15,000 men were investing the fort

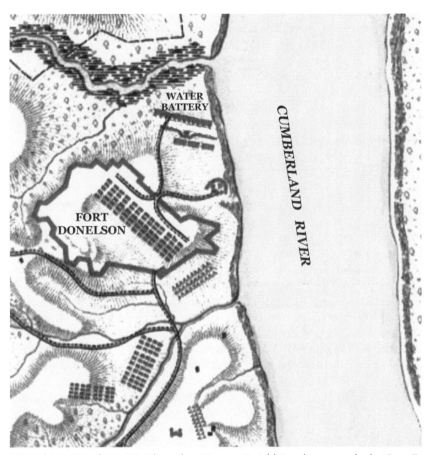

Map of Fort Donelson. OR Atlas, *plate XI, map 5. Additional cartography by Gary D. Joiner.*

on February 13, Walke decided to fire some rounds to test its batteries and to announce to Grant that he had arrived. He then retired downriver to await either Grant or the flotilla.[25] Floyd brought the remainder of his men inside, unmolested. Grant intended to begin the action after the remainder of the gunboats arrived; however, that did not occur. McClernand, seeing Floyd's men entering, impetuously attacked the outer works and was repulsed with heavy losses.[26] It was the first time that Grant was irritated with the political general. It would by no means be the last.

Now that the Confederates knew the Union forces were preparing to attack, Grant believed he needed to begin the operation, with or without the comfort of the bow batteries of the massed Pook Turtles. He ordered Walke to bring up the *Carondelet* and commence bombardment of the fort.

Walke steamed out in the channel, leaving the tug, *Alps*, to act as a sentinel. Before he steamed into range, Walke examined the works by using a spyglass through the narrow slits of his Texas deck pilothouse. He did not like what he saw. The upper belt of gun emplacements was dug into the face of the hill, described as "dismal-looking sepulchres cut into the rocky cliffs near Jerusalem."[27] The elevated positions meant two things. First, the Confederate artillery could fire down upon Walke's vessel, exposing his most vulnerable areas. Second, it would be more difficult for him, with his limited elevating capabilities, to strike at the battery.

Walke brought the *Carondelet* to within a mile of the fort and began firing with Division 1, his bow battery (Division 2 consisted of his broadside guns, and Division 3 were his aft guns). The fort's batteries were silent. As the *Carondelet* slowly steamed forward and raked the emplacements, there still was no response. Walke's guns fired 139 shells into the batteries, disabling a Rebel gun carriage. Then the fort opened up as the gunboat drew near. Many rounds missed, but two hit the vessel. One was from the 10-inch Columbiad. Its 128-pound shell ripped through the casemate and bounded around the interior unimpeded, chasing the jack-tars like "a wild beast pursuing its prey." The round shot smashed into the engine room and ruptured a steam heater. Walke kept the shell as a souvenir.[28] The single round severely wounded seven men and slightly wounded five others. Walke dropped the *Carondelet* downstream to the *Alps*, which now became a floating hospital. The carpenters and mates repaired the damage, and the gunboat steamed back, disheartening the Confederate gunners who were sure that the ironclad had been knocked out of action.

Photo # NH 49991   USS Carondelet tied up to the river bank, during the Civil War

Stern view of the USS Carondelet. U.S. Naval Historical Center image NH 49991.

Union gunboats attack Fort Donelson on February 14, 1862. Harper's Weekly *engraving. U.S. Naval Historical Center image NH 58898.*

The weather had turned cold, and Grant wanted to finish off the fort as soon as possible. Now with snow and freezing rain falling, his men were miserable. In the short march, many had stupidly dumped their heavy winter gear, including their blankets.[29] These soldiers had not yet suffered the rigors of winter in war.

About 11:30 P.M. on the night of February 13, Foote arrived with the *St. Louis, Louisville, Pittsburg, Lexington, Tyler,* and *Conestoga*. Foote used the remainder of the night and most of the next day to ensure that all the vessels were resupplied, all the crews rested, and the boats prepared for battle. He was still uneasy about the fort and the state of preparedness of his flotilla. Foote gave the order to attack at 3:00 P.M. on the afternoon of February 14. The *Louisville* steamed up near the western bank of the river. The *St. Louis*, with Foote aboard, steamed up the center of the channel. The *Pittsburg* and *Carondelet* advanced along the eastern bank. The three timberclads formed a second line about half a mile to the rear. The Confederate gunners, now seeing the foe multiplied many fold, began firing wildly at about 3:30 P.M. As the boats closed, the ironclads returned fire with better accuracy.[30] One of the spectators within the fort was the great cavalryman Colonel Nathan Bedford Forrest, who turned to one of his officers, the Reverend Major D. C. Kelly, and shouted, "Parson, for God's sake pray! Nothing but God Almighty can save that fort."[31]

As ferocious as the battle had been, it was about to get worse. Foote made a terrible mistake. The ironclads approached within a quarter mile of the fort. With the fort's elevation advantage and almost point-blank range, even the 32-pounder carronades were effective. They simply made plunging shots down on the vessels. The disaster Walke feared earlier occurred. Although one of the Confederate gunners accidentally disabled his cannon, the others fired round after round into and around the ironclads in a fierce exchange of heavy-caliber gunfire. A 10-inch shell from the Columbiad smashed the *Carondelet's* heavy wrought-iron anchor.

A round from a smaller artillery piece pierced the pilothouse, mortally wounding one of the vessel's pilots. Other rounds ripped away all four of the *Carondelet*'s landing boats. About this time, one of the bow guns exploded, wounding a dozen sailors and filling the open interior with smoke. The screams of the wounded added to the brilliant flashes and roaring din of the guns as the crew went about their deadly business. All four of the turtles were repeatedly struck. Panic and inattention among the pilots caused additional chaos as the *Pittsburg* rammed the *Carondelet*'s stern, disintegrating its starboard rudder. It maintained steerage and continued the fight. The *St. Louis*'s pilothouse took a direct hit that shattered the 1.25-inch iron plating, killed the pilot, and wounded Captain Foote in the foot. The shell also knocked down one of its funnels. Additionally, the *Louisville* lost its tiller, the *Pittsburg* was hit in the bow and its tiller ropes were shredded by shell fragments, and the *St. Louis* lost a funnel and its boats.

The firing remained intense, with the Confederate gunners getting the best of the ironclads. The *Louisville, Pittsburg,* and *St. Louis* were all forced to allow the current to carry them out of range, leaving Walke and the *Carondelet* to carry on the fight. The timberclads, positioned behind the ironclads, added their heavy guns to the fray, but one 8-inch round from the *Tyler* fell short and slammed into the *Carondelet*. It seemed the hapless ironclad could not be in a worse situation. Confederate gunners in the lower battery began a favorite tactic of southern artillerists: they skip-bombed shells across the water in the same manner one would skip a stone

across a pond. Two 32-pound shells, thus lobbed, pierced the *Carondelet* between its iron plates and wooden hull, holing it. The ironclad began to wallow and became increasingly unmanageable. Walke had no other choice but to retreat. The *Carondelet* had been hit thirty-five times when the battle ended at 5:00 P.M. with the ironclad's departure. The Union navy suffered eight killed and forty-seven wounded. The Confederates had none.[32]

Bow image of the USS Louisville. *U.S. Naval Historical Center image NH 49996.*

This failed attempt at reducing the fort caused Foote great consterna-
tion and destroyed Grant's idea about how the fort could be reduced.
Grant realized that naval firepower alone would not be the answer. Mc-
Clernand had been repulsed, the Confederates outnumbering him 21,000
to 15,000. The Rebel batteries were intact, the Union flotilla was not in
good shape, Grant's men were cold and miserable, and, finally, he had
made no real attempt at investing the outer works of the fort. Just as the
situation seemed the bleakest, he received reinforcements in the form of
Brigadier General Lew Wallace and his division. Grant then prepared for
a siege. Foote sent a message to Grant's headquarters telling him of his
wound and asking the general to come to the *St. Louis* for a conference.
Foote explained that the gunboats must return to Mound City for repairs
but that they would return in about ten days. There was little Grant could
do. He hated to see Foote and those huge guns leave, but there was no
other option.

Just when Grant's chances of success seemed limited, Providence came
from an unlikely source. Prior to the gunboats' bombardment, General
Floyd had held a council of war within the fort. The Confederate generals and their staffs knew that Grant was receiving reinforcements, and
they were aware of what the ironclads had done to Fort Henry. They
overestimated Grant's strength to be between 30,000 and 50,000 men, and
they decided to abandon the fort and cut their way out.[33] Floyd believed—and the other generals agreed—that Grant would only get
stronger. They decided that Pillow's division would attack McClernand
while Buckner withdrew, covered the road to Charlotte, and proceeded
to Nashville. Nathan Bedford Forrest's cavalry was to assist if needed.
Pillow attacked the next morning at dawn. With the aid of Buckner's and
Forrest's men, his force pushed McClernand's division back and secured
the Charlotte road.[34] In fierce fighting, McClernand and Wallace re-
grouped and retook the ground they had lost. One road on the bank of
the river was left open. Floyd, by that time deeply depressed, did nothing to evacuate his men.[35]

On Sunday morning, a Confederate steamer, the *General Anderson*, arrived with 400 men. Floyd requisitioned the vessel and left with only
his brigade of Virginians. General Pillow and his staff escaped across
the river in an old boat.[36] When asked what he would do, Forrest answered, "I did not come here for the purpose of surrendering my command, and I will not do it if they will follow me out."[37] Forrest led his
command (and many others who would follow him) out that one open
road. Buckner attempted to surrender to Grant with some options but
did not get any terms, except for the reply that catapulted Grant to
fame. In a terse response to Buckner's request, after conferring with

Brigadier General Charles F. Smith, his subordinate and former teacher, Grant responded,

GENERAL S. B. BUCKNER,
Confederate Army.
Sir: Yours of this date, proposed armistice and appointment of commissioners to settle terms of capitulation, is just received. No terms except an unconditional surrender can be accepted. I propose to move immediately on your works.
I am, sir, very respectfully,
Your ob't se'v't,
U.S. Grant,
Brig. Gen.[38]

Buckner surrendered the fort without resistance.

Swiftly, the news of the fort's surrender spread north and south, east and west. Grant became the darling of the northern press, and Halleck became even more jealous of him. Major General Don Carlos Buell at the head of the Army of the Ohio marched into Nashville unopposed on February 25, opening even greater areas of Tennessee. Fort Donelson was the first great victory of the North. With it, a Rebel army was captured almost intact, and Grant would be forever remembered as "Unconditional Surrender" Grant. The fact that his initials were "U. S." made it even better in the news-hungry North. Perhaps the most important factor, not really brought forward, except in Grant's later *Memoirs*, was that the general could rely on the navy to do its job, even under the most dire of circumstances. His confidence in them would be confirmed many times. The attack on the forts showed that the ironclads could do much damage to well-protected fortifications. Unknowingly, the ironclads changed the mind-set of the Confederate high command. General Johnston sent a dispatch to Richmond, reporting that "the best open earthworks are not reliable to meet successfully a vigorous attack by gunboats."[39]

It is difficult to assess the loss of the two forts, particularly Fort Donelson, on the fortunes of the South.[40] The loss of the garrison was grievous: 2,000 killed or wounded and 12,000 to 15,000 captured out of a total of 19,000 to 21,000 troops present.[41] The loss of the lower reaches of the Cumberland and Tennessee rivers opened the gates for future Union operations. Confederate Nashville became vulnerable and was lost within days without a fight. Kentucky was all but lost. The first and second defense lines of the South were compromised and almost abandoned, and the fantasy of the Ohio River as a national boundary was destroyed forever. The internal line within Kentucky based on Bowling Green to Columbus evaporated with the loss of the two forts. Island No. 10 became the next vital strongpoint on the Mississippi River. The loss of Fort Donelson opened the door for a desperate gamble by General Johnston to seek retribution from Grant, to gain back much of the lost territory, and attempt to reestablish a more northern defense line. The result would be the first great bloodbath of the war, the Battle of Shiloh.

Soon after the fall of Fort Donelson, Foote took his damaged flotilla back to Mound City for extensive repairs. He knew he had a chance to disrupt Confederate activity on the Mississippi after the loss of their Cumberland and Tennessee River forts. Foote took the Pook Turtles and two mortar rafts down to Columbus on February 23 but did not realize that the Rebels were withdrawing to Island No. 10 after the remaining artillery crews fired a few rounds in their direction. Foote tried to take Columbus again on March 5, this time encountering the Confederate gunboat *Grampus*. The Rebel gunboat struck its colors when confronted by the ironclads but left quickly when the ironclads seemed paralyzed. The crew did not fire or approach. Foote gave chase, only to find the boat under the shelter of the heavily fortified island. He immediately sent the gunboats to the bases at Cairo and Mound City and ordered the ironclads fully repaired, their pilothouses strengthened, and their engine rooms and boiler areas better protected. He did not want a repeat of Fort Donelson. This refurbishing and augmentation was the primary reason that only the *Tyler* and *Lexington* were available at the Battle of Shiloh. While the ironclads were repaired at Mound City, the task of patrolling the Ohio, Cumberland, and Tennessee rivers continued. The three timberclads shouldered this responsibility. The *Tyler* and *Lexington* were assigned primary responsibility for the Tennessee River. At the same time, Grant prepared his army for a push to the next large objective near the river, Corinth, Mississippi, with it the major railroad intersection and supply depots. The Tennessee was still unpredictable, rising and falling erratically as winter gave way to spring. During February and March, the gunboats patrolled the Tennessee as far as Florence, Alabama, where the river became too shallow to navigate, even for the six-foot-draft vessels.

On March 1, the *Tyler*, under Lieutenant William Gwin's command, and the *Lexington*, under Lieutenant James Shirk, carried infantry units toward Savannah, Tennessee, on the Tennessee River. Proceeding up river, the gunboats passed Diamond Island and noted the bluffs ahead on their starboard sides. As they approached, cannon fire erupted from the heights. The commanders decided to press the attack once they recognized the notch in the riverbank nearby as a steamboat landing and determined that the road leading up from the landing offered a direct route to Corinth, Mississippi. [42] Firing from a range of 1,000 yards, the boats silenced the six to eight field artillery pieces within thirty minutes.[43] Gwin sent four small boats ashore with a contingent from the 32nd Illinois Infantry detachment. The 18th Louisiana Infantry attacked them and forced their retreat. After the shore party shoved off, heading for the gunboats, the 18th Louisiana opened up on them again. Gwin and Shirk returned fire, but Gwin reported that his landing boats were "perfectly riddled with balls."[44] The 18th Louisiana retired to the relative safety of the heights, and the Union shore party returned to the safety of their gunboats. The *Tyler* fired 202 rounds of ammunition and the *Lexington* eighty-six during the attack on the battery and the Louisiana infantry. The Union suffered two killed, six wounded, and three missing. One Union soldier wrote his parents about the action, saying that the gunboats "paid them [the Confederates] a visit one day and shelled them to atoms."[45] These southerners were more than an advance party of Rebels. During the coming weeks, Gwin paid particular attention to the landing, known as Pittsburg Landing, and returned often to check on it. He reported this activity to Foote, who thought it important enough to dispatch the *Cairo*, which was patrolling the Cumberland at the time and could not arrive until the end of March.[46]

The army generals understood that moving troops and supplies up the Tennessee without gunboat escort was foolish. Grant, Sherman, and McClernand were all in agreement on this principle.[47] During the upcoming campaign, the Navy and the Army Quartermaster Corps utilized up to 174 vessels for convoying, ferrying, and landing 50,000 troops as well as performing artillery support and interdiction duties.[48]

On March 13, the Army of the Tennessee began its efforts in the region in earnest. Major General Lew Wallace's division left Crump's Landing on

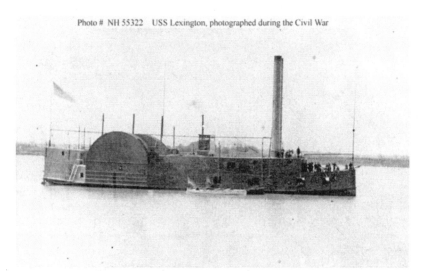

Photo # NH 55322   USS Lexington, photographed during the Civil War

USS Lexington. U.S. Naval Historical Center image NH 55322.

the west side of the river and ripped up some of the Mobile and Ohio Railroad. Brigadier General William Tecumseh Sherman raided south of the landing on March 15, doing damage to the Memphis and Charleston Railroad, across the line in Mississippi. Sherman believed he must have gunboat support to secure his rear and to perform forward reconnaissance. Gwin volunteered the *Tyler*.[49] The great number of vessels, particularly the Army Quartermaster Corps transports, occasionally caused logistical problems on the Tennessee River. The lack of suitable landings on the stretch above Savannah meant that troops must be deployed several miles downstream from or at Pittsburg Landing. The lack of available space at the landing caused severe delays. At times, the boats pulled up to the landing in as many as three layers; some unloaded, while most anchored or turned their wheels to keep in place with the current.[50] On April 1, the *Cairo, Tyler,* and *Lexington* accompanied another of Sherman's raids up the Tennessee. While no Confederates were seen, the expedition was cut short because the Tennessee began to drop precipitately. The vessels could then reach only the small town of Hamburg, a few miles south of Pittsburg Landing.

All the riverine raids toward Corinth ended on April 6, 1862, when the Union Army of the Tennessee was completely surprised by a full-scale Confederate attack on their steamboat landing base. Johnston gambled everything on an Armageddon-like thrust into the Federal camps, and Grant and Sherman were unaware that the Rebels had amassed forces. No attempt was made to reconnoiter or to protect the Union camps.

The *Tyler* was at Pittsburg Landing at dawn on April 6. The *Lexington* was six miles north at Crump's Landing. Both Gwin and Shirk heard the initial attack and quickly responded. Gwin steamed the *Tyler* south about a mile to provide cover for the 71st Ohio Infantry on the Union left flank, who were pinned. The *Lexington* steamed up to the landing, arriving about 10:15 A.M., but the crew could see nothing because of the high bluffs. Shirk took the gunboat back to Crump's Landing to provide support to General Lew Wallace's division.[51] Gwin and his crew aboard the *Tyler* received no pleas from the army for assistance but only watched Federals retreat. Some Confederate artillery fire overshot their targets and splashed in the river around the gunboat, but the *Tyler* received no damage.

About 1:30 P.M., Gwin sent an officer ashore to ask for orders from Brigadier General Stephen Hurlbut. The general ordered Gwin to commence firing and, more important, told him where *not* to fire. After receiving this message, Gwin opened up with his 8-inch and 32-pounder at 2:50 P.M. and later reported that he silenced several Rebel batteries. Hurlbut confirmed Gwin's claim, stating that the naval fire was "most effectual."[52] Gwin moved the *Tyler* back to the landing about 4:00 P.M. and attempted to contact Grant for orders. Grant responded that Gwin should use his own judgment. The *Lexington* arrived almost immediately in order to help the *Tyler*. Shirk was to support Wallace, but the latter marched along inland roads to assist Grant, so the *Lexington* steamed from Crump's Landing against an increasing current and a rising river toward Pittsburg Landing.

What happened next was the most famous naval incident at the Battle of Shiloh and also the most misunderstood, not from controversy but from how it was accomplished. Shortly after 4:00 P.M., the *Tyler* and *Lexington* steamed south about three-quarters of a mile from the landing and engaged Confederate batteries operating on the bank. The Rebels lobbed shells at the gunboats, but they did no damage. The return fire from the boats silenced the batteries. They waited to see if other targets would present themselves, and when they did not, the boats steamed north to a position opposite the steep ravine of Dill Branch, just south of Pittsburg Landing. Beginning about 5:30 P.M., the gunboats worked with field artillery batteries to stem a Confederate attack by crossing the ravine in an attempt to attack the landing. The Confederates were stymied and then repulsed. The gunboats continued the fire until no targets presented themselves, and the supporting Confederate artillery was silenced.[53]

The *Tyler* then initiated harassing fire as night descended. Brigadier General William "Bull" Nelson ordered Gwin to fire selectively on different areas of the battlefield to support the Union troops and keep the Confederates off balance. Gwin began the fire about 9:00 P.M. and continued until 1:00 A.M., when the *Lexington* took over. The *Tyler* fired one of its heavy guns every ten minutes, never consecutively at the same target. To confuse the Confederates, Gwin sometimes interspersed his heavy ordnance with "an occasional shrapnel from the howitzer." The *Lexington* continued the practice from 1:00 A.M. until dawn at fifteen-minute intervals.[54] The Confederates, who had halted their attacks as twilight descended, were kept up all night, never knowing if the screaming, hissing rounds would be aimed at them or another group of men nearby.

The next day, April 7, with the assistance of 20,000 reinforcements under Major General Don Carlos Buell and the Army of the Ohio, Grant and Sherman pushed the Confederates back. General Johnston had been mortally wounded in the first day's fighting, and his replacement, General P. G. T. Beauregard, was not up to the task of completing the destruction of the Union army and withdrew his battered army to Corinth, where the issue would be decided in a few weeks with a Rebel loss. Several Confederate commanders credited the gunboats with providing covering fire, protecting the Union transport vessels, and adding greatly to the Union defenses.[55]

One of the great questions of the Battle of Shiloh remains: how did Gwin and Shirk provide the harassing fire? Gwin explained that he set his

Bluff above Dill Branch overlooking the Tennessee River. Photography by Gary D. Joiner.

fuses at various lengths, thus providing for range differences of the shells.[56] But that does not solve the problem. An understanding of the to- pography of Dill Branch yields other answers and adds to an appreciation of Gwin's genius. At first, it appears the *Tyler* and *Lexington* fired blindly into Dill Branch that night. Fragments of naval rounds and fuses have been found in Fraley Field and at Shiloh Churchyard, placing shells 12,000 feet from the river at Dill Branch ravine and well beyond the effec- tive range of the guns.[57] Several fragments have also been discovered in the ravine.[58] This is because the boats had no idea of their aim, and if the gunfire were at too flat an angle, the rounds would lodge into the ravine. Gwin had been told to fire on Confederates who were in the Union camps, but there was no line of sight. The gunners "walked" rounds by elevating their guns and then incrementally dropping them, perhaps one-half of a degree at a time, until the low point of aim was achieved and then re- versed the method, in effect, "hosing" a target. The northern side of the ravine makes a deflection to the south near its western end, thus allowing Gwin and Shirk to aim at that point, changing their elevation and trajec- tory angle with each shot.[59] The effect was to spread their rounds over a great area, over the heads of the Union soldiers and certainly many Con- federates as well. The former were comforted by the tremendous noise; the latter certainly were not.

The average height of the river in summer is about 342 feet above sea level (ASL). Flood stage is about 360 feet ASL. In April 1862, the river was running about 370 feet ASL.[60] The ravine is about eighty feet deep with a gradient slope of 40 to 70 percent.[61] This means that during the battle, the ravine was partially filled with river water and that the river was at least ten feet above flood stage. If the water level had been lower, the boats' chances of achieving great range with their rounds would had been vastly diminished. The gradient of the ravine made "skipping" the shells more effective. If the powder was heavily packed into the smoothbores, the ranges achieved were well within reason.

Grant and Sherman had nothing but praise for the navy in this campaign. The mutual trust between the western generals and their naval counterparts cemented their relationship, setting the stage for upcoming successes in the Mississippi Valley.

NOTES

1. Ezra J. Warner, *Generals in Gray: Lives of the Confederate Commanders* (Baton Rouge: Louisiana State University Press, 1959), 242–43.

2. *OR* 3: 167–68; Jack D. Coombe, *Thunder along the Mississippi: The River Battles That Split the Confederacy* (New York: Sarpedon, 1996), 40.

3. *OR* 3: 151–52.

4. *OR* 3: 398.

5. *ORN* 22: 356–57.

6. *ORN* 22: 427–28.

7. Captain Jesse Taylor, "The Defense of Fort Henry," *Battles and Leaders* 1: 368–73.

8. Taylor, "Defense of Fort Henry," 368.

9. Ulysses S. Grant, *Personal Memoirs of U. S. Grant* (New York: Da Capo, 1982), 147.

10. *OR* 7: 121.

11. *OR* 7: 121; Grant, *Personal Memoirs of U. S. Grant*, 147.

12. *OR* 7: 120–22; Naval Historical Division, *Civil War Naval Chronology 1861–1865* (Washington, D.C.: U.S. Government Printing Office, 1971), pt. 2, 15–17.

13. David Dixon Porter, *The Naval History of the Civil War* (New York: Appleton, 1886), 147.

14. Bruce Catton, *This Hallowed Ground* (New York: Pocket Books, 1982), 114–15.

15. Catton, *This Hallowed Ground*, 143; Bern Anderson, *By Sea and by River: The Naval History of the Civil War* (New York: Knopf, 1962), 94; Henry Walke, "The Gunboats at Belmont & Fort Henry," *Battles and Leaders* 1: 362.

16. *ORN* 22: 577.

17. Walter J. Buttgenbach, "Coast Defense in the Civil War," *Journal of the United States Artillery* 39 (March–April 1913): 210–16.

18. Buttgenbach, "Coast Defense in the Civil War," 210–16.

19. B. F. Thomas, "Soldier Life: A Narrative of the Civil War." Privately printed, unpaginated. Archives and collections of Shiloh National Military Park Library.

20. Buttgenbach, "Coastal Defense in the Civil War," 211–13.

21. Otis Edward Cunningham, unpublished doctoral dissertation, Hill Memorial Library, Louisiana State University, Baton Rouge, Louisiana, 50.

22. Alfred Roman, *The Military Operations of General Beauregard in the War Between the States* (New York: Harper, 1884), 1: 225.

23. Charles Whitlesey, *War Memoranda: Cheat River to the Tennessee, 1861–1862* (Cleveland, 1884), 33, as described in Cunningham dissertation.

24. *OR* 7: 170; Grant, *Personal Memoirs of U. S. Grant*, 152.

25. *ORN* 22: 587–88; H. Allen Gosnell, *Guns on the Western Waters: The Story of the River Gunboats in the Civil War* (Baton Rouge: Louisiana State University Press, 1949), 59–60.

26. *OR* 7: 72–73. Grant, *Personal Memoirs of U. S. Grant*, 153.

27. Henry Walke, "The Western Flotilla at Fort Donelson, Island Number Ten, Fort Pillow, and Memphis," in ed. Robert Underwood Johnson, *Battles and Leaders of the Civil War*, vol. 1: Opening Battles (new edition Edison, N.J.: Castle/Book-Sales, 1990; orig. pub. Century Company, 1883), 431.

28. Gosnell, *Guns on the Western Waters*, 60. Grant states in his memoirs that Ledyard Phelps commanded the *Carondelet*. He was mistaken. See Grant, *Personal Memoirs of U. S. Grant*, 153–54.

29. Grant, *Personal Memoirs of U. S. Grant*,153.

30. Gosnell, *Guns on the Western Waters*, 61–62.

31. John Wyeth, *That Devil Forrest: Life of General Nathan Bedford Forrest* (New York: Harper and Brothers, 1959), 40.

32. *ORN* 22: 585–94; *OR* 7: 262–63; Gosnell, *Guns on the Western Waters*, 61–62.

33. *OR* 7: 330.

34. *OR* 7: 175; Wyeth, *That Devil Forrest*, 45–46.

35. Wyeth, *That Devil Forrest*, 50.

36. Cunningham, doctoral dissertation, 70–71.

37. R. S. Henry, *"First with the Most" Forrest* (Indianapolis: Bobbs-Merrill Company, 1944), 57, 59; *OR* 7: 288.

38. Grant, *Personal Memoirs of U. S. Grant*, 159.

39. Naval Historical Division, *Civil War Naval Chronology*, pt. 2, 21.

40. Excellent critiques are found in Benjamin Franklin Cooling, *Forts Henry and Donelson: The Key to the Confederate Heartland* (Knoxville: University of Tennessee Press, 1987), and Kendall Gott, *Where the South Lost the War: An Analysis of the Fort Henry-Fort Donelson Campaign, February 1862* (Mechanicsburg, Pa.: Stackpole, 2003).

41. *OR* 7: 169. Figures vary but do not differ greatly.

42. *ORN* 22: 643; F. Y. Hedley, *Marching through Georgia: Pen-Pictures of Every-Day Life in General Sherman's Army, from the Beginning of the Atlanta Campaign until the Closing of the War* (Chicago: Donohue, Henneberry & Co., 1890), 37; Timothy B. Smith, *The Untold Story of Shiloh: The Battle and the Battlefield* (Knoxville: University of Tennessee Press, 2006), 56.

43. *ORN* 22: 643–45, 783.

44. *ORN* 22: 644.

45. Christian Zook to Father, March 24, 1862, 46th Ohio Infantry File, Shiloh National Military Park.

46. *ORN* 22: 644–47, 784; Edwin C. Bearss, *Hardluck Ironclad: The Sinking and Salvage of the* Cairo (Baton Rouge: Louisiana State University Press, 1966), 46.

47. *OR* 10: 9–10, 22–23; Naval Historical Division, *Civil War Naval Chronology*, pt. 2, 34.

48. Charles Dana Gibson and E. Kay Gibson, *Assault and Logistics: Union Army Coastal and River Operations, 1861–1866* (Camden, Maine.: Ensign Press, 1995), 78–79; Smith, *Untold Story of Shiloh*, 58.

49. *OR* 10: 22; unsigned, undated memoir in USS *Tyler* file at Shiloh National Military Park.

50. *OR* 10: 27; Christian Zook to Father.

51. *ORN* 22: 762, 764; *OR* 10: 259, 261.

52. *ORN* 22: 762–63; *OR* 10: 205.

53. *ORN* 22: 763–64; Mildred Throne, ed., *The Civil War Diary of Cyrus F. Boyd: Fifteenth Iowa Infantry, 1861–1863* (Baton Rouge: Louisiana State University Press, 1953), 34.

54. *ORN* 22: 763–64.

55. *OR* 10: 385–87, 397, 418, 423, 425, 432, 455, 480, 499, 534, 582, 601, 616, 622.

56. *ORN* 22: 763–64.

57. Personal conversation with Stacy Allen, historian at Shiloh National Military Park, July 22, 2005.

58. Various archaeological reports in the archives of Shiloh National Military Park.

59. U.S. Geological Survey's 7.5-minute topographic quadrangle map of Pittsburg Landing, Tennessee; National Geographic TOPO! Tennessee 3-Dimensional seamless digital topographic data.

60. Personal conversation with Stacy Allen.

61. Pittsburg Landing 7.5-minute topographic quadrangle map; National Geographic TOPO! Tennessee data.

4

✝

Striking South

. . . by the force of circumstances, the city is in your power.

—John Park, mayor of Memphis

Four days after the Battle of Shiloh, Henry Halleck, a two-star general with a legendary reputation for brilliance but only a modest history as a commander, demonstrated that he might have seen a threat in the military hierarchy from U. S. Grant, another major general who had proven himself as a decisive, tough leader. Halleck, more like McClellan in the East, organized and minutely examined every possibility while opportunities slipped through his fingers. Such an opportunity existed for the Union forces immediately following the Battle of Shiloh, but it was one that he squandered. General Halleck moved his headquarters to Pittsburg Landing to exercise his command of the forces. The press was enamoured with Grant, and Halleck wanted to steal some of that glory for himself. He commanded three full mobile field armies: the Army of the Tennessee, the Army of the Ohio, and the smaller Army of the Mississippi. Two of the three were with him at Pittsburg Landing, and the third would arrive ten days later, giving him 104,162 men to Beauregard's 52,700 Confederate effectives.[1] Although many in the military had high hopes for Halleck, others, like British General Marshall-Cornwall, believed he was "no Napoleon."[2]

An example of Halleck's failure to act is evident in his encounter with Confederate General P. G. T. Beauregard, an overly cautious commander in his own right, as he retreated to Corinth, Mississippi. Halleck arrived at Pittsburg Landing and could have pursued the Rebels with three-to-two odds before the southerners had a chance to dig in. Instead, he planned, fretted, and cautiously crept his way to besiege the Mississippi supply depot, thus failing to eliminate Confederate resistance in the eastern Mississippi Valley. Just when it appeared that a mighty battle would be fought, Beauregard evacuated the army to Tupelo, leaving only the sick and seriously wounded. Beauregard and Halleck failed to act aggressively. Neither would achieve lasting fame as a daring risk taker or master on the field of battle.

In his memoirs, Grant wrote bitterly about Halleck's failure to pressure Beauregard after the Battle of Shiloh and described with crystal-clear hindsight that Chattanooga, Chickamauga, and Stone's River probably would not have been fought had Halleck followed through. He indicated that Burnside would not have been besieged in Knoxville with no opportunity for relief and that "positive results might have been: a bloodless advance to Atlanta, to Vicksburg, or to any other desired point south of Corinth in the interior of Mississippi."[3]

If Halleck had quickly pushed forward to Corinth and removed the Rebel army as a threat, perhaps he would have been considered a great general, and Grant would have been relegated to a mediocre position in the history books. Instead, Halleck's lack of decisiveness ensured that events would play out in an entirely different manner.

Halleck's third mobile field force was the short-lived Army of the Mississippi, commanded by the extremely controversial Major General John Pope. Perhaps historian Allan Nevins penned the best summation of Pope's personality: "Actually, incompetence and timidity offer a better explanation of Pope than treachery, though he certainly showed an insubordinate spirit."[4] Pope forced Confederate major general and former governor Sterling Price and his force south, taking 1,200 prisoners in a small action at Blackwater, Missouri, on December 18, 1861. In twenty-first-century terms, Pope was a "spin master" seeking headlines to further his career. Halleck appointed Pope commander of the District of the Mississippi, Department of the Missouri, and gave him command of the Army of the Mississippi with 25,000 men and orders to clear all Confederate obstacles in his district. Pope quickly focused on New Madrid. He believed he could conduct his operations alone, with no need to involve the navy. He was wrong. The navy would be a critical component of the operation.

Pope surprised the Confederate garrison at New Madrid on March 14, taking the town with relative ease. He did not want to share glory with the navy in his attempt to neutralize Island No. 10 but could not avoid it. He needed to cross the Mississippi to the Tennessee side and take out the artillery batteries and the garrison there. The river rose rapidly and cut off the Confederates. Although Island No. 10 guarded the Mississippi from both upstream and downstream approaches, most of its batteries faced upstream. Pope wrote Halleck on March 19, "Is it not possible for a couple of gunboats to run past Island No. 10 so I can cross my command over the river? Have urged Foote to try."[5] He wanted Halleck to pressure Foote into what appeared to be an almost suicidal attempt.

Island No. 10 was an elongated oval about two miles long and one mile wide.[6] Located in the middle of a hairpin "S" curve, or "Devil's Elbow," of the Mississippi River, it was upstream but south of New Madrid, Missouri, which had its own fortifications.[7] Like Fort Henry, the island's batteries were at shore level. General Beauregard lavishly endowed the island and the adjoining banks with guns and men. At that time, the island had a garrison of 6,000 troops and seventy-five guns in eleven batteries, mounting 32-pounders and heavier guns up to 100-pounders.[8] Ashore, the batteries contained another forty-seven heavy guns and thirty-five field pieces. In addition, the *Grampus* and four transports were under the protection of the guns. The Confederates had sunk a hulk to limit navigation in the main channel north of the island and also positioned a floating battery with nine guns at the northwest tip.[9]

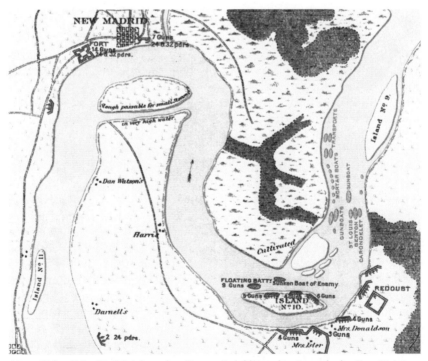

Map of Island No. 10. OR Atlas, plate X, map 1. Additional cartography by Gary D. Joiner.

On March 14, Foote took nine gunboats, ten mortar rafts, and 1,500 army troops to capture Hickman, Kentucky. He then moved down to extreme range of Island No. 10.[10] Foote made another attempt the next day, anchoring the mortar rafts at Island No. 9, within range but out of sight of Island No. 10. Their fire was impressive but only splashed mud without doing damage to the batteries, which remained silent.[11]

Foote faced a tactical problem not present at either Fort Henry or Fort Donelson. There, the rivers' currents had worked to his advantage. If a gunboat were damaged, the current simply floated it out of harm's way, but this was not the case on the Mississippi. If damage occurred and a vessel's engines or steerage were disabled, the current would take it closer to imminent danger. Foote decided on a conservative but powerful alternative.

The next attempt to capture Island No. 10 occurred on March 17. This time, Foote lashed his flagship, the *Benton*, between the *St. Louis* and *Cincinnati*.[12] This combined ten-gun battery would steam down the east bank to combat the island's batteries. Six other gunboats were to steam down the west bank. The newly repaired *Pittsburg* moved to the east just before the boats opened fire. The island's batteries answered in a heated exchange with geysers of water erupting up and down the 2,000-yard interval. A round-shot struck the *Benton*'s forward casemate but did little damage. The *Benton* was hit four times that day, and the *Cincinnati* suffered damage to one of its engines. Then one of the *St. Louis*'s 42-pounder rifles exploded, killing two and wounding thirteen.[13] The island had suffered little damage, and Foote declined to send the Turtles into harm's way against a foe with superior firepower. He ordered the mortars to pound the fort until another solution could be found.

Pope could not sit back and watch the navy steal his glory. His staff reviewed their options. Some controversy exists about who came up with the next idea to capture the island. Colonel J. W. Bissel reconnoitered in the swamp above the mortar boat anchorage and found an old road that connected with a waterway, Wilson's Bayou, that emptied just east of New Madrid. He theorized that using the bayou, a canal could be cut to bypass Island No. 10 completely.[14]

Pope had 20,000 men with adequate materiel, and he ordered them to work. Men were sent in to cut the trees down to trunks and push the debris aside. Others came behind and dug out the road, while even more troops used underwater circular saws to make the waterway about four-and-one-half-feet deep. On April 4, after only nineteen days, the Mississippi flowed through the twelve-mile-long, fifty-foot-wide chute. Pope moved his men, transports, and field pieces to New Madrid via the new waterway.[15] The canal was cut too shallow for the gunboats to navigate, however, and this placed the naval firepower upstream and the army downstream. Pope was no closer to winning than he was nineteen days earlier.

The navy provided the solution, as ingenious as it was daring. While the army was building the canal, the navy, recognizing the canal's shortcomings, considered other strategies. On March 20, in response to Pope's letter to Halleck and the department commander's response calling for action to support the army, Foote held a meeting with his staff and the captain of each ironclad. Captain Walke, commanding the *Carondelet*, offered to take the ironclad through the gauntlet at night, provided certain tasks were accomplished. He requested that the crews bolster the fore and upper decks with wood from a barge, drape anchor chains over the decks and exposed areas aft, surround the pilothouse with an eleven-inch hawser chain, and stack cordwood around the boilers. Walke would also lash a barge, filled with coal and hay bales, on the port side, which would face the island's batteries. He also wanted the crews to transfer the hay from the barge to the stern after the vessel passed the batteries. Additionally, Walke requested that the steam from the ironclad's pop-off valves be diverted into the wheelhouse to reduce the chugging noise of the engines. Finally, as an added measure to prevent boarders, army sharpshooters were carried and a hose from the boilers was made ready to scald any intruders. If the *Carondelet* had mechanical problems or was disabled, Walke was to scuttle it.[16] Another precaution was undertaken on the night of April 1. Colonel George Roberts and fifty men from the 42nd Illinois Infantry made an amphibious raid to spike the guns of the upper battery on the Tennessee side, which the Confederates called Battery No. 1.[17] The men rendered six guns useless and returned without injuries.

April 4, the same day water was directed into the canal, was chosen for the run. A fierce electrical storm set the stage for the nighttime maneuver and aided the *Carondelet*. At 8:00 P.M., the barge was attached, and at 9:00 P.M. the river pilot, First Master William R. Hoel, came aboard. As 10:00 P.M. arrived, Hoel shoved off, and the muffled, much-modified gunboat began her journey. Just as the vessel passed shore Battery No. 2, both chimneys flared with spouts of flame from soot ignited by the intense heat of the boilers. The lightning from the storm hid the light show by providing brighter flashes. Apparently, the Confederate gunners did not see the vessel. The crews lit the chimneys again as the *Carondelet* pulled up even with the island. This time, the artillerymen in the batteries saw the gunboat and began firing. All the *Carondelet*'s gun ports were closed, and the cannon were pulled in to keep the vessel blacked out. This way the *Carondelet* could not return fire. Walke pushed the gunboat as fast as it could go. One round landed in the coal barge but did no damage. The *Carondelet* passed the floating battery, which made only a halfhearted response to the gunboat's run. Walke then brought the *Carondelet* to New Madrid's waterfront amid the cheers of the soldiers. The ironclad spent the next few days shelling batteries and harassing the Confederates, who were now in a precarious position since their escape route was eliminated. On April 6, the *Pittsburg* made an identical run with the same results. The two iron-clads provided protection for Pope's forces to cross over to the Tennessee side on April 6, when Grant and Sherman were caught off guard at Pittsburg Landing. The garrison on Island No. 10 surrendered to Foote on the night of April 7.[18]

News of the victory spread quickly across the North. Foote was hailed for his work on the Cumberland, Tennessee, and now the Mississippi rivers. Secretary Gideon Welles wrote Foote, "Your triumph is not the less appreciated because it was protracted, and finally bloodless."[19] Banner headlines recorded the triumph: the *New York Times* led with "Island No. 10 is Ours!" One-hundred-gun salutes were fired in Boston and in Providence, Rhode Island, in honor of the victory.[20]

Although complimentary of the navy, Pope downplayed its role. A furious set of letters was passed back and forth from St. Louis to Washington among various officers. On April 10, Welles thanked the flotilla and particularly Walke and Hoel. On April 11, President Lincoln gave the navy the thanks of a grateful nation. On April 15, Welles requested Hoel's full name so that he could be promoted. On May 11, William D. Porter, recuperating from his earlier wounds, sent a private letter to Foote concerning Pope's official report. The always-blunt Porter clearly stated what he thought of the report and added, "I sincerely hope you will compel General Pope to make some explanation which may do away with the implied imputations he has made on yourself, as well as others, by implying

Currier and Ives lithograph of the naval bombardment and capture of Island No. 10 on April 7, 1862. U.S. Naval Historical Center image KN-969.

that the fleet was useless and the chief of it afraid to do his duty, etc."[21] On July 11, Foote was given the thanks of Congress for his gallantry at Fort Henry, Fort Donelson, and Island No. 10.[22] On November 13, 1862, Foote put the army's role in the battle in perspective in his report to Welles by remarking, "It is a singular fact that in the captures of Fort Henry and Island No. 10, not a gun was fired by the army."[23]

Below Island No. 10, the city of Memphis, Tennessee, dangled as a tempting prize. Guarding Memphis from the north was the heavily defended Fort Pillow, located at another sharp bend of the river about fifty miles south of Island No. 10 and about eighty miles north of the city. Fort Pillow consisted of some five miles of breastworks from riverbank level up to high bluffs that were armed with forty guns, including five or six 8-inch and 10-inch Columbiads with the remainder 32-pounders.[24]

Foote and Pope decided on a joint operation similar to that at Island No. 10. Foote was to take the flotilla downriver near Fort Pillow on April 12, and the army transports would follow the next day. The flag officer gathered the vessels at New Madrid and shoved off. The ironclads *Cairo*, *Cincinnati*, *Mound City*, and *St. Louis* were soon joined by the *Carondelet* and *Pittsburg*, which had been anchored at Tiptonville, and all moved downstream in single file. Of course, the turtles moved with their entourage of supply vessels, coal barges, mortar scows, dispatch boats, tugs, and a floating machine shop.[25] Most of the flotilla ran the fifty miles of river that day and anchored in the evening a short distance upstream from the fort. Before the flotilla's departure on April 12, Foote was aware that Confederate gunboats had been seen fifteen miles south of New Madrid. In his official report of that date, he told Welles that his intelligence source indicated that there were "some seven rebel gunboats, mounted with six and seven rifled and large caliber guns, upon an average; these are *General Polk*, *Pontchartrain*, *Livingston*, *McRae*, *Ivy*, and one other, name not known. It is hardly probable that these boats will make a stand, but will run as we approach them till they reach the cover of their heavy batteries."[26] Pope arrived with his tugs, mortar rafts, troop transports, and 20,000 men shortly after dawn on April 13, and at 8:00 A.M., five Confederate cottonclad rams rounded the bend. The cottonclads were early versions of tinclads but had, in this case, tightly compacted cotton bales packed in the spaces around the engines and boilers, plus four inches of oak beams laminated together around the exterior of the boats. The outside featured one inch of iron plating, which was enough to stop musket and rifle fire but not field artillery or naval ordnance. They also were outfitted with iron beaks that made them deadly projectiles.[27] The *Benton*, *Cincinnati*, and *Carondelet* moved forward to engage the intruders, and after an exchange of about twenty rounds, the cottonclads turned around to wait under the protection of the bluffs at Fort Pillow.[28] Pope tried to find a place to land behind the fort the next day but could not locate a suitable site. Foote ordered the mortars to fire to soften the defenses, but they did little damage.

Halleck ordered Pope to abandon the plan to occupy Fort Pillow and leave only two regiments in case the situation changed there. Pope left on April 16 and proceeded to Pittsburg Landing, arriving at Halleck's headquarters on April 24 so that he and his troops could participate in the operations in northern Mississippi.[29]

On April 17, Foote reported to Welles that the Rebels had ten gunboats at Memphis and that ten others were en route. He knew that he might reduce the fort but that he could not occupy Memphis without the army. The loss of Pope's 20,000 soldiers was devastating to the most successful inland naval campaign, but it was only the beginning of problems.[30] The Mississippi River began rising suddenly and endangered the Union complex at Cairo, as the water flooded the magazines and approached the tops of the levees. All of the powder, shot, and shells were put on vessels. Additionally, Foote's intelligence sources provided information that the Confederates were completing a very powerful ironclad, the *Louisiana*, at New Orleans in order to assist Fort Pillow. These reports were partially correct: the *Louisiana* was one of two giant ironclads under construction at New Orleans, but on April 23, neither one had engines. Foote had no way to identify the truth. The posed threat from New Orleans made him increasingly nervous about his lack of assistance from the army.

Rear Admiral Andrew Hull Foote in 1862. U.S. Naval Historical Center image NH 61932.

Moreover, Foote's leg and foot became greatly inflamed. In his April 13 report, he complained to Welles that his wound was swelling and was not getting the attention it needed.[31] The fleet surgeons feared for his life if did not receive treatment. He requested and was granted a leave of absence. He turned over what he thought was temporary command of the Western Gunboat Flotilla to Captain Charles H. Davis, but he would never see his beloved flotilla again.[32] After receiving medical treatment, he was given command of the blue water South Atlantic Blockading Squadron besieging Charleston. Before he could assume command, however, he died on June 26 of Bright's disease, which harmed his liver and kidneys.[33] On Foote's death, Davis's command became permanent. Promoted to the rank of commodore, he was soon designated flag officer.

Like Foote, Davis made the *Benton* his flagship. After Foote had gone to Washington, Davis placed his gear aboard and assessed the operations against Fort Pillow. The next morning, he ordered the *Louisville* to join the flotilla from its patrol position at Hickman, Kentucky. Each morning, one of the gunboats, accompanied by a mortar raft, descended the river. The pair anchored around the bend from the fort, in range but out of sight of the guns on the bluffs. The raft pounded the fort until its ammunition was expended or until relief arrived. On the morning of May 10, this duty fell to the *Cincinnati*, commanded by Commander Roger Stembel, and to *Mortar Boat No. 16*, under Second Master T. B. Gregory. The *Cincinnati* tied up to the bank and the mortar boat, located farther out in the channel, began lobbing shells at 6:00 A.M. The other turtles were tied to the bank about three-eighths of a mile upstream, three on the eastern bank and four on the western.[34]

Gregory saw telltale columns of smoke rising from the chimneys of the Confederate Defense Fleet before he caught sight of the rams. He warned Stembel, who immediately ordered oil poured into the *Cincinnati*'s fireboxes to create a head of steam, which had not built up before then. The commander then signaled the fleet of the approaching danger. The first of the City-class ironclads to respond was the *Mound City*, under Commander Augustus H. Kilty. Within thirty minutes, the remainder of the ironclads built up steam and joined the fray.[35]

Bearing down on the *Cincinnati* and the mortar raft were eight cottonclad rams under the command of James Edward Montgomery. These were the same vessels Foote had seen, but now they were anything but timid. Making the attack were the *Little Rebel, General Beauregard, General Bragg, General Earl Van Dorn, General Lovell, General M. Jeff Thompson, General Sterling Price,* and *General Sumter.* Four were fitted with iron rams, and most carried from one to five guns, ranging from 12-pounders through 42-pounders. They were an odd mixture of types, but all were fast, making from eight to ten knots.[36] Their crews, trained in theory and tactics under Montgomery, knew they could use their rams to disable and perhaps sink the Union ironclads.

Stembel moved the *Cincinnati* away from the bank and prepared to meet the speeding gunboats, but the cumbersome, unwieldy giant was at a disadvantage. The *General Bragg* steamed a straight course, striking the ironclad on the starboard side. Stembel fired a broadside into the *Bragg* just as the *General Sterling Price* rammed the *Cincinnati* in the stern and destroyed one of its rudders. The *Mound City* moved to protect the mortar raft and

Naval battle between Union and Confederate rams at Memphis, Tennessee, in June 1862. Currier and Ives Lithograph. U.S. Naval Historical Center image NH 42367.

block the charging cottonclads. Aboard the raft, Gregory reduced the powder charges in the mortar, lowered the elevation as far as it would go, and fired fragmentation rounds into the Confederates. The *Mound City* and *Carondelet* approached, and both fired into the *Bragg*, which wheeled away downstream, out of control. The *General Sumter* rammed the *Cincinnati* so hard that it opened the hull; water poured in, and the ironclad sank in eleven feet of water. The rams also carried sharpshooters who fired at targets of opportunity. They severely wounded Commander Stembel and mortally wounded Acting Fourth Master G. A. Reynolds. The *General Earl Van Dorn* moved up to the mortar boat and fired a pair of 32-pound rounds through its blinds and then rammed the *Mound City* almost at the same moment the *General Sumter* hit the ironclad. Lieutenant Phelps, commanding the *Benton*, moved his giant ironclad into the fight and blasted both the *General Lovell* and the *General Van Dorn*. The *Mound City*, which had not seemed to be in dire trouble, began to wallow, and Commander Kilty moved as close to the bank as he could before it sank, settling in twelve feet of water. The *Carondelet* fired on and destroyed a cottonclad,[37] and with that, the first purely naval battle of the war in the West was over.

Montgomery withdrew his little fleet to the protection of the guns at Fort Pillow. Stembel was taken to Cairo, where he recovered from his wounds. Unfortunately for the Confederates, the *Mound City* was raised the next day and the *Cincinnati* soon afterward with the help of one of James Buchanan Eads's inventions, the diving *Bell Boat No. 8*, and the stern-wheeler pump boat *Champion*, using 20-inch high-pressure pumps. The two stricken ironclads were towed back to Cairo. The *Mound City* was soon on patrol with the fleet, but the *Cincinnati* took somewhat longer.[38] One consequence of this fight was that the Union fleet incorporated anti-ramming measures, and railroad iron was added around the bows and sterns of the turtles. In addition, from that point, logs were suspended down each side to ward off all but perpendicular ramming hits whenever the threat of rams persisted.[39]

Montgomery believed the attack was a success. He had sunk two of the feared Union ironclads, and his losses were acceptable in light of this tremendous accomplishment. The cottonclads withdrew to Memphis and awaited the additional gunboats coming up from New Orleans. He believed that when the Yankees tried again, he would be able to stop them just as he had at Plum Point, the name by which this battle would be known.

After all the effort to take Fort Pillow, there was to be no climactic battle. Nothing of significance happened at the fort for almost three weeks. Halleck inched toward Corinth, Mississippi, and prepared extensive siege lines with his 120,000-man army. Beauregard prepared to meet him but then unexpectedly decided to evacuate to a safer haven at Tupelo, Mississippi. With Corinth taken, Fort Pillow's importance, ninety miles above Memphis, declined. The Confederates began their evacuating on the evening of May 29 and continued until June 3, but not before they destroyed or dismantled anything the Union forces might find useful.[40]

Before the evacuation of Fort Pillow, the Confederates on the bluffs watched as a new type of Union vessel appeared on the waters of the Mississippi. Not only were they peculiarly shaped, but the flotilla to which they belonged was perhaps the oddest on either side during the war. The new boats were the rams of the Mississippi Ram Flotilla, later to become the Mississippi Marine Brigade. This unit was the brainchild of Colonel Charles Ellet Jr., a civil engineer who had proposed a series of manmade reservoirs on the Mississippi and Ohio rivers to alleviate flooding and increase water levels during droughts. In addition, he designed locks and dams and was extremely knowledgeable about the western rivers. Ellet had served as an observer to the Russians during the Crimean War and had suggested the use of rams there to thwart the British and French. They ignored his suggestion. He brought the same concept to the navy after the *CSS Virginia* damaged the wooden warships in Hampton Roads prior to her encounter with the *Monitor*. Again his idea was rejected. Ellet finally found an ally in Secretary of War Edwin Stanton. Ellet was made a colonel in the army and then told to create a ram fleet for western use.[41] With this action, Stanton added to the complex command relationship in the West. The army bought and paid for the ram fleet and supplied the army personnel to staff it, the officers in command were primarily from the Ellet family, and the fleet was to be used in conjunction with the Western Gunboat Flotilla; however, it was not to be under the authority of either branch of service. Although it was eventually known as the Mississippi Marine Brigade, it was not part of the U.S. Marine Corps.[42]

Ellet purchased the nine fastest steamers available on the Ohio River and converted them to his specifications at available shipyards. The *Lioness*, *Sampson*, and *Mingo*, all large stern-wheeler towboats, were converted at Pittsburgh. The *Queen of the West*, *Monarch*, and *Switzerland* were large side-wheelers, while the *Lancaster* was a smaller side-wheeler. The *Dick Fulton* and *T. D. Horner* were smaller stern-wheelers. The *Lancaster* and *Queen of the West* were retrofitted at Cincinnati; the *Switzerland* at Madison, Indiana; and the *Monarch* at Albany, Indiana; the *Dick Fulton* and *T. D. Horner* were completed at Cincinnati.[43] The *Switzerland* was designated the flagship. The *Dick Fulton* and *T. D. Horner* became tenders for the ram fleet. Later, other vessels were added: the tugs *Alf Cutting*, *Bell Darlington*, and *Cleveland*; the hospital vessel *Woodford*; and the transports *Autocrat*, *Baltic*, and *Diana*.

Ellet's original idea was for the rams to be so fast (averaging ten to twelve knots each) that none would need guns. This was illogical, and some were armed. The boats were extremely sturdy after retrofitting. The rams' protection against self-injury consisted of three solid timber bulkheads attached with iron rods to the keel, hull, and decks. Each bulkhead was from twelve to sixteen inches thick and four to seven feet high. Each was cross-braced forward and aft to form a single unit. A central beam was installed from the bow to the stern, and the bow was packed with laminated oak. Iron stays, bolstered in all directions, secured the boilers and machinery. The pilothouse was reinforced with additional planks, and the boilers and engines were sheathed in two-foot-thick oak timbers that were bolted together.[44] The bows mounted iron beaks. On impact from a ramming maneuver, the entire vessel's weight concentrated on the beak, providing a tremendous amount of energy in a very small surface area. Ellet slung a large ornament consisting of the first letter of each boat's name from the spreader bar or spanner cables between the chimneys. The side-wheelers also carried the name painted in large letters on their wheel boxes. Each vessel carried a contingent of sharpshooters, and, eventually, mounted marines on their own vessels were attached to the unit. This was truly a hybrid unit like nothing else in the U.S. armed forces.

On arriving above Fort Pillow on May 16, Flag Officer Davis and Charles Ellet initially were wary of one another. Davis was dismayed to learn that the rams were not under his direct control. Ellet, who was excitable and tended to be erratic and impulsive, developed a closer rela-

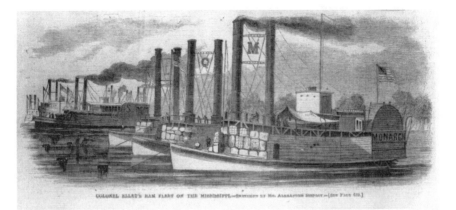

Vessels of the Ellet ram fleet. The vessels are (right to left) Monarch, Queen of the West, Lioness, Switzerland, Sampson, *and* Lancaster. Harper's Weekly *image. U.S. Naval Historical Center image NH 59007.*

tionship with Davis once the ram commander agreed to cooperate and not create his own missions. The rams played no major part at Fort Pillow, but that changed dramatically downstream.

Memphis was not simply the next big target of opportunity below Fort Pillow but was also vital to the Confederacy. The city was the largest population center between St. Louis and New Orleans, with a population of about 33,000 people.[45] Railroads connected it to Savannah, Georgia, via Chattanooga and to New Orleans. Across the river, railroads and roads connected the city with Little Rock, Arkansas. Men, cattle, and produce— all vital to the Confederacy—flowed from the Department of the Trans-Mississippi to supply the Army of Northern Virginia and the Army of Tennessee. The city also boasted a shipyard; just like New Orleans and other internal river ports including Shreveport, Louisiana, the shipyard saw the construction of two large Confederate ironclads, the *Arkansas* and the *Tennessee*.[46] After Island No. 10 fell, the *Arkansas* was moved down to Yazoo City for completion, and the *Tennessee* was moved across the river and then taken to safety.

Just a few months earlier, Memphis was thought to be so isolated that it needed little immediate protection. The Confederates believed that Fort Pillow to the north and "Fortress Vicksburg" to the south would protect it. That faulty logic dearly cost the South. The Confederate Defense Fleet, riding high on its recent victory at Plum Point, provided the main defense of Memphis, and it was about to be tested.

June 6, 1862, dawned bright and sunny. A festive atmosphere was pervasive in the city. Captain Montgomery aligned his eight remaining cottonclads abreast across the Mississippi, awaiting the turtles. Between

5,000 and 10,000 citizens of Memphis lined up to watch the great specta-cle, which they hoped to be a replay of the sinking of the ironclads at Plum Point.

Davis and his flotilla had no intention of allowing the people of Mem-phis that pleasure. The ironclads had a full head of steam, and the new rams were to be used. On the prior evening, Davis anchored his fleet four miles upstream at Paddy's Hen and Chickens, an oddly named sandbar. Early the next morning, he gave the signal, and the great van of vessels steamed southward. The ponderous ironclads led with Davis in the flag-ship *Benton*, the rams to their rear, and the auxiliary boats following like a great school of fish. Gun ports were open, cannons loaded and reeled out, and gun crews poised to begin their deadly business. All command-ers had their orders and took their jobs seriously. There would be no re-play of Plum Point, no humiliation this time.

Davis harbored the same concern as Foote about fighting the turtles on the Mississippi, especially since the Plum Point fiasco. He knew that if disabled and rendered unmanageable, the boats might float down with the current, giving the Rebels the chance to capture them and use them against him later. He chose a different tactic. The ironclads would expose their stern batteries downstream, and the vessels would make just enough speed to steer but not enough to counter the current. If they took hits and were damaged, the captains were to increase speed and move the gun-boats out of harm's way.

Ellet stood between the chimneys of his flagship, the *Queen of the West*, and chafed at not leading the charge. As the Rebel flotilla came into sight, he took off his hat, waved, and pointed to his brother, Alfred, who was commanding the *Monarch*. At that signal, Davis's majestic precision de-scent along the river ended. The eyewitnesses on the scene do not agree about the order in which events next occurred. With the field of action ob-scured by the heavy veil of smoke from each vessel, the action can be de-scribed as a melee. On Charles Ellet's signal, both the *Queen of the West* and the *Monarch* charged through the line of Union ironclads. The gun crews aboard the ironclads could not then fire directly into the Confeder-ate vessels without endangering the Union rams. The southern boats were taken completely by surprise, and the situation at Plum Point was avenged.

The *Queen of the West* and *Monarch* charged toward the Confederates at flank speed. As they did, the ironclads fired rounds at targets of opportu-nity that were rapidly traversing their fields of fire. Ellet aimed at the *Gen-eral Lovell* in a bow-to-bow attack. At the last moment the *Lovell* veered, and the *Queen* struck it full bore amidships. The *Lovell* rolled to starboard with such force that one of its chimneys broke and fell across the *Queen's* bow. The *Lovell*'s crew abandoned ship, most jumping into the churning waters and swimming for the Arkansas shore. Ellet pulled the *Queen*'s beak out of the *Lovell*, and the latter had enough speed left to inch closer to the Arkansas shore, sinking into the shallow mud. The *General Beauregard* then rammed the *Queen*, wrecking one of its side wheels. Ellet moved the *Queen* to the Arkansas bank and beached it, while the *Monarch* aimed at the *General Sterling Price*. After the *Beauregard* hit the *Queen*, it bounced off and aimed at the *Monarch*. Alfred Ellet used greater speed to his advantage and slipped between the two Confederate cottonclads, which then collided. The *Beauregard* sheared off one of the *Price*'s side wheels, rendering it useless. Alfred Ellet then wheeled the *Monarch* sharply around in time to ram the *Beauregard*. One of the ironclads fired a shot into the *Beauregard* just as it was rammed, bursting its boiler. The cottonclad had enough steam and momentum to approach the Arkansas bank. Just before it reached safety, it sank.[47] The *Monarch* then chased down Montgomery's flagship, the *Little Rebel*, which the gunboats had already pummeled. Hitting the cottonclad with the force of a flank-speed ram, the *Monarch* completely pushed the Confederate vessel out of the water onto the bank. The *General Bragg* grounded itself to keep from being sunk, and the *General Jeff Thompson* exploded on the riverbank with enough force that it blew out windows in downtown Memphis. The *General Sumter*, riddled by the ironclads and grounded, sank in very shallow water. The *General Earl Van Dorn*, the fastest of the Rebel gunboats, cut and ran, leaving her pursuers behind after a chase of ten miles.[48] Later that day, Flag Officer Davis demanded the surrender of Memphis. Mayor John Park stated, "In reply I have only to say that the civil authorities have no resources of defense, and by the force of circumstances, the city is in your power."[49]

At some point during the frenetic river ballet, a pistol ball from a Confederate sharpshooter wounded Charles Ellet in the leg, and he collapsed.[50] His wound did not appear particularly serious. He was moved aboard the *Switzerland*, which was then acting as a hospital ship, and taken to Cairo. He wrote reports and remained as head of the ram fleet, but he later took a turn for the worse and died on June 21. His body was taken to Independence Hall in Philadelphia, after which he was given a state funeral. Alfred Ellet then took command of the unit.

Davis received a request for help from General Halleck shortly after Memphis fell. General Samuel Curtis, who had been fighting the Rebels in southern Missouri and northern Arkansas since the previous year, believed he was in serious trouble. Curtis thought that new troops from Texas had reinforced the Confederates under General Thomas Hindman and that their strength was greater than his own. He gathered his men at Batesville and asked for reinforcements and supplies as soon as possible. The army quartermaster corps, already using their transports elsewhere, could not meet his needs.

Davis was happy to help Halleck. He feared that the *General Earl Van Dorn* might be hiding up one of the tributary rivers and would pounce when given the chance. The most obvious hiding places were the Arkansas and White rivers. Davis wanted to clear the river of opposition before the flotilla contended with Vicksburg, its toughest challenge of the war. He made plans for the expedition while the army gathered its relief force and supplies. If the operation succeeded, Curtis would be reinforced and the rivers cleared of Rebel gunboats.

The Confederate commander of the Department of the Trans-Mississippi, General Hindman, did indeed have engineers survey the Arkansas and White rivers to prevent such an incursion up either. The Arkansas was running low that summer, making its upper reaches impassable, so Hindman concentrated on the White River, which normally was open to navigation for the lower 300 miles of its length. His engineers chose a location near the town of St. Charles, Arkansas, at Devall's Bluff. They created an impromptu artillery emplacement on the bluff and just above river level below it. Two 42-pounder rifled seacoast howitzers, brought upriver by the steamer *Pontchartrain*, and two 3-inch rifled cannon, hauled in from the Little Rock arsenal, were placed on the bluff. The lower battery consisted of two 9-pounder Parrott rifles and two brass 12-pounder field guns taken from the steamer *Maurepas*.[51] The engineers used pile drivers to pound logs into the river bottom, then they sank the steamers *Eliza G.*, *Mary Patterson*, and *Maurepas* to block the stream. Then they waited.

Davis chose the *Mound City*, commanded by Augustus Kilty, as his flagship and also selected the *St. Louis*, *Lexington*, and the armored tug *Spitfire* to sweep down the river. Other vessels would join the core group later. Kilty and his cohorts left Memphis on the morning of June 12 and reached the mouth of the St. Francis River that afternoon. He sent the *Spitfire* up the stream while the others waited. The captain of the tug reported seeing no vessels, but he did find cotton ready for shipment. The location was noted, and at 3:00 P.M., the squadron proceeded downstream. They encountered the steamer *Clara Dolson* moored at Helena, Arkansas, but before they could capture it, the steamboat cast off. The *Lexington* pursued but could not catch it. June 13 passed uneventfully, but the boats reached the mouth of the White River the next day. They had traveled 180 miles and met no resistance. Kilty sent the *Spitfire* on a reconnaissance mission in advance of the squadron, which entered the river in single file. They were shortly greeted by the *Spitfire* with the *Clara Dolson* in tow.[52]

A brief distance up the White River is an ancient crossover channel that connects it to the Arkansas River; this was known as the "Arkansas River Cutoff." Kilty anchored there to await the other vessels. The *Conestoga* and the transports *New National*, *Jacob Musselman*, and *White Cloud* joined him. The squadron moved upstream with the *Mound City* leading, followed by

St. Louis, the timberclads, and the transports. Scouts reported the Rebel works at Devall's Bluff, and Kilty called a halt for the night.

Kilty decided to advance with the *Mound City* and the *St. Louis*, not wanting to risk the timberclads or the tug if met with surprise fire. Some distance below the bluff, Kilty disgorged Colonel Graham Fitch's 46th Indiana Volunteer Infantry, which had been aboard the transports, in order for them to approach while he kept the artillery busy. The two ironclads moved up to the bluff and opened up on the river battery at 600 yards. The Rebel gunners answered with deadly fire. Kilty, not paying attention to the gun battery on the higher elevation, believed he had almost silenced the paltry obstacle of his mission. Then the ironclads received fire from the battery on the bluff. A well-placed round from the 42-pounder seacoast howitzer slammed into the *Mound City*, penetrating its port casemate immediately in front and a little above a gun port. The round did unbelievable damage as it passed through the iron and the oak behind it; it killed three men while still in flight and then exploded the steam drum, scalding the majority of the crew.[53] As many of the sailors jumped into the water to escape almost certain death, Confederate riflemen fired at them, killing them as they floated or swam away. The *St. Louis* and *Lexington* moved forward and provided covering fire while the *Conestoga* attached lines to the *Mound City* and moved the stricken ironclad out of the way. Union gunboats picked up the wounded sailors. Confederate troops tried unsuccessfully to board the *Mound City*, and Fitch's Indianans took the batteries and scattered the Confederate defenders. Of the *Mound City*'s crew of 175 men and officers, eighty-two were buried at the site, forty-three drowned or were shot while in the water, and twenty-five were scalded, including Commander Kilty. Only twenty-five (three officers and twenty-two men) were uninjured.[54]

Additionally, a severely wounded gunner in his death throes aboard the *Mound City* rolled over and pulled the lanyard on a primed 8-inch bow gun. The grape shot penetrated the *New National*, rupturing a steam pipe and disabling one of its side wheels. First Master John A. Duble was placed in charge of the ironclad.[55] Many of the survivors opened the liquor locker, drank themselves into oblivion, and looted the officers' cabins on the *Mound City*.[56] The transports took the wounded back to Memphis.

The mission continued for another sixty-five miles to Crooked Point, where the water became too shallow to navigate. Kilty was brave beyond reproach but foolish in his attempt to win the battle single-handedly. The infantry reached the position and would have accomplished the mission given enough time. Davis reported that the White River was clear of Rebels, and Curtis's condition was eased. He pronounced the mission a success with the sole exception of the *Mound City* tragedy. New, very

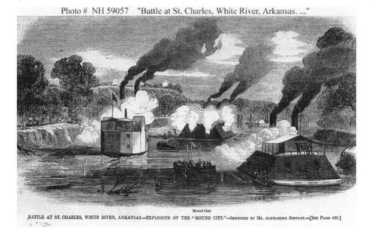

Photo # NH 59057 "Battle at St. Charles, White River, Arkansas. ..."

Explosion aboard the USS Mound City at the Battle of St. Charles on the White River in Arkansas. Harper's Weekly engraving. U.S. Naval Historical Center image NH 59057.

hard lessons were learned, but the navy and the army further realized the importance of cooperation. New campaigns would only solidify this awareness.

NOTES

1. Ulysses S. Grant, *Personal Memoirs of U. S. Grant* (New York: Da Capo, 1982), 193n. Beauregard's total includes General Earl Van Dorn's troops that arrived after the Battle of Shiloh.

2. James Marshall-Cornwall, *Grant as Military Commander* (New York: Van Nostrand Reinhold, 1970), 66.

3. Grant, *Personal Memoirs of U. S. Grant*, 199.

4. Allan Nevins, *The War for the Union, Vol. I: The Improvised War 1861–1862* (New York: Charles Scribner's Sons, 1959), 378. Pope, a native of Kentucky, was a friend of Abraham Lincoln and was Mary Todd Lincoln's second cousin. He commanded the District of North and Central Missouri. Pope had a very contentious relationship with General Frémont and actively worked against the department commander to have Frémont removed from command.

5. *OR* 8: 625.

6. Island No. 10 no longer exists. The Mississippi River has destroyed all traces of it.

7. See *OR Atlas*, plate 10.

8. *ORN* 22: 316.

9. *OR Atlas*, plate 10.

10. *ORN* 22: 315.

11. William M. Fowler Jr., *Under Two Flags: The American Navy in the Civil War* (Annapolis, Md.: Naval Institute Press, 2001), 152.

12. Henry Walke, "The Gunboats at Belmont & Fort Henry," *Battles and Leaders* 1: 439–40.

13. Bern Anderson, *By Sea and by River: The Naval History of the Civil War* (New York: Knopf, 1962), 104.

14. *ORN* 22: 731–34; J. W. Bissell, "Sawing Out the Channel Above Island Number Ten," in *Battles and Leaders of the Civil War*, vol. 1: *Opening Battles*, ed. Robert Underwood Johnson (Edison, N.J.: Castle/Book Sales, 1990; orig. pub. Century Company, 1883), pp. 460–62.

15. *ORN* 22: 732.

16. Anderson, *By Sea and by River*, 105–6; Jack D. Coombe, *Thunder along the Mississippi: The River Battles That Split the Confederacy* (New York: Sarpedon, 1996), 90–91.

17. *OR* 8: 119.

18. *ORN* 22: 734–35.

19. *ORN* 22: 724.

20. *ORN* 22: 730; Larry J. Daniel and Lynn N. Bock, *Island No. 10: Struggle for the Mississippi Valley* (Tuscaloosa: University of Alabama Press, 1996), 142; Spencer C. Tucker, *Andrew Foote: Civil War Admiral on Western Waters* (Annapolis, Md.: Naval Institute Press, 2000), 188.

21. *ORN* 22: 730–31.

22. *ORN* 22: 728–35.

23. *ORN* 22: 316.

24. *ORN* 23: 3–4.

25. Walke, "Gunboats at Belmont & Fort Henry," 446.

26. *ORN* 23: 3.

27. Paul H. Silverstone, *Warships of the Civil War Navies* (Annapolis, Md.: Naval Institute Press, 1989), 226–27.

28. *ORN* 23: 4.

29. *ORN* 23: 6–7. After McClellan's Peninsular Campaign in Virginia failed, Pope was ordered east to command the Army of Virginia. Frémont, then operating poorly in the Shenandoah Valley, resigned over the assignment. Pope led his forces to disaster at the Second Battle of Manassas on August 30. He was relieved of command on September 12, and the Army of Virginia was merged into the Army of the Potomac. When Pope went east, the command of the Army of the Mississippi was turned over to Major General William S. Rosecrans. Its last operations were at Corinth and Iuka before it was decommissioned on October 26, 1862. The bulk of its troops were placed in the 13th Army Corps.

30. *ORN* 23: 7–10.

31. *ORN* 23: 5.

32. *ORN* 22: 316.

33. Tucker, *Andrew Foote*, 202–3.

34. *ORN* 23: 13–16.

35. *ORN* 23: 13–16.

36. Silverstone, *Warships of the Civil War Navies*, 226–27.

37. At the time, the cottonclad was thought to be the *General Sumter*; however, since this vessel was seen some days later, it is unclear which vessel the *Carondelet* destroyed.

38. *ORN* 23: 13–17; Silverstone, *Warships of the Civil War Navies*, 170; Coombe, *Thunder along the Mississippi*, 125.

39. Anderson, *By Sea and by River*, 111.

40. *OR* 10: 901.

41. William D. Crandall and Isaac D. Newell, *History of the Ram Fleet and the Mississippi Marine Brigade in the War for the Union on the Mississippi and Its Tributaries: The Story of the Ellets and Their Men* (St. Louis, Mo.: Society of Survivors, 1907), 9–13.

42. For a modern treatment of the unit, see Chester G. Hearn, *Ellet's Brigade: The Strangest Outfit of All* (Baton Rouge: Louisiana State University Press, 2000).

43. Silverstone, *Warships of the Civil War Navies*, 161–62; Crandall and Newell, *History of the Ram Fleet*, 27.

44. Crandall and Newell, *History of the Ram Fleet*, 28–29.

45. Untabulated returns from the Eighth Decennial Census (1860) for Memphis, Tennessee, Western Tennessee Historical Society Library, University of Memphis, McWherter Library Special Collections, Memphis, Tenn.

46. *ORN* 23: 132–34.

47. *ORN* 23: 907–8.

48. Walke, "The Gunboats at Belmont & Fort Henry," 452–62; Anderson, *By Sea and by River*, 113–14; H. Allen Gosnell, *Guns on the Western Waters: The Story of the River Gunboats in the Civil War* (Baton Rouge: Louisiana State University Press, 1949), 94–99; *OR* 10: 906–10.

49. *ORN* 23: 122.

50. *ORN* 23: 907–8.

51. *Mobile Daily Tribune*, July 2, 1862; *ORN* 23: 166.

52. *ORN* 23: 152–59, 164–66.

53. *ORN* 23: 166.

54. *ORN* 23: 196.

55. *ORN* 23: 167.

56. *ORN* 23: 168–69.

5

✛

The Lower River

. . . no one will do wrong who lays his vessel alongside the enemy or tackles the ram. The ram must be destroyed.

—Flag Officer David Glascow Farragut

Any discussion of the efforts of the brown water navy in the Mississippi River Valley is incomplete without knowledge of the Union's blue water naval activities on the lower river. Those efforts are remarkable because the vessels participating were inappropriate for the missions. The twin sagas of the brown and blue water forces are inextricably intertwined.[1]

New Orleans was one of the greatest prizes of the Civil War. The French founded the city on a crescent bend of the Mississippi, ninety miles above its mouth, near Lake Pontchartrain. In 1860, it was the largest and most cosmopolitan city in the South and home to 170,000 people of various nationalities.[2] All the cotton grown in the Mississippi River Valley was processed in New Orleans, making it an extremely wealthy community. At the time of the war, New Orleans was the second-greatest port in the United States after New York.

The greatest battle of the War of 1812 was fought just south of the city, and New Orleanians never forgot that their city had stopped a southern invasion by the British. They believed that any Yankee invasion would meet with the same results. During the War of 1812, Fort St. Philip, located seventy miles below the city on the east bank of the river, was strong enough to deter most of the British fleet. After the war, the U.S. government built other forts below the city and at approaches to the lakes and waterways to its east. Fort Jackson was constructed across the river and downstream a short distance from Fort St. Philip. Two other emplacements, forts Pike and Macomb, guarded the eastern approaches to the city. The Confederates occupied these forts at the beginning of the war and built a huge boom across the river between forts St. Philip and Jackson. Because the government thought these forts were sufficient, New Orleans itself was almost completely unfortified. That belief dearly cost the city; large military contingents were not brought in to its defense.

Most troops raised by the state of Louisiana during the first year of the war were sent to Tennessee and Virginia and to coastal forts. Major General Mansfield Lovell commanded the local forces of about 4,000 men, most of whom were poorly equipped or unarmed. Despite the lack of soldiers and munitions in Louisiana, both Confederate officers and citizens of New Orleans mistakenly felt secure, putting their confidence in the river forts below.

Because so much faith was placed in the forts, numerous projects were undertaken to assure their success, and most were naval. Lightly armed gunboats were built to guard bayous and other approaches downriver and from lakes Pontchartrain and Borgne. These vessels carried few guns, but they were able to operate in the shallow depths of the swampy streams. Other projects were more advanced. The Confederates converted a boat into the *Manassas*, a cigar-shaped semisubmersible, and mounted on it a single 64-pounder cannon that fired through a forward port. Although it resembled a submarine, it was not designed to operate beneath the surface.[3] At the same time, two giant ironclads, the *Louisiana* and the *Mississippi*, were under construction. Had they been completed, they would have commanded the Mississippi River, serving as a threat to any force below as well as to the Western Gunboat Flotilla. These were the gunboats that Foote had expected to challenge him at Island No. 10, but at that time the manufacturers were behind schedule; neither vessel had been equipped with engines, and both had lacked full armor and armament.

The Union navy in the Gulf of Mexico blockaded the multiple mouths of the Mississippi River until late September 1861, when the *Richmond*, followed by the *Vincennes*, *Preble*, *Water Witch*, and *Frolic*, slowly moved up to the Head of the Passes, the southernmost point on the river before it split into its several exit channels. This action prevented blockade runners from using the Mississippi. The small flotilla had no intention of taking New Orleans but rather to enforce the blockade from a central point.

The Confederates waited until the evening of October 11 to force the issue. The Confederate ram *Manassas*, accompanied by several towboats and fire rafts, descended on the Union warships. The Rebels found the vessels anchored in a haphazard manner with their crews simply conducting onboard duties.[4] The *Manassas* tried to ram the *Richmond* but glanced off a coal barge before penetrating the hull of the sloop. Had the collier had not absorbed most of the blow, it is likely the concussion would have sunk the *Richmond*. The ram lost its smokestacks from the impact but continued to fight. The Rebel towboat crews ignited pine knots and other combustibles on fire rafts and sent them against the wooden-hulled blockaders, but all missed. At the same time, the Union vessel captains, fearing for the safety of their crews, tried to escape. Both the *Vincennes* and the *Richmond* ran aground in the soft mud. As the Rebel towboats fired at targets of opportunity, Captain Robert Handy of the *Vincennes* panicked; he first ordered his crew to abandon ship and then ordered them to return. Cooler heads prevailed, and both sloops were hauled off the muddy bottom of the river. The Union vessels suffered minor damage and retreated into the broad waters of the Gulf. The actions of the captains disgusted Secretary Gideon Welles, and he removed both Captain John Pope of the *Richmond* and Handy from command in disgrace.[5]

Union officials turned their attention to plans that would give them control of the lower Mississippi. Gideon Welles, Gustavus Fox, and Commander David Dixon Porter were the first Federal officials to suggest taking New Orleans with a fleet.[6] In late 1861, Fox proposed that the blue water fleet blockade vessels steam upstream, neutralize the forts, and join the Western Gunboat Flotilla and thus control the river.[7] Porter outlined the plan, but he was not allowed to lead the operation.[8] The scenario had three components. First, naval vessels from the blockade would provide the firepower and mobility to control the lower river. Next, a flotilla of mortar schooners, each equipped with a single huge weapon, would reduce forts Jackson and St. Philip and allow the blockade ships to reach New Orleans. Finally, an army force of 20,000 soldiers would attack and occupy the city after landing downstream. Welles selected Captain David Glascow Farragut to lead the operation and had him designated as a flag officer. To preserve secrecy, Welles divided the Gulf Blockading Squadron into two parts: the East Gulf Blockading Squadron was responsible for the coast east of Pensacola to Cape Canaveral, Florida, while the West Gulf Blockading Squadron lined the Alabama, Mississippi, Louisiana, and Texas coastlines.[9] Farragut was given command of the latter.

Farragut quickly assembled his fleet of screw sloops, gunboats, and auxiliary vessels. Additionally, he had thirteen mortar schooners, commanded by Porter, his foster brother. Farragut's flagship was the *Hartford*, which was thereafter linked to the future admiral. The fleet staged from Ship Island, south of Biloxi, Mississippi. They encountered difficulty entering the Mississippi when the *Colorado* grounded on the sandbar at the channel's mouth. Following the laborious work of hauling the deep-draft ship over the sandbar, the column proceeded unimpeded and occupied the Head of Passes. Farragut then ordered crews to prepare the vessels for the operation. The bow of each vessel was lowered to prevent the ships from slipping sideways in the currents. Chains were hung over the sides to deflect artillery shells, and ladders were positioned so that carpenters could be dropped over the sides to repair shell holes. Hawsers were prepared to establish towing capability should a vessel become disabled. The crews also covered all the white paint on the ships' sides with mud to make the vessels less visible. Finally, the tops of the mortar schooners were adorned with trees to hide them from the forts.[10] Surveyors prepared seven anchorage sites for the mortar schooners on the west bank below Fort Jackson and six on the east bank below Fort St. Philip. The mortars began bombarding the forts on April 18, 1862, and for five days they poured about 16,800 rounds into and around the forts, damaging but not reducing them.[11]

Farragut finally lost patience and decided to attack the forts. In order to do so, he knew the vessels would have to break the boom, which the Confederates had covered with chains and cables before they stretched it across the river. He sent gunboats to sever it on the night of April 20. They breached the boom, but the Confederates drove them back and repaired the damage almost immediately. Farragut made another attempt to break the boom during the night of April 24. This time he was successful, and the fleet proceeded en masse.

Two small sloops led the way and engaged Fort St. Philip. The second group consisted of the *Hartford*, *Brooklyn*, and *Richmond*, which were to move against Fort Jackson. The third wave was to compromise the boom and support the first two groups. At 3:30 A.M., after an hour and a half of steaming, the forts began firing on the first two groups, and cohesion of movement was lost in this attack. The *Hartford* ran aground near Fort St. Philip and soon was struck and set afire by a torched raft. Flames ran up the side and licked at the masts before being extinguished. The Confederate gunboats made futile attacks on the Union sloops, and most were destroyed or fled upstream. The *Manassas*, which had remained upstream under the protection of the forts' guns, joined other more conventional rams, fire rafts, and the unfinished *Louisiana*, which formed a floating battery. Moving downstream, the *Manassas* tried to ram several targets before it struck the *Brooklyn* and suffered extensive damage. The captain beached the vessel before it sank. The *Louisiana* added to the confusion by firing at every vessel that passed nearby. By 4:40 A.M., every Union vessel had received hits, but the fleet had moved above the forts. The *Hartford* itself had been struck thirty-two times, but only the gunboat *Varuna* was lost after the Confederates rammed it repeatedly. Farragut sent word for Porter to demand the surrender of the forts, while the flag officer assembled the warships at Quarantine Station. He left two gunboats to protect the army and told Major General Benjamin F. Butler to land his troops at Breton Sound, near the station. The sloops reached the War of 1812 battlefield and received heavy artillery fire, which each vessel in the line returned. The Confederates desperately filled some older vessels with cotton, set them on fire as giant fire rafts, and set them adrift. These did no damage, and no other opposition was encountered as the Union fleet anchored near the levees of New Orleans.[12]

The forts did not immediately surrender. Porter sent a demand that the Rebels ignored, and he then continued the bombardment the next day. The sloops that passed the forts and received fire from the *Louisiana* were unsure whether it was powered. Porter sent six of his schooners downstream for safety and demanded the forts' the surrender again on April 27. Many of the Rebel soldiers in the forts mutinied that night, and they surrendered the following day. As negotiations continued aboard Porter's flagship, the unmanned *Louisiana* floated downstream, engulfed in flames, before exploding near Fort St. Philip. The battle for New Orleans was over, and after the navy contended with a threatening mob, General Butler took control of the city on May 1. With his mission accomplished, Porter took the schooners to Ship Island. Although Mobile, Alabama, might have been an easy target, he reoccupied Pensacola, Florida, and most of his schooners were sent to strengthen the blockade.

The fleet then advanced in a series of rapid leapfrog actions. Farragut had orders to control the Mississippi River north of New Orleans and join with Flag Officer Charles H. Davis's ironclads at Memphis. The *Richmond*

Farragut's Fleet Passing the Forts below New Orleans *by Mauritz Frederik Hendrik De Haas. Historic New Orleans Collection.*

forayed on May 3 but ran aground in an attempt to reach the Louisiana capital at Baton Rouge. Four days later, the *Iroquois* arrived there and demanded the capital's surrender. Although the city featured no practical defenses, it refused to surrender. Commander J. S. Palmer sent a shore party to the former Federal arsenal and raised the U.S. flag. The *Iroquois* moved close into the bank with its guns loaded, guarding the small group of Union sailors ashore. Farragut arrived at Baton Rouge on May 10 and immediately sent the *Oneida*, under Commander S. P. Lee, upriver to demand the surrender of Natchez, Mississippi. Because the town's citizens could not bear to see naval gunfire destroy its magnificent homes, they surrendered immediately.[13] On May 18, Lee steamed farther upstream to take Vicksburg, Mississippi. This all seemed unbelievably easy, and up to that point, it was. The navy sloops steamed hundreds of river miles above New Orleans with only token resistance, but the blue water vessels were moving into a narrowing river without knowing its depth.

Lee arrived at Vicksburg on May 18 and observed for the first time the already fortified bluffs that rose 290 feet above the river. When the commander demanded the town's surrender, James L. Autry, the post's military commander, replied tersely, "I have to state that Mississippians don't know, and refuse to learn, how to surrender to an enemy. If Commodore Farragut or Brigadier General Butler can teach them, let them come and try."[14] Confederate Brigadier General Martin Luther Smith responded to Lee's demand, stating, "Regarding the surrender of the defenses, I have to reply that having been ordered here to hold these defenses, it is my intention to do so as long as in my power."[15] The mayor of Vicksburg responded that he had created no defenses. The bluffs provided massive defensive capability. Lee then gave the authorities twenty-four hours to evacuate the women and children because if he attacked, the navy could not avoid damage to the town.[16] The naval vessels did nothing, and the Rebel gunners on the bluffs watched them. On May 24, Farragut arrived with army transports filled with 1,500 of Butler's soldiers. After conferring, the officers decided that nothing could be done. The Confederates had more than enough men and guns. Worse, the navy's guns could not be elevated to meet the threat atop the bluffs. Farragut returned to New Orleans on May 30, leaving Butler's troops in Baton Rouge. Farragut wanted to leave the river with its fickle currents and too-close banks. The first attempt at taking Vicksburg was a failure.

President Lincoln put great pressure on Gideon Welles to have Farragut join Flag Officer Davis and to take the city. Accordingly, Farragut returned to the area below Vicksburg on June 26 with three of his sloops and several auxiliary vessels. Porter assisted with seventeen of the mortar schooners, and Butler sent 3,000 men under Brigadier General Thomas Williams. The mortar boats initiated a brisk but ineffective bombardment

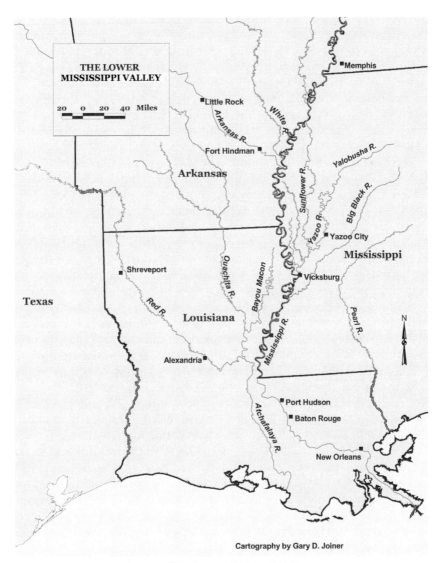

THE LOWER
MISSISSIPPI VALLEY

20 0 20 40 Miles

Map of the lower Mississippi Valley.

since the bluffs obscured the city from the navy's vantage point. After two days of steady firing, the observers saw little damage to the defenses. Farragut realized he should land the soldiers, but he saw no viable place. Williams reported to Farragut that he commanded far too few men to take Vicksburg. Not wanting to withdraw a second time, Farragut decided to run past the batteries to join Davis, whom he hoped was near.

General Williams was under orders from Butler to land on the Louisiana side and cut a canal to bypass the batteries if he could not take Vicksburg directly. Several commanders had similar ideas, but Williams was on the scene and began cutting a big ditch across the De Soto peninsula.[17] He used his own men plus slaves from nearby plantations. The normal summer drop of the river's level, a problem very apparent to Farragut, made the arduous work even more difficult. Mosquitoes infested this swampy region, and the men quickly fell ill. The canal was destined to fail.

The sloops steamed upstream in the early-morning hours of June 28. Rebel batteries spotted the intruders and began firing down on them. The sloops returned fire as best they could, while the mortar schooners, anchored below, poured spectacular but ineffective fire over the bluffs. By dawn, *Hartford, Iroquois,* and some of the support boats had passed the batteries, but the *Brooklyn* and two other vessels had not and turned back. Farragut was pleased that the *Hartford* had received only minor damage but was dismayed that his force was severed. Prior to the attempt, Farragut had made contact with some of the Ellet rams by land reconnaissance and joined three of them. He requested that they send one ram back to Memphis to have Flag Officer Davis bring the gunboat flotilla and also that they wire Halleck to send a force of infantry to assist in capturing Vicksburg.[18] Davis complied, and all the gunboats that were not on the White River expedition joined Farragut. Among these were four mortar rafts that began firing on the bluffs in concert with Porter's schooners. Halleck replied that he could not spare any men from Corinth, which he had occupied a month earlier. The department commander had not decided what to do next, but Vicksburg was not on his agenda.

Even with the additional boats, both Davis and Farragut decided that the navy could not take Vicksburg alone, and Farragut wired this decision to Welles. Several days later, Welles responded by ordering Porter and twelve of his schooners to proceed to Hampton Roads, Virginia. Farragut requested that he be allowed to take the sloops downriver past the batteries to a place where the water was deeper.[19] Several days would pass before a reply arrived.

While waiting, the rams *Lancaster, Monarch,* and *Queen of the West* went on a reconnaissance mission to find the CSS *Arkansas,* which was believed to be nearby. The *Arkansas,* commanded by Isaac Brown, was an unusual ironclad. The armor was tilted at a forty-five-degree angle unlike that of other Confederate vessels, and this gave it the appearance of a house on a raft. The boat sported twin propellers, but the powerful engines raised from a sunken steamboat never worked properly and often died. Conversely, the ram alone was sixteen feet long and ten feet wide and attached to ten feet of solid timber. Armament consisted of two 9-inch smoothbores, two 64-pounders, two 6-inch rifles, and two 32-pounder smoothbores. The eighteen-inch-thick iron plate and railroad iron casemate were from salvaged metal and colored a rusty brown.[20] The *Arkansas*'s rusted brown iron made it all but invisible when the vessel was near a riverbank. This would be a benefit in the days to come.

On the morning of July 15, the *Arkansas* moved downstream near the mouth of the Yazoo River. A Union tug saw it and turned around to warn the fleet. The nearest warships were the ironclad *Carondelet*, the timberclad *Tyler*, and the ram *Queen of the West*. The *Carondelet* and *Tyler* fired at the Rebel ironclad at close range with no visible effect. The *Arkansas* fired point-blank into the *Carondelet*, doing heavy damage. Commander Walke nursed his stricken vessel to shore, grounding before it sank. Both the *Queen of the West* and the *Tyler* fled before they could fall victim to the powerful intruder. The *Arkansas* chased the boats out into the Mississippi, where the remainder of Farragut's fleet kept up just enough steam to maintain the engines.

Despite all the firing heard from upstream, the fleet of thirty vessels was caught unaware. Davis's ironclads were anchored on the east bank of the river. Ellet's rams were near the mouth of the Yazoo, the army transports were tied up to the Louisiana side, and the mortar schooners were downstream. Brown had few choices. He chose to steam as quickly as possible through the middle of the Yankee fleet and to seek the protection of the batteries on the bluffs. The *Arkansas*'s stack was damaged from the

CSS Arkansas. *Watercolor by R. G. Skerrett. U.S. Naval Historical Center image NH 61912-KN.*

last encounter, and its steam pressure was low; however, the river current added speed. Brown fired into targets as they appeared, severely damaging the *Lancaster*. The *Arkansas* also received hits from the *Hartford* and exchanged rounds with the *Benton*. Then the Confederate ironclad seemed to disappear against the bluffs. It arrived at the wharfs and was among the protective batteries. Farragut was "mortified" by the action.[21] He asked Davis to help him take out the ironclad, but the other commander was reticent. Davis reconsidered and allowed the *Essex*, *Queen of the West*, and *Sumter* to make an attack. The group closed in near the bank under the guns on the bluffs. As the *Essex* approached, it exchanged fire with the *Arkansas* and was damaged. The *Queen of the West* rammed the ironclad, but it took a hard pounding from the shore guns before finally running aground. The ram was able to extricate itself and move upstream to safety. The *Essex* and *Sumter* were forced to run the gauntlet to achieve safety downstream, while the *Arkansas* remained at the wharf.[22] The pair was now cut off from Davis's command. Additionally, the river continued to fall, and Farragut was forced to move his squadron downstream on July 24. The army transports picked up General Williams with his sick and disgusted men, leaving the slaves to whom they promised freedom without it. The second attempt to take Fortress Vicksburg had failed miserably.

The Confederates planned to recapture Baton Rouge. They wanted the *Arkansas* to reinforce the army and keep the Union navy occupied. On August 5, the Rebels attacked their former capital. The *Arkansas*, on its way to assist them, suffered engine problems and grounded itself on the west-

USS Essex. *Library of Congress image LCB816-3134.*

ern bank just upstream from Baton Rouge. After helping repulse the Confederate attack, the *Essex* steamed upstream to attack the *Arkansas*. As it approached, the crew set the *Arkansas* ablaze to keep it out of Union hands.

With this final action, Farragut pulled the fleet back to New Orleans. Thankful to be leaving the tortuous river, he earnestly began preparations for the fleet's next mission, which he believed would be an attack on Mobile, Alabama. Farragut left the failed attempts to capture Vicksburg behind him as the vessels pushed out of the Mississippi River into the deep, blue water of the Gulf.

NOTES

1. The efforts of the U.S. Navy on the lower Mississippi River are not, strictly speaking, within the focus of this book. The events recounted in this chapter are included to provide the reader with a summary of the actions under Admiral David G. Farragut and do not constitute a full history the battles involved. For a more complete history, see Charles L. Dufour, *The Night the War Was Lost* (Garden City, N.Y.: Doubleday, 1960); John D. Winters, *The Civil War in Louisiana* (Baton Rouge: Louisiana State University Press, 1963); Ivan Musicant, *Divided Waters* (New York: HarperCollins, 1995); and Bern Anderson, *By Sea and by River: The Naval History of the Civil War* (New York: Knopf, 1962), among others.

2. Eighth Decennial Census (1860), untabulated returns for Orleans Parish, Louisiana.

3. Silverstone, Paul H. *Warships of the Civil War Navies* (Annapolis, Md.: Naval Institute Press, 1989), 203.

4. Winters, *Civil War in Louisiana*, 50–52.

5. Winters, *Civil War in Louisiana*, 53.

6. Gideon Welles published his account of the plans that he and Fox created in the November and December 1871 issues of *Galaxy* magazine. Porter published his account in *Incidents and Anecdotes* in 1885. Porter, addicted to hyperbole, took too much credit but certainly had a central role in the operation.

7. Howard P. Nash Jr., *A Naval History of the Civil War* (New York: A. S. Barnes and Company, 1972), 122.

8. Musicant, *Divided Waters*, 218–22.

9. Anderson, *By Sea and by River*, 118.

10. Anderson, *By Sea and by River*, 119.

11. *Battles and Leaders* 2: 34; Jack D. Coombe, *Thunder along the Mississippi: The River Battles That Split the Confederacy* (New York: Sarpedon, 1996), 106.

12. Winters, *Civil War in Louisiana*, 85–102.

13. *ORN* 18: 490–91.

14. *ORN* 18: 492.

15. *ORN* 18: 492.

16. *ORN* 18: 493.

17. Commander H. H. Bell transmitted such an idea on June 14, 1862. See *ORN* 18: 582. The De Soto peninsula was on the Louisiana side. It forced the river to make a hairpin turn near the base of the bluffs. By cutting a canal across its base, the Union navy would be able to bypass the Vicksburg batteries in relative safety.

18. Although Farragut could have ordered rather than requested, this was a courtesy. Davis was of parallel rank, but it was granted at a later date, making Farragut the senior officer. Davis's rank as flag officer was not confirmed until the death of Rear Admiral Foote on June 26. Halleck was the department commander. Although Farragut was of parallel rank, he had no sway over the recalcitrant army general.

19. *ORN* 18: 579–80.

20. Silverstone, *Warships of the Civil War Navies*, 202.

21. Anderson, *By Sea and by River*, 133.

22. Isaac Brown was wounded in the action and requested leave to Grenada, Mississippi to recuperate. He would never see his vessel again. Coombe, *Thunder along the Mississippi*, 162.

6

✛

The Mississippi Squadron

Audacity and drive are born of the soul, and do not die ever in some
great leaders.

—Naval Historical Division,
Civil War Naval Chronology 1861–1865, part 2, 100

Although not recognized for its significance at the time, the Union
navy's aborted attempt to capture Vicksburg heralded a turning
point in the war in the West. The continued separation of the blue and
brown water squadrons, the lack of cooperation from the army, and the
expanding strength of the Vicksburg fortifications all forced Abraham
Lincoln and his planners to make some tough decisions. In the following
months, both the army and the naval forces in the West would see radical
changes not only in who led them but also in how and where they would
fight.

The Union navy was instrumental in rupturing the forts that guarded
the navigable approaches to the southern heartland, and great expanses
of the Mississippi River Valley had been opened. The lower Mississippi
was under Federal control, but General Butler had squandered a golden
opportunity to bring New Orleans and the surrounding area into the
Union fold as a model for easy reconstruction. His lack of cooperation
with the navy not only doomed the Vicksburg expedition but also forced
a reconsideration of all future efforts in the lower river valley. Major General Nathaniel Prentiss Banks, another political general from Massachusetts, replaced Butler in November 1862. Banks's assignment reflected
Lincoln's hope that Butler's ill will could be overturned and that the

southern states could be repatriated with relative ease. This model, later termed the "ten percent plan," was the core of Lincoln's formula for ending the war and reuniting the nation.[1]

Efforts north of Vicksburg included even greater changes. General Halleck's refusal to send land forces to assist Flag Officer Charles H. Davis in taking the bluff fortress forced the Western Gunboat Flotilla into a defensive stance. The flotilla, minus the *Essex* and *Sumpter*, patrolled the Tennessee and Cumberland rivers in addition to the Mississippi River north of Vicksburg. The Confederates harassed the Union army transport convoys with guerrilla raids and mobile artillery batteries as the transports headed into northern Mississippi to supply Halleck's army.

Without naval escort, the great army was in danger of being cut off or at least forced to fight its way back to safe Union-held territory, but Halleck insisted that the inland navy was a subordinate arm of the land forces. Secretary Gideon Welles had guaranteed this relationship with his prior orders; however, the flotilla's success in opening long reaches of southern rivers, sometimes without the army's assistance, forced Welles to rethink his position. After Halleck and Butler had refused to supply adequate support for the naval missions, Welles and Assistant Secretary Gustavus Fox urged the president, the cabinet, and Congress to move the fleet under the direct control of the Navy Department. These intense lobbying efforts were successful, and in August, Congress passed legislation transferring the Western Gunboat Flotilla to the navy with an effective date of October 1, 1862.[2] The name was changed to "the Mississippi Squadron," reflecting its elevated status and importance, but this was just the beginning of the reorganization.

Welles had radical changes in mind. He wanted Flag Officer Davis transferred to Washington to be chief of the Bureau of Navigation. Welles needed someone he could trust in charge of this important post, and to show that this move was vital and not a demotion or an ill reflection on the flag officer's performance, he named Davis an acting rear admiral.[3] Fox urged that Commander David Dixon Porter be named as the squadron's first commanding officer. Porter had been a favorite of the assistant secretary since his actions at Fort Pickens and the preparation and execution of the plan to capture New Orleans. Welles supported the idea, even though it was unprecedented for a commander to be elevated ahead of all the captains in the navy. He took the nomination to the president, who was wary of the choice. Lincoln believed, with good reason, that Porter was brash and acted impulsively. Porter's enormous drive to succeed was, in fact, exceeded only by his ego, which grew larger as the war was fought.[4] Nevertheless, Welles swayed Lincoln when, in favor of the promotion, he wrote, "His selection will be unsatisfactory to many, but his field of operations is peculiar, and a young and active officer is required for the duty to which he is assigned."[5] Both Lincoln and Welles wanted a man in command who was fearless, thought unconventionally, and could work within the spheres of naval and army command. They could not have picked a better candidate. Porter possessed the vital ability to identify a problem and create a solution, regardless of what effort was required. Although this sometimes placed him and his forces in dire straits, it gave him success more often than not. Once Porter was promoted, many senior officers were upset since they had waited decades for a promotion, but Porter also had waited twenty years between promotions from lieutenant to commander.[6] He took command on October 15 with the rank of acting rear admiral.

After a short inspection of his resources, the new admiral immediately bombarded Washington with a long list of needs: more gunboats, more auxiliary craft, more artillery, more officers, more crewmen, and more of anything and everything with which he was to wage war on the western waters. He quickly assessed the gunboats under his command and realized that the next phase of the war required a new type of craft that would be better suited for the shallow bottoms and narrow widths of smaller streams. The City-class ironclads were by no means obsolete, but their use in narrow southern streams would be as constrictive as Farragut's screw sloops were in the Mississippi River. Porter was willing to send them into harm's way, but he wanted new vessels that would be more versatile hybrids, carrying adequate weapons with lighter armor and having a shallower draft. The primary missions of this new type of vessel would be convoy protection and infantry support.

The resulting vessels were tinclads. These were mostly sternwheelers that carried one-and-one-quarter-inch armor plating. The new tinclads were even more versatile than expected. Eventually, the U.S. Navy had sixty-three of these tough craft, and some of the vessels, particularly the *Marmora*, *Fort Hindman*, *Juliet*, *Cricket*, *Covington*, and *Signal*, became known for their exploits. The *Cricket* was a typical example of a stern-wheeler tinclad. The navy acquired it in November 1862, two years after its construction in Pittsburgh. The boat was 154 feet long with a width of twenty-eight feet and

Rear Admiral David Dixon Porter. U.S. Naval Historical Center image NH 47394.

Mississippi Squadron at anchor, possibly at Memphis. Library of Congress image LCB816-3132.

two inches, a draft of four feet, and two engines and two boilers for power. In January 1863, it mounted six 24-pounder howitzers. In August 1864, the armaments consisted of two 20-pounder rifles, one 12-pounder, and four 24-pounder howitzers.[7]

For additional vessels, Porter was open to new ideas, particularly those of James B. Eads, the mastermind behind the Pook Turtles. After meeting with Porter, Eads and others designed and built a series of exotic craft for river use. Eads built the *Neosho* and *Osage*, the only two stern-wheeler monitors of the war. Each boasted a seventy-eight-ton turret, which mounted two 11-inch smoothbore guns, near the bow. The decks were curved downward on both sides, giving them the nickname "turtle backs." The turrets carried six-inch armor plating. The decks and other surfaces sported two-and-one-half-inch-thick armor.[8] To equalize the weight, the engine and wheel were mounted close to the stern, making the monitors very powerful but also difficult to handle in tight turns. Additionally, Porter's brother, William, designed two powerful but exceedingly odd vessels, the *Choctaw* and the *Lafayette*. These were originally clad with India rubber as armor because the rubber was flexible, and it was easier to work with on complex surfaces. Designers felt that cannonballs would simply ricochet off the rubber, doing no damage. Unfortunately, they failed to consider that it was impossible to calculate in which direction the still-deadly projectile would go, leading to fear among crews on other vessels. In addition, the designers failed to consider the fact that rubber rotted rather quickly in the moist southern climate. The vessels

Photo # NH 55524   USS Cricket (1863-65) during the Civil War

USS Cricket. *U.S. Naval Historical Center image NH 55524.*

were converted to ironclads, while the rubber remained intact.[9] The largest of the ironclads was the *Eastport*, captured by Seth L. Phelps on an earlier mission. After it was redesigned, the side-wheeler was 280 feet long with six-and-one-half-inch-thick armor and eight guns, including two 100-pounder rifles.[10] The use of these guns as bow guns displayed the intent for the gunboat to be an ironclad killer.

Certainly, there were vessels that did not perform up to expectations, particularly three ironclads quickly designed, built, and launched in 1862. These were the *Tuscumbia, Indianola,* and *Chillicothe.* All three gunboats were side-wheelers and suffered from poor design, inadequate armor, and fickle propulsion systems. Another boat that approached the status of albatross was the *Ozark,* a hybrid monitor with a revolving turret supplemented by single guns fore and aft. It was underpowered, and because of its design, the turret was effective only when firing at targets on either side. Porter referred to it as "a miserable vessel."[11]

The admiral's favorite boat was the side-wheeler *Black Hawk,* which was classified as a large tinclad. Measuring 260 feet in length, it was 100 feet longer than a typical tinclad. Porter made the *Black Hawk* his flagship. Its extra length and unique black-and-white paint scheme made it easily recognizable. Originally named the *New Uncle Sam,* it had been a luxurious river cruise boat before the war. The vessel was renamed on December 13, 1862. After conversion, the *Black Hawk* mounted thirteen guns. It is

USS Neosho. *Image misidentified as USS Osage. U.S. Naval Historical Center image NH 49997.*

unclear whether it bore the typical one-and-one-half-inch armor.[12] Porter kept some of the cruise ship amenities such as the rich wood paneling and the chandeliers in "officer country." It included stalls for horses, and there are many accounts of Porter riding a horse down the gangplank for excursions ashore.[13]

The squadron also possessed a number of river auxiliary and service vessels needed to repair and replenish the war craft and also to feed and tend to the crews. Among these unsung craft were the tugs *Fern*, *Dahlia*, and *Thistle*; the *Red Rover*, which was the navy's first dedicated hospital ship; the ordnance boat *Judge Torrence*; the *Samson*, a floating machine shop; the mail/supply vessel *New National*; pump boats *Champion No. 3* and *Champion No. 5*; and the river service vessels *Benefit* and *William H. Brown*. These vessels operated at the rear but were also deployed within the squadron as necessary. Each was a target of enemy fire, and some were lost.

This buildup of the fleet took several months and occupied most of the available shipyards in the upper Mississippi River Valley. Porter's rapid acquisition of new or captured vessels along with the refitting of all the boats into a new type of naval strike force forever changed the war on the western waters. Once the Mississippi Squadron was rightly placed under the jurisdiction of the U.S. Navy, one troublesome question nagged at Porter: what should be done with Ellet's ram fleet?

USS Black Hawk. *Admiral Porter's flagship. U.S. Naval Historical Center image NH 49993.*

Porter did not intend to allow an independent naval force to operate within his jurisdiction. The army quartermaster boats ferried men and supplies, but combatant vessels were another matter entirely. The rams had proven very effective against the Confederate defense fleet at Memphis, but Porter had no way of knowing if any other vessels were arrayed against him. The admiral's nature was to control all available assets completely; thus, he requested that a new entity be created and that the rams be folded into it. The squadron needed an amphibious force of marines to secure steamboat landings in forward areas, to conduct limited onshore reconnaissance missions, and to assist in patrol duties. The force would be semi-independent but operate under naval orders. This brigade would have its own support vessels under the naval umbrella.

Alfred Ellet, commanding the ram fleet, agreed to the idea. He was made a brigadier general and ordered to build the unit, which he called the Mississippi Marine Brigade. Since Ellet was not allowed to transfer marines from existing units or raid army or navy recruiting billets openly, he recruited from hospitals. Looking for veterans who wanted to come back into service, he promised the men bonuses, the advantage of going into missions aboard clean vessels with good conditions and food, and fame.[14] The hybrid brigade consisted of an infantry regiment and a cavalry battalion. Ellet procured several vessels to support the rams. Among them were the transports *Autocrat, B. J. Adams, Baltic, Diana,* and *T. D. Horner;* the commissary and quartermaster boat *Fairchild;* the tugs *Alf Cutting, Cleveland,* and

Brigadier General Alfred Ellet. U.S. Naval Historical Center image NH 49621.

Bell Darlington; the hospital boat *Woodford*; and the gunboat *Little Rebel*. Although the brigade was very effective in conducting near-shore reconnaissance and inter-diction duties, it earned a well-deserved reputation for being un-ruly, undisciplined, and prone to use incendiary tactics and for being dis-ease ridden, often with smallpox. The Mississippi Marine Brigade was also widely known for treating civil-ians harshly ; committing atrocities; burning Austin, Mississippi, to the ground in 1862; and decimating the lower Red River Valley below Alexandria, Louisiana, in the spring of 1864.[15] By mid-1864, neither the navy nor the army trusted them completely.

When Porter was ordered to take the mortar schooners east to Hamp-ton Roads, Virginia, he had ample time to visit the naval headquarters at Washington, D.C., and attend to his social obligations. At Lincoln's request, Porter met with Major General John McClernand, a political general and friend of the president.[16] President Lincoln gave McClernand authority to raise an army in the West and to act independently in capturing Vicksburg. Realizing the general's con-nection to the president, Porter saw the benefits of cooperating and ini-tially offered to help. After he reached his command, however, he had sec-ond thoughts and attempted to back away, believing that the scheme would compromise the efforts of Major General Ulysses S. Grant. By that time, Grant had succeeded Halleck in command of the western theater af-ter Halleck moved east to become chief of staff of the army.[17] Grant had little use for McClernand, and this only deepened when it became appar-ent that the new army was being raised from the region where he pro-cured recruits.

Grant pleaded to Halleck for help. Halleck viewed McClernand as a threat to the war effort in the West, and he lobbied the president on Grant's behalf, strongly suggesting that Grant be placed in overall com-mand in the West and that McClernand be made one of Grant's subordi-nates. The president listened to reason and acquiesced.[18] As Grant learned about Lincoln's deal with McClernand, he put a new plan in action. It was hastily conceived and not fully developed. He informed Halleck of his intentions but received no reply from the slow-moving, wary general-turned-bureaucrat. Two separate columns were to strike south in an overland attack to draw the Confederates out into the open, engage and destroy them, and then take Vicksburg. William T. Sherman was a major general in command of one of Grant's corps based in Memphis and was to lead the smaller of the columns. Grant moved to Holly Springs, Mississippi, and established a large supply depot. No word arrived from Washington as November passed.

Eventually, Halleck sent his reserved blessing to the operation. Grant then changed his mind about using three columns and sent Sherman, who was waiting near Holly Springs, back to Memphis to descend the Mississippi River in conjunction with Porter. Sherman was ordered to march 32,000 men down the eastern wall of the Mississippi Valley, cooperate with Porter when needed, and attempt to draw the Confederates out of the fortifications at Vicksburg. The Rebels would then be caught between the hammer of Sherman's Corps and the anvil of Grant's two other corps. Grant pushed into north-central Mississippi in an attempt to crack the Confederate defensive line based on the Yalobusha River near Grenada, Mississippi. When Porter was notified of the mission, he was not very pleased about it, as he had conflicting orders from the secretary of the navy to cooperate with McClernand in any manner possible.

In November, Porter staged his forces at Helena, Arkansas. As per his orders, he awaited McClernand, who had notified the admiral that he intended to strike into the Yazoo River basin to attack Vicksburg from the north, beyond the area, it was hoped, that the Confederates had well fortified. McClernand sent Porter a message that he did not intend to arrive with his force until sometime in December. Porter did not want to be late in his first large-scale effort to assist the army, especially after he rashly rescinded a report previously sent to Secretary Welles that stated that the squadron would be unable to resume operations against Vicksburg until early 1863. He moved most of the fleet to the mouth of the Yazoo prematurely, but he never liked to be inactive. Usually this served Porter well, but at other times it caused a great deal of trouble.

Porter ordered Captain Henry Walke to take the Pook Turtles with some escorts to the mouth of the Yazoo and probe up the stream as far as possible to identify what, if any, resistance the Rebels might offer. Not willing to send his heavy ironclads into the tight confinements of the Yazoo, Walke chose a more cautious approach. After an initial foray by the tinclads *Signal* and *Marmora*, he determined that the river had sufficient depth for the ironclads to operate but that the Confederates had sunk barges to block the channel at various points and had sown numerous torpedoes.[19] Torpedoes were what would later be termed "mines." Not a new invention, they dated back to at least the American Revolution; however, the Confederates improved on earlier designs and named them for a species of stingray from the family *Torpedinidae*.[20] These "infernal machines," as the Union navy called them, were typically three feet long, and the Confederates could detonate them remotely by using insulated wires tied to the mine and strung to galvanic batteries onshore. The system used a telegraphy key as a trigger switch. Others could be detonated by impact via a percussion plunger or with a clock mechanism.[21] The percussion variety was the type used in the Yazoo more than the others.

The pair of gunboats returned with this information, and Walke reconsidered his options. He met with Porter and the newly arrived Sherman, both of whom wanted to use the Yazoo to bypass the already formidable Vicksburg defenses if at all possible. Both the admiral and the general were under the impression that timing was critical. They believed that if Union forces could gain the Chickasaw and Haynes' bluffs before the Confederates could strengthen their positions, the Union could turn the Vicksburg defenses. They also felt that if Grant would adhere to the schedule, the Rebels might be distracted from defending Vicksburg. Porter ordered Walke to ascend the Yazoo again. This time, the *Marmora* and *Signal* made the attempt with the ironclads *Pittsburg* and *Cairo* and the Ellet ram *Queen of the West*. Walke believed that the mines were sown primarily in side channels and that the barges could be pushed away. If

USS Signal. *U.S. Naval Historical Center image NH 49977.*

he found mines, he intended to retrieve them and destroy them safely.[22] The mission began on the morning of December 12, 1862.

Although Porter and Sherman were not in a position to know what was occurring, Grant had moved his force south toward Grenada. Everything worked according to plan until disaster struck on December 20. Confederate General Earl Van Dorn, in what was undoubtedly his best effort in the war, raided Grant's supply depot at Holly Springs. Using 3,500 troopers, the cavalry raid destroyed the bulk of Grant's equipment needed to sustain his column. Almost simultaneously, another raid under Confederate General Nathan Bedford Forrest destroyed seventy miles of railroad track and threatened Memphis. Grant had suddenly lost one of two primary supply depots as his army was striking deep into Rebel territory. His only option was to withdraw his army to Grand Junction in southern Tennessee, where he prepared to meet an attack from either Van Dorn or Forrest. A battle never occurred. Porter's boats were far up the Yazoo without knowing that the primary Union force needed to draw off the Confederates was heading in the wrong direction. Although Porter and Sherman were notified the day after the raid, no recall orders were issued by Grant.[23]

The vessels of the Yazoo River expedition moved into the narrow channel in single file, probably to reduce the likelihood of collateral damage if a torpedo exploded and damaged one of the vessels. The *Marmora* led the column with the *Signal* trailing. The ram followed these, and the heavy ironclads brought up the rear. The column moved slowly, occasionally blasting the woods to scatter sharpshooters and discourage potential attackers. Acting Volunteer Lieutenant Robert Getty, commanding the *Marmora*, encountered a small boat with two men aboard, one white and

USS Marmora. *U.S. Naval Historical Center image NH 52798.*

the other black. Getty interrogated the pair and discovered that the white man knew about the mines. In order to keep the man from notifying the Confederates about the Union vessels, Getty arrested him and placed him in chains, letting the man know that if something happened to his vessel, it would also happen to him.[24]

The vessels moved up the river eighteen to twenty miles from the mouth, where they encountered a large cluster of mines. Getty ordered a small landing craft, known as a cutter, to be detached. He anticipated that he would tie a line ashore and then move in a semicircle to trap any attached lines to the mines. The *Signal* and *Queen of the West* joined the *Marmora*, adding their cutters to the job of clearing the mines. Union sharpshooters exploded the mines as they were brought to the surface.[25]

Lieutenant Commander Thomas O. Selfridge, Jr., commander of the *Cairo*, heard the musketry and believed the gunboats were under attack. He moved the ironclad up to protect the boats and began shelling the woods with canister. Getty indicated to Selfridge that they had found torpedoes, specifically the high explosive percussion-detonated versions.[26] The ironclad captain lowered a boat to inspect the mines. The channel depth at that point was about thirty-six feet with plenty of water under the ironclad's keels. As the *Cairo* steamed slowly into the middle of the channel, a torpedo, possibly two, exploded under its port bow, creating a gaping hole. All hands were removed from the stricken vessel, and everything of value that could be stripped from it was taken in the twelve minutes the ironclad remained afloat. Only the tops of the chimneys showed

USS Cairo. *Vicksburg National Military Park archives.*

USS Cairo *showing damage from the torpedo detonation. USS* Cairo *Museum, Vicksburg National Military Park. Photography by Gary D. Joiner.*

above the water, displaying its distinctive grey stripes.[27] The chimneys were toppled to prevent the Rebels from identifying the location.[28] The *Pittsburg*, commanded by Lieutenant Hoel, landed boats and found the torpedoes under construction behind the levee very near where the *Cairo* was sunk. He also found the batteries and equipment to detonate them. The *Pittsburg* destroyed them, and the vessels then descended the river, occasionally blasting the banks as Rebel sharpshooters appeared.

Porter ordered the gunboats to continue to clear the torpedoes out of the Yazoo. By the fourth week of December, the river was clear to a point near Haynes' Bluff, located less than fifteen miles north of the Vicksburg defenses. This mission included the *Benton*, commanded by Lieutenant Commander William Gwin, and the timberclads *Lexington* and *Tyler*. Gwin was confident that the Rebels had been thwarted in their attempts to reseed the river with torpedoes. The gunboats had fired at irregular intervals to drive sightseers away from the operation.

Porter met Sherman in Memphis, where they decided to renew the effort against the bluffs. Both commanders were to employ naval assets, Sherman using fifty-nine quartermaster corps transports to ferry his men and supplies for an assault on the bluffs and Porter taking advantage of the heavy firepower of the squadron to clear the way and provide fire support against any fortifications. Again, the mission was procedurally sound yet hastily conceived. The commanders were still operating under the idea that Grant was on schedule.

Porter distributed his vessels to best provide massive firepower for the column and also ordered the fleet partitioned into two divisions. Four hundred yards separated the leading vessel, a tinclad, from the remainder of the fleet. Porter would not allow the boats to be packed tightly together; the fleet needed such a distance for protection in case the tinclad struck a mine or onshore batteries attacked. Following the tinclad were an ironclad, the *Benton*, twenty transports carrying the first two infantry divisions, an additional ironclad, a second tinclad, another nineteen transports with the other two infantry divisions, and the remainder of the guard vessels.[29] Captain Henry Walke, aboard the *Carondelet*, commanded the first division, while Lieutenant Gwin, aboard the *Benton*, commanded the second division. The divisions would also trade places; therefore, Captain Walke would lead one day and Lieutenant Gwin the next.

The flotilla entered the Yazoo on December 23 and slowly ascended the narrowing river for the next few days, occasionally firing canister rounds into the woods to scare away any Confederates who might be present. On December 27, the second division of Porter's flotilla led the column. The second division, with the *Benton* in the lead, slowly moved up the river and cleared the area of torpedoes as some of Sherman's men landed on the left bank to help push the Confederates back. Haynes' Bluff and the Walnut Hills loomed ahead of the flotilla, with the former well fortified with at least eight large-bore guns.[30] The Confederate fortifications extended south from Haynes' Bluff across a saddle in the ridge to Snyder's Bluff. From there it continued southward to Drumgould's Bluff, the latter two separated by Virginia Bayou. All three bluffs were well fortified.[31]

As the *Benton* fished for torpedoes, the *Louisville* and *Cincinnati* made a feint on the bluffs to keep the Confederates' attention occupied. The *Baron De Kalb* assisted the *Benton* in removing torpedoes.[32] Throughout the morning and early afternoon, the gunboats fished for and snagged torpedoes. The guns on the bluffs were ominously silent. Sherman's men pushed forward, but too few were sent to make a serious threat on the heights. The boats were warned not to fire in the direction of the infantry in order to prevent deaths from friendly fire.[33]

The *Benton* pushed to within 1,200 yards of the bluffs, and at 2:30 in the afternoon, the Rebel guns opened up on the ironclad. The *Benton*, as well as the *Cairo* and other ironclads, had been recently "shot-proofed," their iron plates augmented with railroad iron in sensitive areas. This method worked on the vertical surfaces and pilothouses but had no effect on plunging fire from above or from torpedoes in the water. A lack of funding and initial rush to complete the ironclads precluded iron plating the decks; this had plagued them at Fort Donelson and did so again on the Yazoo. The Confederates' fire was very effective, and almost every round fired struck the *Benton*. The arcing fire struck several iron plates, unhinging some and cracking others. Some of the shells penetrated the upper deck, wreaking havoc below as they struck boilers and wounded some of the crew.

Lieutenant Gwin disregarded the pleas of his second in command, Acting Lieutenant George P. Lord, and stood on the deck outside the protected pilothouse, shouting orders. Porter later described that Gwin "was of [the] opinion that a pilot-house or casemate was no place for the commander of a ship of war in battle."[34] Gwin believed his place was on the quarterdeck. This was a brave but foolish notion, as a Confederate sharpshooter wounded the lieutenant. The round tore into his chest and ripped away most of the muscles in his right arm, mortally wounding him.[35] Gwin was taken to Porter's cabin and died two days later. In addition, Lord was seriously wounded in the foot, and nine other crewmen were killed or wounded.[36] On that same day, Porter wrote to Sherman, "The *Benton* has been a good deal cut up by the fort, which has heavy rifled guns mounted."[37] Regarding the fort and his greatest fear at the moment, he added, "I was in hopes they [the Confederates] would burst their guns. There were 10 killed and wounded on board the *Benton*. They struck her almost every time they fired. It will be well not to mention this, as the rebels will hear of it and find out the vulnerability of our vessels."[38]

USS Benton *at Vicksburg in 1863. Carte de Visite image in the collection of the author.*

Confederate General Van Dorn's destruction of Grant's supply depot at Holly Springs allowed General John C. Pemberton, the Confederate commander at Vicksburg, to withdraw his troops from the Yalobusha Line and reinforce the already strong defenses surrounding Vicksburg. Sherman's 32,000 troops were not enough to carry the day against the strongly entrenched and heavily armed Rebels. Sherman made futile attempts to attack at nearby Chickasaw Bluffs and suffered 1,776 casualties compared to 187 for the Confederates.[39] Although Sherman complained that some of his brigade commanders were not aggressive enough, he shouldered the blame. Porter withdrew the gunboats, correctly believing that the bluffs could not be taken. Sherman arrived at the same conclusion. The general wrote to his wife a few days later, "Well, we have been to Vicksburg, and it was too much for us, and we have backed out."[40]

The disgruntled Sherman knew he must do something to salvage the horrific loss and possibly his career. He and Porter mused over the matter, and Porter offered to go anywhere to help him. Sherman replied, "Then let's go and thrash out Arkansas Post."[41] This was a Confederate fort called Fort Hindman, located about fifty miles north of the mouth of the Arkansas River. This was a star fort, measuring 300 feet in diameter with twenty-foot-thick walls and an eighteen-foot ditch. It contained eight large guns, and a mile of rifle pits supported it. If taken, they might be able to capture Little Rock, the capital of Arkansas, and possibly salvage the bad situation in which the two commanders found themselves.

Porter's meetings with General McClernand in Washington had been all but forgotten. Much had happened since the beginning of Grant's overland campaign to take Vicksburg to deflect any problems that the political general might cause. McClernand had raised an army of 40,000 raw recruits that he placed into forty-nine regiments. He notified President Lincoln that he had sent them from Springfield, Illinois, to prepare for operations against Vicksburg on December 12, 1862.[42] The troops moved via transports to Memphis, and he asked permission to be placed in overall command of the operations against Vicksburg. He steamed downstream along the Mississippi River toward Memphis with his new army as Porter and Sherman were working their way up the Yazoo to Haynes' Bluff.

As McClernand moved his force to Memphis, Grant received orders that he had been placed in full command over the Vicksburg operation. Grant then sent orders to McClernand at Springfield, Illinois, explaining that McClernand was now under Grant's command as of December 18. McClernand was to be one of four corps commanders under Grant, with General George W. Morgan's and General Andrew Jackson Smith's divisions beneath him. Sherman's corps would consist of General Steele's and General Morgan Lewis Smith's divisions.[43] McClernand, Sherman, and Porter knew nothing of this order. Although Grant's order was sent to McClernand, it took weeks to reach him since he was almost constantly on the move. Sherman and Porter were up the Yazoo River, and neither of them received information of the changes since both were dealing with adversities. The result was confusion and misinformation.

Sherman and Porter reached the mouth of the Yazoo about the same time as McClernand arrived aboard Grant's old flag boat, *Tigress*. McClernand was irate about the Yazoo expedition because his appointment as major general took precedent over Sherman's rank. McClernand took command of all forces and issued orders stating that there had been a change of command, and he was assuming authority over them.[44]

Porter's cordial relationship with McClernand disintegrated. The admiral had worked closely and cooperatively with Sherman, and the two men had bonded under circumstances wrought only by sharing the hardships of command through very adverse conditions. Porter now despised McClernand, especially since the political general had chosen to berate both the admiral and Sherman over their joint expedition. Porter was loyal and valued that characteristic in others. In a single childish fit, McClernand had not only made an enemy of Porter, but he also cemented Porter's formerly remote and rather impersonal working relationship with Grant. Most of the fleet remained at the mouth of the Yazoo, but Sherman, Porter, McClernand, and a sizable contingent of gunboats and transports steamed upstream to Young's Point, just below Milliken's Bend on the Louisiana side of the Mississippi. This became the operational base for future operations.

Although it remains unclear who first decided to attack Fort Hindman, it appears that Porter and Sherman had the greatest sway as to how the operation was to be conducted. Sherman made no mention of the operation in his report to Grant prior to undertaking it. McClernand may have heard about the need for it when he stopped at Helena, Arkansas, during his descent of the river. Porter only mentioned it as Sherman's idea in his postwar books.[45] McClernand certainly viewed it as a path to glory. Sherman and Porter saw the attempt as a practical necessity to clear their back door before resuming operations against Vicksburg and to redeem them from the Haynes' Bluff debacle.

Porter took the lead defining the naval forces. He allocated the ironclads *Baron De Kalb*, *Cincinnati*, and *Louisville*; the Ellet ram *Monarch*; his flagship *Black Hawk*; the timberclad *Tyler*; and the tinclads *Glide* and *Rattler*. Sherman allocated 30,000 men who were moved aboard army transports. This mighty array of vessels was to move against an anticipated garrison of 5,000 Confederate troops.[46]

The fleet left Young's Point on January 4, steaming to the mouth of the White River, to the Arkansas cutoff, and up the Arkansas River. The fleet dropped anchor three miles south of the fort on January 10. Sherman's men deployed on both banks in order to prevent a Confederate escape.

They set up a two-gun section of 20-pounder Parrott rifles on the opposite bank that began firing at the water battery and lower rifle pits. If the project was designed to give McClernand glory or to rehabilitate Sherman's image, it did not unfold as anticipated. On January 11, Porter's vessels' guns blasted the rifle pits and the fort itself, silencing the big guns. Sherman's men stormed the outer rifle pits and moved close to the ramparts. As the Union troops moved steadily forward and Porter's gunboats blasted away, several Confederates in either the 17th and 18th or the 24th and 25th Texas Dismounted Cavalry regiments raised white flags.[47] They were acting without orders; this, in effect, was a mutiny. Sherman's men overran the ramparts and parapet, and the garrison had no choice but to surrender the fort. Perhaps out of necessity or shame at giving up to Sherman's men, the fort surrendered to the navy rather than the Union army.

Both Sherman and Porter made much of this battle, spinning the victory for all it was worth. McClernand did not have a chance to brag much about his portion of the effort. When Grant learned about the battle at Arkansas Post, he railed against McClernand for conducting an unauthorized raid and usurping his authority. He backed off this criticism when Sherman explained what really happened. Grant went to Memphis and assumed his command of all land forces arrayed against Vicksburg and presented McClernand with his new subordinate position. A disgruntled McClernand was now forced to be a closely watched team player. By the end of January 1863, Grant, Porter, and Sherman were all prepared to resume operations against the "American Gibraltar."

NOTES

1. James P. Hollandsworth Jr. *Pretense of Glory: The Life of General Nathaniel P. Banks* (Baton Rouge: Louisiana State University Press, 1998), 84–85.

2. Naval Historical Division, *Civil War Naval Chronology 1861–1865* (Washington, D.C.: U.S. Government Printing Office, 1971), pt. 2, 100; Bern Anderson, *By Sea and by River: The Naval History of the Civil War* (New York: Knopf, 1962), 137.

3. Effective to full rank February 7, 1863. William B. Cogar, *Dictionary of Admirals of the U.S. Navy, Volume I: 1862–1900* (Annapolis, Md.: Naval Institute Press, 1989), 41–42. The timing was important. Davis's rank of rear admiral technically made him the third man to hold that rank, following his successor, David Dixon Porter, who was made acting rear admiral on October 15, 1862, but effective full rank on July 4, 1863. Cogar, *Dictionary of Admirals of the U.S. Navy*, 131–33.

4. Historians have long held Porter's writings with suspicion. The most factual accounts are generally found in the Mississippi Squadron Papers in the National Archives and Records Administration in Washington, D.C. His later reports and certainly his postwar volumes, *Incidents and Anecdotes* (New York: Appleton, 1885) and *The Naval History of the Civil War* (New York: Appleton, 1886), should be viewed as starting points for the reader but are not to be taken as gospel. Porter

viciously protected officers he liked and became a scourge to those individuals who crossed him. His penchant for self-aggrandizement saw few parallels during and after the Civil War.

5. Naval Historical Division, *Civil War Naval Chronology*, pt. 2, 100.

6. Porter was promoted to the rank of lieutenant on February, 27, 1841, and commander on April 22, 1861. Cogar, *Dictionary of Admirals of the U.S. Navy*, 131.

7. Paul H. Silverstone, *Warships of the Civil War Navies* (Annapolis, Md.: Naval Institute Press, 1989), 170.

8. Silverstone, *Warships of the Civil War Navies*, 149.

9. Silverstone, *Warships of the Civil War Navies*, 157–58.

10. Silverstone, *Warships of the Civil War Navies*, 156.

11. Silverstone, *Warships of the Civil War Navies*, 147–48; personal communication with Edwin Cole Bearss, chief historian emeritus of the National Park Service, October 14, 2005.

12. Silverstone, *Warships of the Civil War Navies*, 164.

13. Silverstone, *Warships of the Civil War Navies*, 164; Anderson, *By Sea and by River*, 138; Porter, *The Naval History of the Civil War*, 494–533.

14. George E. Currie, *Warfare along the Mississippi* (Mount Pleasant: Central Michigan University, 1961), 59–62; William D. Crandall and Isaac D. Newell, *History of the Ram Fleet and the Mississippi Marine Brigade in the War for the Union on the Mississippi and Its Tributaries: The Story of the Ellets and Their Men* (St. Louis, Mo.: Society of Survivors, 1907), 129–52.

15. Currie, *Warfare along the Mississippi*, 59; Gary D. Joiner, *Through the Howling Wilderness: The 1864 Red River Campaign and Union Failure in the West* (Knoxville: University of Tennessee Press, 2006), 52–53, 58, 67, 71, 76, 171.

16. For McClernand's actions at the Battle of Shiloh, see chapter 4.

17. Terrence Winschel, "Fighting Politician: John A. McClernand," in *Grant's Lieutenants from Cairo to Vicksburg*, ed. Steven E. Woodworth (Lawrence: University Press of Kansas, 2001), 129–50; Anderson, *By Sea and by River*, 137–38.

18. *OR* 17, part 2: 420.

19. James Russell Soley, "Naval Operations in the Civil War," *Battles and Leaders* 3: 559.

20. Jack D. Coombe, *Thunder along the Mississippi: The River Battles That Split the Confederacy* (New York: Sarpedon, 1996), 172.

21. For a thorough examination of the Confederate torpedo program, see Milton F. Perry, *Infernal Machines: The Story of Confederate Submarine and Mine Warfare* (Baton Rouge: Louisiana State University Press, 1965). For Federal countermine operations, see Tamara Moser Melia, *"Damn the Torpedoes": A Short History of U.S. Naval Mine Countermeasures, 1777–1991*, Contributions to Naval History, no. 4 (Washington, D.C.: Naval Historical Center, Department of the Navy, 1991). For the most complete account of the operation from the Confederate perspective, including very specific information on the Confederate Secret Service Crew in the operation and details of the torpedo construction, see John C. Wideman, *The Sinking of the USS* Cairo (Jackson: University Press of Mississippi, 1993).

22. *ORN* 23: 546–47.

23. Terrence J. Winschel, *Chickasaw Bayou: A Battlefield Guide* (Washington, D.C.: National Park Service, n.d.), 1.

24. Winschel, *Chickasaw Bayou*, 5.

25. Porter, *The Naval History of the Civil War*, 284–85.

26. *ORN* 23: 550; Wideman, *Sinking of the USS* Cairo, 26–31.

27. *ORN* 23: 552; Porter, *The Naval History of the Civil War*, 285. Selfridge was initially accused of acting rashly, bringing the *Cairo* too far forward with abundant mines in the river. Porter, aboard his flagship *Black Hawk* at the naval base at Cairo, interviewed Selfridge and agreed that he was imprudent but extended his protection to the ironclad captain. He later stated that the incident was "an accident liable to occur to any gallant officer whose zeal carries him to the post of danger, and who is loath to let others do what he thinks he ought to do himself." Selfridge was immediately cleared of any improprieties and given command of the *Conestoga*.

28. This was successful. The hulk rested there undisturbed for 100 years. For the recovery efforts, see Edwin C. Bearss, *Hardluck Ironclad: The Sinking and Salvage of the "Cairo"* (Baton Rouge: Louisiana State University Press, 1980).

29. Bearss, *Hardluck Ironclad*, 564. Captain Walke's first division included the new ironclad *Chillicothe*, the timberclad *Lexington*, and the City-class ironclads *Cincinnati*, *Louisville*, and *Baron De Kalb*. The City-class ironclad *St. Louis* was renamed the *Baron De Kalb* when it was noted that the U.S. Navy already had a USS *St. Louis* on active duty. Lieutenant Gwin's second division included the timberclads *Tyler* and *Conestoga*, the ironclad *Indianola*, and the City-class ironclads *Pittsburg* and *Mound City*. *ORN* 23: 565.

30. *ORN* 23: 575; Anderson, *By Sea and by River*, 140.

31. William L. Shea and Terrence J. Winschel, *Vicksburg Is the Key: The Struggle for the Mississippi River* (Omaha: University of Nebraska Press, 2003), 45, 51–52.

32. *ORN* 23: 571–72.

33. *ORN* 23: 572.

34. Porter, *The Naval History of the Civil War*, 287; *ORN* 23: 573.

35. Porter, *The Naval History of the Civil War*, 287; *ORN* 23: 573. Porter later wrote that the round that hit Gwin was a 50-pound rifle shell, but that is the only instance stating the type of round and is probably incorrect. See Porter, *Naval History of the Civil War*, 287. He stated in his report that it was "rifle shot striking him on the right breast and carrying away the muscle of the right arm." *ORN* 23: 573.

36. *ORN* 23: 574, 576.

37. *ORN* 23: 577–78.

38. *ORN* 23: 577–78.

39. *OR* 17: 625; *OR* 17, part 2, 609–10, 625, 671. An excellent account of this expedition is found is Michael B. Ballard, *Vicksburg: The Campaign That Opened the Mississippi* (Chapel Hill: University of North Carolina Press, 2004), 129–55.

40. William T. Sherman, *Home Letters of General Sherman*, ed. Mark Anthony DeWolfe Howe (New York, 1909), Sherman to Wife, January 4, 1863, 235.

41. Charles Edmund Vetter, *Sherman: Merchant of Terror, Advocate of Peace* (Gretna, La.: Pelican Publishing Company, 1992), 150; Porter, *Incidents and Anecdotes*, 129.

42. *OR* 17, part 2: 401.

43. *OR* 17, part 2: 425.

44. *OR* 17, part 2: 534.

45. Ballard, *Vicksburg*, 148.

46. *ORN* 23: 166; W. T. Sherman, *Memoirs* (New York: The Library of America, 1990), 320–21.

47. For an account of the Union army's effort at Fort Hindman, see McClernand's report in *OR* 17: 702–9.

7

✛

Vicksburg

The scene while the fleet was passing the batteries was grand in the extreme . . .

—Admiral David Dixon Porter

The Union commanders focused all their efforts on taking Vicksburg and wresting control of the Mississippi River following the fall of Fort Hindman. Generals U. S. Grant and William T. Sherman still had no clear concept of how to breach the Vicksburg defenses. Although Sherman was but one of four corps commanders in Grant's army, the two sought each other's counsel and were close friends. Admiral Porter was admitted into this inner circle after the Yazoo fiasco. His loyal support of Sherman cemented the relationship, which lasted throughout the war and beyond. In the upcoming months, Sherman's and Porter's forces would work closely together in the initial attempts on Vicksburg.

The Vicksburg defenses were strong and the prospects of a frontal assault, at least from the river, appeared nonexistent. At the same time, the Confederates were fortifying two strong positions downstream at Port Hudson, Louisiana, and Grand Gulf, Mississippi. Port Hudson, located upstream from Union-held Baton Rouge, served as the southern anchor in the Confederates' strategy to hold the vital stretch of the river separating the Mississippi Squadron from Farragut's blue water navy. Grand Gulf, located on lower bluffs than Vicksburg, offered the Rebels another point to thwart the Union navy. Between these two new obstacles lay the mouth of the Red River and entry into the greatest cotton-growing region in the South. A significant number of Confederate troops were located west of the Mississippi, but commanders were not ordered to transfer them to the east. While troops were not being sent across the river at that time, materiel and cattle were being sent to Vicksburg and points to the east. Steamboats based on the Red River transported these supplies to landings on the eastern bank of the Mississippi between Vicksburg and Port Hudson.

Efforts to bypass the great artillery-studded bluffs at Vicksburg seemed to offer the best opportunities for the Union. If the bluffs could not be taken, then circumventing movements might render them useless. The swampy lands on the Louisiana side remained a problem. The area was unsuitable for large-scale movements by field forces. The Confederates managed only to station a few small units between the Red and Mississippi rivers. Geography seemed a greater foe than the Rebels on and near the western approaches to the Mississippi River.[1]

Porter's mission was more easily defined. The Mississippi Squadron patrolled the areas that the navy controlled and won, sometimes at great cost. The Cumberland, Tennessee, upper portions of the Mississippi, and lower reaches of the Arkansas and White rivers all received attention. Another aspect proved more problematic. The Confederate forces in and near Vicksburg received vital supplies from the Red River Valley. Porter decided to halt or at least thwart this traffic. Of course, the squadron was still above Vicksburg; therefore, some of his boats would need to run the gauntlet of the bluff batteries to conduct the mission. Another issue loomed: if the boats successfully passed the defenses, how were they to be supplied?

On February 2, 1863, Porter sent Colonel Charles Rivers Ellet, aboard the ram *Queen of the West*, past the batteries. The ram carried cotton bales over its wooden sheathing to absorb or deflect the solid rounds from the Rebel artillery. The *Queen* also mounted a 30-pounder bow gun and three 12-pounder howitzers.[2] The difficult passage was made with minor damage. Porter stationed observers to watch the run to ascertain the strength of the defenses on the Vicksburg bluffs. What they saw surprised the admiral, as he reported to Secretary of the Navy Gideon Welles:

> On the morning when the ram *Queen of the West* went by the batteries I had officers stationed all along to note the places where guns were fired from, and they were quite surprised to find them firing from spots where there were no indications whatever of any guns before. The shots came from banks, gulleys, from railroad depots, from clumps of bushes and from hilltops 200 feet high. A better system of defense was never devised.[3]

Ellet's orders were to interdict Confederate boat traffic, specifically to destroy the Confederate vessel *City of Vicksburg* and perform a reconnaissance of the lower Red River.[4] Ellet found the Confederate steamer tied up at a wharf near the middle of the Vicksburg batteries. The ram steered directly for the *City of Vicksburg*, firing its bow gun before ramming the hapless vessel. The attempt damaged the steamer, though not fatally. Ellet then drifted downstream. Before he could make another attempt, an artillery round slammed into some of the cotton bales aboard the *Queen*, setting it ablaze, and another Rebel shell dismounted one of the howitzers. Ellet then wisely put the crew to use as firefighters and headed the *Queen* downstream past the lower batteries of the fortress city.[5] He then steamed a safe distance to make repairs. Next, Porter ordered a mission, brilliant in its simplicity and inexpensive to conduct. He ordered a collier barge filled with 20,000 bushels of coal to run the batteries at Vicksburg. Unpowered, unmanned, and unescorted, allowing the current to guide it, the barge floated past the batteries in the middle of the channel, apparently unnoticed by the gunners on the bluffs.[6] The barge traveled ten miles unmolested. Ellet snagged the collier, and the *Queen of the West* had plenty of fuel to conduct the mission. He then conducted a sweep of the river below.

The *Queen of the West* steamed downstream that evening and night, passing the newly constructed defenses at Grand Gulf. The Confederates paid no attention to the ram, either not seeing it or believing that it was a friendly craft. At night, with no bonfires lit on the opposite shore as backlighting, the radically different superstructure of the *Queen* went unnoticed. Ellet passed Natchez, Mississippi, at midnight with the same results.[7] The ram had yet to encounter any opposition.

The Confederates operated at least thirty vessels based in the Red River at Alexandria and Shreveport. Most were river packets used as transports, and others were armed. These included the high-speed ram *William H. Webb*, the tinclad *Grand Duke*, and armed tender *Mary T*, also known as the *Cotton II*.[8] The transports carried

CHARLES RIVERS ELLET

Charles Rivers Ellet. U.S. Naval Historical Center image NH 49622.

much-needed supplies to Port Hudson, as well as Port Gibson and Vicks-burg. Ellet steamed about fifteen miles below the mouth of the Red River and encountered the steamers *A. W. Baker* and *Moro*. He captured both as prizes. Returning to the mouth of the Red, he seized another packet, the *Berwick Bay*. The passengers of the three vessels netted seven Confederate officers, "7 or 8 ladies," and the cargoes consisted of "110,000 pounds of pork, 500 hogs, and a large quantity of salt, . . . 200 barrels of molasses, 10 hogsheads of sugar, and 30,000 pounds of flour, and 40 bales of cotton."[9] Ellet entered the Red River and destroyed 25,000 pounds of meal.[10] He re-leased the civilians and attempted to return with his prizes; however, he was running low on coal and was forced to burn the three boats, although he kept the cotton. Ellet reported his good fortune to Porter, who imme-diately informed Secretary of the Navy Gideon Welles, "I would recom-mend that an agent of the Navy Department be appointed out here to pro-tect the interests of the Navy. If the Department will permit me, I will appoint a suitable person."[11] Welles then acquiesced to the admiral's re-quest under the Naval Prize Law.

The capture of the steamboats alerted the Confederates of the *Queen*'s presence. Messengers were sent to units operating near the area of the at-tacks on the steamboats. Confederate commanders moved cavalry squadrons and artillery batteries to points along the river to engage the ram if it were sighted. They also planned a mission to either capture or de-stroy the *Queen of the West*. The formerly safe waters between Vicksburg and Port Hudson were no longer comforting for the Confederates. The se-cure supply lines were disrupted, and although the Confederates believed only one rogue vessel was in their midst, they were uncertain because nei-ther Port Gibson nor Natchez had reported sightings of roving Union gun-boats. Neither side could boast of dominating the mouth of the Red River.

Porter managed to float another coal barge past the Vicksburg defenses. Ellet retrieved the much-needed fuel and used the *DeSoto* as a collier ten-der. Ellet steamed into the Red River for about four miles to the small town of Simmesport and decided to investigate the upper reaches of the Atchafalaya River. The Atchafalaya, an ancient channel of the Mississippi, served as a diversion channel for the Red River's water. On February 12, Ellet steamed down the Atchafalaya about six miles. There, he discovered and destroyed twelve wagons. He then returned to his tender, the *DeSoto*, at the mouth of the Red River. At Simmesport, Ellet destroyed a cache of barrels on the wharves filled with beef and burned houses in retaliation for gunfire that wounded one of his officers.[12] Admiral Porter contributed to his success by sending the ironclad *Indianola*.

The *Indianola*, under the command of Lieutenant Commander George Brown, passed the Vicksburg batteries on the night of February 13. Strapped to the ironclad were two coal barges with enough fuel for two

USS Indianola. *Water color by Oscar Parkes. U.S. Naval Historical Center image NH 59549.*

months. The Confederate gunners sighted the *Indianola*, and although they opened fire on the vessel as it passed through the gauntlet, they did not strike it. Porter reported to Secretary Welles the next day, "This gives us entire control of the Mississippi, except at Vicksburg and Port Hudson, and cuts off all the supplies and troops from Texas. We have below now 2 XI-inch guns, 2 IX-inch guns, 2 30-pounder rifles, 6 12-pounders, and 3 vessels. They have orders to burn, sink, and destroy."[13]

Porter's orders to Brown were very specific. He was to protect the *Queen of the West* and *DeSoto* from the *William H. Webb*. The admiral was certain that the Confederate ram would not attack both vessels.[14] The *Indianola* was ordered not to patrol below the mouth of the Red but to hold the *Queen*'s rear area safe while Ellet reconnoitered Port Hudson. Brown was also to take cotton from Jefferson Davis's plantation and from Davis's brother's plantation as well.[15] The cotton and as many single male slaves as possible were to be placed aboard a captured steamer and sent through the Vicksburg batteries to Porter. The *Queen* and *Indianola* were then to foray up the Red River and destroy as many of the enemy's stores as possible. Porter admonished Brown, "Whatever you undertake try and have no failure. When you have not means of certain success, undertake nothing; a failure is equal to a defeat."[16] Finally, Porter ordered Brown to "tell Colonel Ellet when he gets to Port Hudson to send a communication in a barrel (barrel to be marked '*Essex*'), and tell the commander in said communication that I direct him to pass Port Hudson on a dark night and join the vessels above."[17] Had the *Essex* received the order and its commander, William Porter, been able to comply, the Mississippi Squadron would have a formidable force operating between Vicksburg and Port Hudson. Were the admiral to resupply his vessels below the bluff defenses, Vicksburg's fortunes would have diminished rapidly. This grand plan never had a chance of success.

On February 13, the *Queen* steamed up the Red River about fifteen miles to the mouth of the Black River.[18] Ellet halted there as night fell before proceeding farther up the Red the next morning. The ram ventured another fifteen miles and captured the *Era No. 5*, filled with 4,500 bushels of corn. One of the captured crewmen told Ellet that three steamers were tied to the bank at Gordon's Landing, another fifteen miles upstream.[19] The navy received intelligence that the Rebels had positioned a battery at the landing and were perhaps building a fort. The fort, still unfinished but fortified with a powerful water battery, was Fort DeRussy.[20] It proved to be Ellet's undoing. A man that Ellet did not trust piloted the *Queen*, as his preferred pilot had fallen ill. The new man moved into view of the battery and ran the vessel hard aground. The Confederate gunners damaged the ram with almost every shot. Ellet and his crew were forced to abandon ship, floating down the Red on the cotton bales they used for armor. The *DeSoto*, waiting downstream out of range, rescued them.[21] Believing that the three Rebel boats would soon be in pursuit, Ellet took command of the tender and returned to the *Era No. 5*. The two vessels made a dash for the mouth of the Red. About fifteen miles south of the rendezvous point, the *DeSoto* lost its rudder, and Ellet burned the boat. The same river pilot that grounded the *Queen* also grounded the *Era No. 5* at the mouth of the Red. Ellet arrested him and placed the pilot in chains.[22] He then steamed north to a point about ten miles below Natchez, where he met the *Indianola* on the morning of February 16.

Ellet's elation meeting Lieutenant Commander Brown and the ironclad *Indianola* was short lived. The Rebels repaired the *Queen of the West* faster than anyone thought possible. They intended to put the sturdy ram to good use to wreck Porter's plan to dominate the Mississippi River between Vicksburg and Port Hudson. In the process, they hoped to add the ironclad to their fleet.

Brown received intelligence that the *Queen* was not as badly damaged as Ellet believed, with the primary harm limited to its steam and escape pipes. Brown and Ellet decided to find the ram and either recapture or destroy it. The next day, the *Indianola* headed downstream with the *New Era No. 5* in the lead. Fog slowed them down, and visibility was restricted. Ellet, aboard the *New Era*, signaled the ironclad of danger ahead, and Brown saw the *Webb* appear out of the fog. He fired the *Indianola*'s 11-inch bow guns, and the *Webb* retreated. Later that day, the pair arrived at the mouth of the Red River. No river pilots who knew the Red could be found, so on February 18, Ellet took the *New Era* upstream with prisoners aboard. The

Indianola blockaded the mouth of the Red until February 21, daring the *Webb* to challenge it. Brown learned that the repairs on the *Queen* were complete and that the ram, the *Webb*, and possibly four cottonclad boats were preparing to engage him. He left the mouth of the river to find baled cotton to use as a barricade in case an attempt was made to board him.[23] Brown steamed north to communicate with Porter. He kept as much coal on board as possible but retained the two barges, one on either side like saddlebags, should other vessels pass through the defenses and need fuel.

On February 24, the *Queen* sailed out of the mouth of the Red River and headed north with her consorts, the Confederate ram *Webb* and the gunboat *Dr. Beatty*.[24] The flotilla was under the tactical command of Confederate Lieutenant Colonel Frederick B. Brand, aboard the *Dr. Beatty*.[25] At about 9:30 P.M., the Confederates found the *Indianola* about thirty miles south of Vicksburg.[26] The battle was fought at night under a nearly full moon. According to his reports, Brand found the *Indianola* tied up at the bank. The ironclad then cast off and steamed into the channel to meet the Rebel flotilla head-on.[27] The *Queen* bore down on the *Indianola*, and in the final yards before impact, the ironclad turned to present one of the coal barges into the ram's path. The *Queen* tore into the barge, rending it into two parts, both still lashed to the vessel. Brand reported the *Queen* was impaled on the ironclad.[28] Brown did not mention it in his report. The *Queen* extricated itself and turned for another ramming attack as the ironclad fired at it but missed. The *Webb* then struck the *Indianola* head-on. Brown reported that the forward eight feet of the *Webb* had caved in, but that seems improbable since the ram was able to function and strike again.[29] The blow disabled the ironclad's starboard engine, jammed the rudders, and separated the port coal barge. The collision also forced the ironclad to steam in tight circles. The *Webb* then struck the *Indianola*'s starboard coal barge, stripping it away. Brown claimed that the fighting was so furious that his crew could not man both the port, starboard, and forward batteries simultaneously.[30]

The *Queen* then made the fourth ram attack, striking the ironclad below the pilothouse and skidding along its flank. This offered the opportunity for the *Indianola*'s stern battery to fire as the ram withdrew for another turn and ramming attack. These blasts hit the *Queen* but did not disable it. It steamed in a tight circle and struck the ironclad in a fifth collision that did little damage.

The *Webb* was conspicuously absent in the battle, perhaps attempting to repair damage sustained in its first attack. It returned for a sixth assault. The high-speed ram crashed into the *Indianola*'s starboard wheel box, shipped the ironclad's rudder, and opened leaks around the shaft. The *Webb* had gained enough speed to steam around and strike the ironclad with a seventh and final devastating crash. This smashed timbers from the stern forward to the starboard wheel box, allowing water to enter in an uncontrollable torrent. The stricken *Indianola* was doomed. When water was two-and-one-half feet deep on the lower deck, Brown tried to spike the guns. He threw the two log books into the river.[31] Brown surrendered the *Indianola*'s colors to Lieutenant Colonel Brand, aboard the *Dr. Beatty*. Brown and the crew were taken to Jackson, Mississippi, and imprisoned.[32] Remarkably, the *Indianola* did not sink. Brand hauled the ironclad upstream to lower Palmyra Island, near Jefferson Davis's plantation, and ran it close in to shore, where it finally settled into the mud. The Confederates intended to repair it there.

Secretary Welles, Admiral Porter, and the squadron captains were at a loss as to what to do about the *Indianola*. If the Rebels repaired the ironclad as they had the *Queen of the West*, the balance of power on the Mississippi River might not be tipped; however, potential consequences were immense. Porter and Admiral Farragut would be less likely to link their forces in the foreseeable future with a formidable Rebel presence between them. Both squadrons might face the specter of an *Arkansas* of their own making. Both commanders knew the capabilities of the *Queen* and *Indianola*. Now they recognized the danger posed by the *William H. Webb* since its whereabouts were unknown. Neither admiral could be certain whether the Rebels had any other surprises in store for them. Porter and Farragut reacted very differently to the situation.

Porter supplied his vessels below the Vicksburg defenses by setting unmanned coal barges adrift in the river's current and having them retrieved. He further expanded this practice, hoping to force the Rebels to destroy the *Indianola*. The plan was hatched at very little expense, and this grand hoax was even more successful than he could imagine. Porter ordered his carpenters and craftsmen to take a coal barge and enlarge its surface area with a log raft. To this, they added a platform that extended the craft to 300 feet. On this platform, the men constructed fake casemates of wood coated in tar to look like iron. Two long smokestacks were created from four long barrels connected to each other. They built a square turret in the front with a blackened log, called a "Quaker gun" because it could do no harm, extending menacingly from a gun port. Large canvas-covered wheel boxes were attached to each side near the stern. Two pots filled with tar and pitch were set afire, providing smoke to stream from the chimneys. Porter's well-known sense of humor was satisfied by the final touches: above the fake turret flew a jack staff sporting the skull and crossbones of a pirate flag. A flagstaff on the stern flew the stars and stripes. Painted on the wheel boxes in three-foot-high letters was the ominous phrase "DELUDED PEOPLE CAVE IN!"[33] The cost for this remarkable hoax was $8.63.[34]

Crews launched the dummy ironclad into the current, and when the gunners on the bluffs saw it, they took aim and fired solid shot. All of them seemingly missed. In fact, one round did damage the vessel near the bow just above the waterline but passed through it.[35] The vessel slowly "steamed" past the batteries and down the river. The *Queen of the West* saw it, turned away, and fled downstream to warn other Confederate vessels to do the same. Porter's fake vessel came to rest only a couple of miles above the damaged *Indianola*. The Rebel engineers attempting to repair the ironclad destroyed it to prevent the vessel from falling into Union hands.[36] The Confederates came on the paper tiger and discovered the deception. The disdain of both the Confederate military and the southern press was best expressed by the *Vicksburg Whig*:

> Destruction of the Indianola.—We stated a day or two since that we would not then enlighten our readers in regard to a matter which was puzzling them very much. We allude to the loss of the gunboat Indianola, recently captured from the enemy. We were loath to acknowledge she had been destroyed, but such is the case.
>
> The Yankee barge sent down the river last week was reported to be an ironclad gunboat. The authorities, thinking that this monster would retake the Indianola, immediately issued an order to blow her up. The order was sent down by a courier to the officer in charge of the boat. A few hours afterwards another order was sent down countermanding the first, it being ascertained that the monstrous craft was only a coal boat. But before it reached the Indianola she

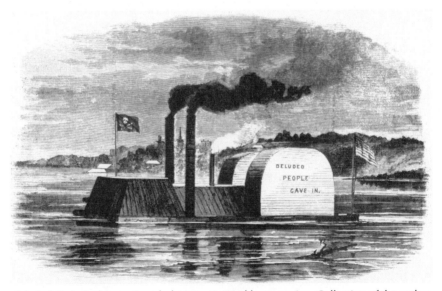

Admiral Porter's dummy ironclad. Harper's Weekly *engraving. Collection of the author.*

had been blown to atoms; not even a gun was saved. Who is to blame for this piece [of] folly? This precipitancy? It would really seem we had no use for gunboats on the Mississippi, as a coal barge is magnified into a monster, and our authorities immediately order a boat—that would have been worth a small army to us—to be blown up.[37]

The Confederates lost a golden opportunity to capitalize on Union misfortune while Porter relished in his success. Admiral Farragut was not privy to Porter's humorous pet project and prepared a much stronger response. Farragut's immediate problem was not Vicksburg but the Confederates' southern anchor complex above Baton Rouge at Port Hudson. When he received information that the *Indianola* had fallen into Rebel hands, he decided to take some of his screw sloops past the Port Hudson defenses and occupy the strategic stretch of the Mississippi River south of Vicksburg. Although he had traversed it before, now the stakes were higher. The Confederates were also much better prepared, and his vessels were not suitable for this type of asymmetrical warfare in closely confined navigable waters. Farragut had an advantage that he did not possess earlier. General Benjamin Butler's replacement, Major General Nathaniel Prentiss Banks, moved the 19th Corps from New Orleans to Baton Rouge. Banks and Farragut met, and the general agreed to move his force of between 15,000 and 25,000 men to Port Hudson as a diversion to allow the oceangoing sloops to run past the river defenses. Like Butler, Banks was a political general from Massachusetts. Unlike Butler, he had aspirations for the presidency and needed a battlefield victory to complete his résumé.[38]

Farragut planned to lead the way with his flagship, the *Hartford*. Lashed to it was the gunboat *Albatross*. Following these were the *Richmond* with the *Genessee* secured alongside, the *Monongahela* with the *Kineo* lashed alongside, and the *Mississippi*. The added power of the gunboats would provide extra propulsion if the screw sloops floundered. The *Essex*, with Farragut since its separation from the Mississippi Squadron, would fire into the shore batteries, providing an additional distraction. Mortar schooners were assigned the task of firing into the batteries and the fortifications to keep the Rebels busy. Everything that could be accounted for in the operation was ready. The run was to begin at 9:30 P.M. on the moonless night of March 14.[39] That afternoon, Banks notified Farragut that he was moving on Port Hudson by land, and although everything seemed to be working, that was not the case.

The meticulous Farragut saw his plans self-destruct almost immediately. The mortar schooners fired sporadically at extreme range with indirect fire; therefore, they did not see their targets. The *Essex* remained with the mortar craft and did not come close to the Rebel batteries. Although the mortars did little damage, their fire alerted the Confederate battery commanders of their presence. The *Richmond* and the other vessels had trouble with the five- to six-knot current and eddies. The channel lay close into the bank on the east side of the river at the fortifications. This brought the sloops so near the bank that that their yardarms sometimes brushed overhanging trees. Adding to the screw sloops' woes were their drafts. When the currents pushed the vessels out of the main channel, their keels sliced into grasping soft mud. The need to power up and move past the ever-changing river bottom stymied every effort to be silent. As the vessels rounded the hairpin bend below the fortifications, Confederate gunners prepared to engage them at short range. The Rebels had prepared for a Union naval attempt to run their batteries and set large piles of dried pitch pine wood ablaze on the western bank.[40] This gave the gunners on shore perfectly silhouetted targets. The pitch pine created large clouds of dense smoke. Added to the smoke from the shore batteries and the return fire from the sloops and gunboats, it created very low visibility.

The Union sloops could only fire their guns as the ships steamed upstream at a snail's pace. They could not fire broadsides without pushing themselves out of the river's current and into the mud; therefore, they fired in sequence, forward cannon to aftmost cannon.[41] The sound of the combined bombardment and return fire was heard in New Orleans, over eighty miles south.[42]

The *Hartford* reached the lower batteries about 11:20 P.M., after steaming about three miles in slightly less than two hours. As the sloop and the attached *Albatross* steamed upstream, the fickle current twisted the pair to starboard with the *Hartford*'s bow scraping the shore before the helmsman could correct the movement.[43] The helmsman brought the sloop back into the main channel, and the vessels proceeded upstream. The two ships passed the upper batteries at 12:15 A.M. Farragut steamed north another two miles and dropped anchor.[44] The *Hartford*'s slow waltz created havoc among the trailing vessels, and this proved to be the mission's undoing.

As Farragut's sloop reeled to the east at about 11:30 P.M., the *Richmond* came to a dead stop to prevent ramming the lead ship. This gave the Rebels ample time to focus on the big screw sloop. Their fire was deadly. Shells entered the *Richmond*'s gun ports, killing and maiming several men. Another shell ripped through an aft bulwark and exploded. Some of the fragments heavily damaged the captain's cabin, but the greatest damage occurred when a shell exploded, destroying a steam valve and filling the lower decks with scalding vapor before all pressure was lost on the starboard boiler. Four crewmen made heroic efforts to save the vessel and stabilize the situation, earning each of them the Medal of Honor.[45] With the starboard engine boiler down, the *Richmond* could not fight the current, and with the help of the *Genessee*, both vessels turned around and allowed the current to carry them out of harm's way. As they moved downstream, little other than the muzzle flashes of the large guns could be seen through the cloud of smoke. The *Mississippi* was engaging the shore batteries, but the *Richmond*'s officers mistakenly believed the firing was coming from the shore batteries and fired into their consort.[46] The *Genessee* attempted to steer the *Richmond* out of the path of the other vessels and grounded it against the western bank. Before the pair moved off the shoal, a shell from the fort holed the gunboat at the waterline. The damage was repaired, and the *Genessee* moved the sloop downstream to the staging area at Prophet's Island, about three miles below the fort. The trek was complete at 1:00 A.M.[47]

The *Monongahela* and the *Kineo* began their run of the batteries at 11:30 P.M. By 12:30 A.M., the pair was opposite the main batteries of Port Hudson; however, the column cohesion had broken down because of the *Hartford*'s navigation problems and the *Richmond*'s damage, and the *Monongahela* steered too far to port. It grounded on the west bank opposite the fort's batteries. The impact was so hard that it tore the *Kineo* loose, grounding it as well. The batteries concentrated on the two unfortunate vessels. One round destroyed the sloop's bridge and severely wounded the captain. The *Kineo* freed itself and then pulled the *Monongahela* out of the muck.[48] The sloop's forward engine overheated and shut down, and the Rebels poured fire into the stricken vessel. The *Monongahela* ceased firing, and as the Confederates attempted to seize it, the sloop and its gunboat drifted downstream to Prophet's Island, out of the range of the Rebel guns.

The last of the great sloops to attempt the passage past the batteries was the *Mississippi*, the only one without an attendant gunboat. The difficulties of the first three sloops forced the *Mississippi* to keep well aft of the column. This was the only side-wheeler sloop in the column with wheel boxes, which extended twenty feet on each side of the hull. Farragut placed it last in the column in case it became disabled.[49] The *Mississippi*'s run past the lower batteries was successful because the Rebel gunners were more interested in the vessels to its front. It did, however, receive damage from the *Richmond* and ran aground, heeling over to port. The Confederates saw a perfect chance to pummel the sloop and made it their primary target. Lieutenant George Dewey, future full admiral of the U.S. Navy and hero of the Battle of Manila Bay during the Spanish-American War, was aboard the stricken vessel. He and Captain Melancton Smith directed the efforts to save the crew who had not already jumped overboard.[50] The Rebels began firing hot shots[51] into the sloop. These ignited the vessel's barrels of turpentine and oil, which began an unstoppable advance to the ship's powder magazine. Dewey was the last man on the deck before he, too, sought safety.[52] Dewey and Smith retreated to a small boat with the lieutenant at the tiller. They reached the *Essex* about 1:15 A.M. The *Mississippi*, eased of much of its burdensome weight, floated off the shoal about 3:00 A.M. On fire, the ghost ship gracefully glided downstream. Its port side guns had been primed, and when the heat reached sufficient intensity, it fired the guns at the Rebel batteries as it passed.[53] The vessel slid downstream, passing the *Essex*, *Richmond*, *Genessee*, and *Sachem*. The magazine finally exploded five miles south of Prophet's Island, near Baton Rouge. The explosion was so large that the flash was seen on the outskirts of New Orleans.[54]

Admiral Farragut now faced a dilemma. The *Hartford* was above the defenses with only its consort, the *Albatross*. General Banks's forward elements approached the outer works of Port Hudson but withdrew to near Baton Rouge on learning of Farragut's problems. The army was of no consequence to the operation. Rather than supporting the admiral, Banks promised to invest the bastion in the near future, apparently when his chances of success were more auspicious. He had, after all, his political ambitions to protect.

Farragut brought the *Hartford* and *Albatross* a short distance below Vicksburg and sent Admiral Porter a dispatch requesting that more gunboats be sent below the Vicksburg batteries to help control the river between that city and Port Hudson.[55] Although Farragut did not know it, Porter was not at Vicksburg but in the maze of bayous north of the city, attempting to find a path to the town's back door. Farragut did receive a response, but it was from the commander of the Mississippi Marine Brigade, Brigadier General Alfred Ellet. The general met with the admiral and offered the assistance of two rams that he would order to run past the Vicksburg batteries. He anticipated that this would provide enough assistance to the admiral in the short term. Farragut considered the offer a violation of the rules of command. Ellet assured the admiral that Porter would agree were he there to offer assistance.[56]

Alfred Ellet ordered his flagship, the ram *Switzerland*, and the ram *Lancaster*, commanded by his brother Colonel John Ellet, to run the gauntlet of the Vicksburg batteries. Alfred Ellet's plan was to let the current move the two rams as far into the deadly zone as possible. He would then start the engines to push them downriver. This worked until the loud popping noise of the steam valves caught the attention of the gunners on the bluffs. The pair of rams proceeded at full speed, the *Switzerland* in the lead. The flagship passed through with little or no damage. The *Lancaster*, however, received three hits. The first shattered the steam drum, scalding some of the crew and slowing the craft down markedly. The second shell hit the ram near the bow at the waterline, passing completely through as water poured in. The third round destroyed the ram's wheel, rendering the boat inoperable. John Ellet ordered "Abandon ship," and the crew, after setting the *Lancaster* afire, complied.[57] Ellet and his crew bobbed in the muddy waters of the Mississippi River until the *Switzerland* picked them up downstream. Farragut ordered another gunboat to patrol the waters of the great river near the mouth of the Red.[58] With a small river force in place, the admiral later ran the batteries to join the squadron, but his focus remained on Port Hudson. Porter was seething about the mission, complaining to General Grant, Secretary Welles, and finally to General Ellet, whom he suspended from command.[59] Porter was in a foul mood not only because of Ellet's blatant usurpation of authority but also because of the circumstances in which he found himself.

Grant, Porter, and Sherman still believed that the bluff and water batteries at Vicksburg were too powerful to confront directly. Grant set his troops to work digging a series of canals on the Louisiana side of the Mississippi River to bypass the defenses. The first was across the river from the batteries on the De Soto Peninsula. The low swampy area was not ideal, and the river's fluctuating depth doomed the project. The second canal was located at Duckport, about twenty miles above Vicksburg. It also failed for similar reasons. The third canal was located at Lake Providence. The idea for this project was to dig a canal the short distance from the Mississippi to the old, meandering oxbow lake and then follow Lake Providence to a drainage stream called Bayou Baxter, which flowed into Bayou Macon. Bayou Macon flowed into the Tensas River, which led to the village of Trinity, where the Tensas River and the Ouachita River formed the Black River. From there the route followed the Black to its confluence with the southern portion of the Red River, which led to the Mississippi. This route bypassed the batteries at Vicksburg and Grand Gulf. If successful, the entire passage encompassed about 400 river miles. Aside from the much longer journey, the problem of the fortifications at Port Hudson must still be addressed. The Union engineers succeeded in dragging a steamboat overland one-and-one-

USS Switzerland. *U.S. Naval Historical Center image NH 55829.*

half miles into Lake Providence to test the route, but Bayou Baxter and Bayou Macon proved to be full of cypress knees and logs. An underwater saw, similar to that used at the Island No. 10 canal, was of little use. Although the project was not completely abandoned for months, it showed little chance of success.

The three commanders also believed that the vast bulk of the batteries faced the river and that the landward perimeter of the city was lightly defended. They felt that if a force could work its way around the north or northeast side of the great bluffs, it might have a chance to take Vicksburg from the east or northeast sides of the city. The problem was in getting enough troops to the proper point to begin the assault. Southern approaches were not viable since Porter's fleet was north of the defenses. That left the northern gunboats, and the Yazoo expeditions had proven that path was untenable. The great Yazoo basin, a product of the outpouring of runoff from the end of the last Ice Age, was sixty miles wide and shaped like an elongated oval. Its interior was a mass of intertwined streams and swamps that could be a green hell without a native guide. On the western rim of the swamp lay the massive Mississippi River levee. On the east was a long line of bluffs, averaging 80 to 100 feet high. Porter and Sherman sent their forces into the swamp.

The Yazoo route would be no less ambitious than the Lake Providence concept. Yazoo Pass was located about 150 miles north of Vicksburg, just below and on the opposite bank from Helena, Arkansas. This "headwater" of the Yazoo swamp fed Moon Lake, which in turn fed one of the myriad cross channels that led to Coldwater River. The Coldwater was a tributary of the Tallahatchie River, which met the Yalobusha River at Greenwood, Mississippi. At this point, the two streams formed the Yazoo River. The Yazoo and all other streams in the basin were actually older channels of the Mississippi River. When the Mississippi flooded, the entire swamp filled with excess water, leading to numerous channels that apparently went nowhere, while only a few moved with enough current to allow for successful navigation. The lower Yazoo basin offered several bayous and rivers, affording alternate routes if one or more were blocked. The approach offered several possibilities for success despite its length of 700 miles. The only way for steamboats to access Yazoo Pass was to blow up the levee. The engineers and commanders knew that this would suck the boats into Moon Lake since the level of the Mississippi River was higher than the swamp, but this was considered to be an aid to navigation rather than a hindrance. The small channel that led from Moon Lake to the Coldwater was lined with a dense growth of trees with overhanging, often intertwining branches. High water actually exacerbated this problem, forcing the vessels to move through the tangle rather than under it.[60]

Map of the streams involved in the Union bayou operations against Vicksburg.

Porter and Sherman gathered their vessels and men at Helena, waiting for their gateway to be opened as the Union engineers blew a hole in the levee on February 3, 1863. The Mississippi poured through the opening, collapsing the levee as it sought the lower level of the adjacent swamp. The resulting flood appeared antediluvian in proportion within the confines of the Yazoo basin. All of the streams in the region were swollen well into central Mississippi.[61] People living in the basin raced for high ground, some taking their possessions, others seeking to preserve only their lives. As one survivor remarked, "It was a weird scene . . . a wild and noisy time, waters roaring, men shouting, cows lowing, pigs squealing."[62] The torrent settled as the river and swamp levels equalized over the next few days.

Watson Smith led the Mississippi Squadron into the breach on February 12. The army Quartermaster Corps transports with 6,000 of Sherman's men aboard arrived at the new opening on February 15. Neither Smith nor the army commanders was interested in tackling the operation. Pioneers[63] were sent in to clear the massive entangling overhangs between Moon Lake and the Coldwater. Work was slow, and it appeared that another stretch of equal or greater hazards followed every mile cleared. This bought the Confederates much-needed time.

Two boats, the *Mary Keene* and the *Star of the West* (of Fort Sumter fame), were sent from the southern end of the basin to help counter the Union threat. The Confederates also prepared a hastily but well-designed fortification built of cotton bales covered with dirt and sand at the confluence of the Tallahatchie and Yazoo rivers. Its flanks were on the banks of both streams, its most powerful salient pointing like a spear at any oncoming threat. Fort Pemberton was in an almost perfect location, offering the Confederate gunners excellent fields of fire with little room to maneuver for any Union gunboat that approached it. The fort sported eight cannon, including a 32-pounder and an excellent Whitworth 6.4-inch breechloader, that were placed in the most advantageous position to do the most damage, pointing straight up the Tallahatchie channel. Several field pieces were mounted in positions outside the walls. Connected to the fort were earthworks reaching out 1,000 yards. A 2,000-man garrison manned the complex.[64] The fort's commander, Major General William W. Loring, ordered the *Star of the West* sunk behind a raft in the Tallahatchie channel in a sharp bend.

The Union force consisted of the ironclads *Baron De Kalb* and *Chillicothe* and the tinclads *Forest Rose, Marmora, Petrel, Rattler, Romeo,* and *Signal*; the Ellet rams *Lioness* and *Fulton*; three coal barges; and Sherman's transports with 6,000 men. The Union pioneers cleared the route into the Coldwater on February 21. From there, the sailing was better and progress more rapid. Moving in single file, the column reached the Tallahatchie on March 5 and confluence of the Tallahatchie and the Yazoo on March 11. The lead vessel, the ironclad *Chillicothe*, sighted Fort Pemberton, only one-half mile in the distance.

The fort's gunners fired, striking the ironclad twice. The first was a glancing blow on the forward casemate, and the second struck the wheelhouse, doing some damage. The *Chillicothe* reversed course, firing as it withdrew to relative safety behind the sharp bend. General Prentiss ordered troops to approach the fort. Almost immediately, they ran into some of the Texans garrisoning the bastion. The area surrounding the fort was inundated, and the Union officers on the scene deemed an infantry assault unwise and potentially disastrous. Watson Smith sent both the *Chillicothe* and the *Baron De Kalb* to pound the fort the next day. The Rebel gunners had the ranges sighted perfectly. As the ironclads advanced, a round sailed through one of the *Chillicothe*'s bow gun ports and struck a gun being loaded. The explosion wrecked the gun and the one next to it, also jamming both gun ports, setting cotton bale armor aflame, killing four men, and wounding nine others.[65] Smith tried again on the next day, sending the two ironclads, a mortar raft, and two tinclads.

The mortar scow was to lob shells into the fort, hopefully reducing it. The two ironclads were placed side by side behind the scow, and each lashed to a tinclad to provide extra power if they were forced to retire quickly. The Rebel gunners seemed to relish firing at the *Chillicothe*, and it suffered more hits. The mortar crew fired forty-nine rounds into and around the fort, doing little damage before the ungainly ensemble retreated. This encounter yielded eighteen casualties.[66] Both sides received supplies, including new artillery pieces. On March 16, the Union tried again, this time with a combined infantry and navy operation that yielded no positive results. A Confederate shell slammed into the *Chillicothe*'s forward casemate, jamming its gun ports closed.[67] This sealed the fate of this portion of the expedition, and Watson Smith, who seemed timid throughout the Yazoo Pass mission, ordered a retreat to Yazoo Pass.[68]

USS Chillicothe. *U.S. Naval Historical Center image NH 264.*

Admiral Porter tried to position the Fort Pemberton debacle in a better light by suggesting a parallel route around the fortification to gain the Yazoo nearer to Vicksburg. This mission, known as the Steele's Bayou/Deer Creek operation, was complex but offered a shorter route than did the first mission. The naval contingent would move up the mouth of the Yazoo near Vicksburg, then upstream to Steele's Bayou, then to Black Bayou, then to Deer Creek. From there, the column would steam south to the Rolling Fork and then the Big Sunflower River to the Yazoo. This contorted path would place the force near Yazoo City. It could then steam north on the Yazoo to cut off Fort Pemberton from the south and deny it supplies, eventually forcing its surrender. Another possibility was to proceed downstream on the Yazoo and flank the guns on Haynes' Bluff and Snyder's Bluff. Porter preferred this plan, as he did all operations that he personally conceived. Grant liked it, but he had reservations after seeing the overhanging tree limbs that would threaten his tall transports with their delicate upper wooden structures and chimneys.[69] Porter chose all his remaining Pook turtles except the *Baron De Kalb*, which was still with the *Chillicothe*. Porter proceeded up the Yazoo on March 12 with the *Carondelet*, *Cincinnati*, *Mound City*, and *Pittsburg*, leaving the *Louisville* to wait for Sherman and lead the army's transports. The turtles moved slowly up the Yazoo, Steele's Bayou, and Black Bayou, as they pushed aside the encroaching branches from the cypress trees. Sherman's force met them as they reached Deer Creek. Sherman did not like the swamp or the close confines of the narrow bayous, but Porter convinced him that it was best to move down Deer Creek.[70]

This stream was wider and deeper, and the cypress trees gave way to willows. The ground became firmer, and the swampy morass changed into cotton fields. Most of the farmers burned the white gold, but the Federals seized or destroyed some of it themselves. Confederate cavalry rode ahead of the column and felled trees into the creek, slowing the boats. Sherman halted his contingent and set up a base camp for reinforcements, who arrived on March 20. The navy was still ahead of his transports, and Porter wished to forge ahead.

The Union pioneers operating with Porter's gunboats were adept at removing the felled trees, and on the same day that Sherman's reinforcements arrived, the *Carondelet*, heading the column, reached the Rolling Fork. The Rebels sent cavalry, artillery, and infantry units to harass the Union navy at the junction of the Rolling Fork, but Porter drove them off.

Porter was aboard the *Cincinnati* at the front of the column when it encountered a 600-yard stretch of willows that choked the stream. The ironclad plowed into them in an attempt to clear the way and not wait for the engineers. Porter later wrote, "And there she stuck; the willow wythes caught in the rough iron of her overhang, and held her as if in a vise. All

STEELE'S BAYOU
EXPEDITION

ARKANSAS

LOUISIANA

Bayou Baxter *Lake Providence* *Black Bayou* *Sunflower River* *Yazoo River* ▪Yazoo City

Rolling Fork

Deer Creek

Steele's Bayou

MISSISSIPPI

▪Haynes Bluff

Tensas River

Mississippi River

Bayou Macon

N

Chickasaw Bayou

▪Vicksburg

Cartography by Gary D. Joiner

Map of Steele's Bayou expedition.

the arts of seamanship could not displace this obstacle; it would have taken weeks to remove the willows."[71] The Rebels landed troops from steamers and set up a crossfire that the ironclads could not return because of the height of the banks. Mortars were the only possible remedy. The ironclads in the rear hauled the *Cincinnati* out of its prison over the course of a day and a night.

Sherman was far behind—according to Porter, some twenty miles.[72] At this point Porter suddenly decided to call off the approach. This change of mind was uncharacteristic of the admiral who, before and after, was the epitome of tenacity. He notified Sherman that he was abandoning the campaign. Porter then ordered his men to swab the hulls and slanted surfaces of the boats with swamp slime to help repel boarders. Porter ordered spare plates attached to the pilothouses of the gunboats. He ordered half rations for all crews and scuttle charges planted on the ironclads and tinclads to prevent their use by the Rebels in the event the gunboats must be abandoned.[73] Once the boats entered a wider channel, Porter ordered the rudders to be removed, and the current took them back downstream. The Confederates moved ahead of the slowly drifting vessels and felled trees along the way. They also positioned sharpshooters and boarding parties in an attempt to pick off unlucky sailors and board the boats. When it seemed that Porter would order the vessels scuttled, Sherman's reinforcements arrived and drove off the Rebels. The column returned to Yazoo Pass on March 26, and the floating engine shops, carpenters, machinists, and boat builders went to work repairing the damage done by the Rebels and clawing swamp trees.[74]

The bayou experiments were all failures to various degrees, but most were unquestionably disasters. Grant, Sherman, and Porter reconsidered their options, and the list was very short. Grant could move all the forces back to Memphis and try an overland march as he had earlier attempted. The commanders agreed that this would be seen as a retreat from Mississippi rather than a repositioning of troops and might cost Grant the command of his army. This idea was dropped quickly. Another possibility was to move all three of Grant's corps of the Army of the Tennessee south on the Louisiana side. The regiments were already spread out from Lake Providence to Young's Point, a distance of over sixty miles. Winter had given way to spring. The land was drying, at least enough to march the units along or beside the levees. Likely places to cross the Mississippi far below Vicksburg were at New Carthage, near Newellton, or Hard Times Plantation, near St. Joseph, both in Tensas Parish.[75] New Carthage was opposite the Confederate fortifications at Grand Gulf. Any plan required the Mississippi Squadron to be in force between Vicksburg and Port Hudson. That meant doing what had been avoided and little discussed: sending the squadron past the gauntlet of the vaunted Vicksburg batteries. The admiral regained his confidence in the presence of his friends Grant and Sherman. Grant was very complimentary of Porter in his *Personal Memoirs*, stating, "The co-operation of the navy was absolutely essential to the success (even to the contemplation) of such an enterprise. I had no more authority to command Porter than he had to command me."[76]

Porter divided the squadron into two flotillas. One was to run the batteries, while the other was to remain above Vicksburg and support a deception operation to draw off some of the Vicksburg defenders from Grant's amphibious assault. The first group would reduce the Grand Gulf fortifications before Grant's infantry could cross the Mississippi. That task alone was monumental and could not be adequately planned before the fate of the flotilla was known. Grant asked his agents to collect yawls and barges in St. Louis and Chicago to transport men across the great river.[77] This was done in distant cities for two reasons. First, the distance from the operation would help to protect their purpose. Second, these two cities were probably the only sites north of Memphis where craft in such large numbers might be collected.

Porter personally volunteered to prepare all vessels, both navy and army, and Grant gladly accepted the proposal. The admiral placed his combined fleet on the Louisiana side above the mouth of the Yazoo, where the dense tree growth protected them from spies. He strengthened the gunboats with additional chains around the pilothouses, draping them over the sides to help deflect the largest-caliber shells. Large logs were strapped together and run along the waterlines. He placed planks atop the wooden decks and added cotton bales and wet bales of hay around the vitals of each vessel to absorb shot and shells.[78] All gun ports were closed until the need to fire was absolute. All internal lights were to be extinguished. Finally, Porter ordered the exhausts diverted into the wheelhouses to reduce the popping noises of the engines as the *Carondelet* had done at Island No. 10.[79] Close attention was paid to the army transports as well. Porter's men packed and stacked bales of cotton and hay several layers deep between the guards and boilers from the boiler deck to the deck above. Sacks of grain were packed tightly in front of the boilers and all around the guards on each boat. The army would need the hay and grain once it reached the assault position, and the roads were too boggy to support the weight of laden wagons.[80]

Lessons learned in prior operations were applied to the first group's plan of movement. A vessel or coal barge would be lashed to each ironclad similar to the tactics used on the attacks on Fort Donelson, Island No. 10, the *Indianola*'s prior run at Vicksburg, and Farragut's passage at Port Hudson. Leading the single-file column was the *Benton* as flagship with Porter aboard. Lieutenant Commander James A. Greer commanded it. Lashed to this vessel was the tug *Ivy*. Next in line was the *Lafayette*, commanded by Captain Henry Walke. This side-wheeler ironclad had the tinclad *General Sterling Price* attached to its starboard side and a coal barge to the port side. A coal barge with 10,000 bushels of coal aboard was attached to each of the following ironclads: the *Louisville*, under Lieutenant Commander E. K. Owen; *Mound City*, under Lieutenant Byron Wilson; *Pittsburg*, under Acting Volunteer Lieutenant William R. Hoel; and *Carondelet*, under Lieutenant Commander J. McLeod Murphy. Next came three army transports packed with needed supplies for Grant's army, followed by the side-wheeler ironclad *Tuscumbia*, under Lieutenant Commander James W. Shirk. The *Tuscumbia*'s task was to prevent the transport captains from turning and running once the batteries began to fire on them.

The passage began at 9:15 P.M. on the night of April 16 with little moonlight and the vessels making just enough steam to keep the wheels turning. This allowed the river current to move them along, just as had oc-

USS Lafayette. *Library of Congress image LCB8184-4584.*

curred with the unmanned coal barges' previous runs. Porter hoped that the batteries would not notice them until the flotilla was well underway, but Confederate scouts spotted the massive dark shapes moving in the night. They ignited dry wood and several abandoned houses on the Louisiana side to backlight the gunboats. The portents were those of Farragut at Port Hudson. The pitch wood fires from the west bank cast a thick pall of smoke, which only the bright yellow and orange flashes punctuated as the guns fired. As the slow, majestic procession moved south, it was perfectly silhouetted for the Confederate gunners. The batteries began firing on the gunboats from seemingly every gun on the bluffs, from the waterline batteries up to the heights of Fort Hill, and down to Warrenton on the southern end of the defense line. Porter's ironclads returned fire, and soon the sky around Vicksburg glowed like the yellow fires of hell. The smoke from the combined guns and the fires from the Louisiana shore created low-hanging, choking, sulfurous clouds.

A ball was held in Vicksburg that evening, and as the alarms went out about the Yankee fleet on the move, officers went to their units and the ladies and gentlemen of Vicksburg ran or rode in their carriages to the best places to view the coming glorious sinking of the hated gunboats. The Sky Parlor on one of the highest bluffs was a popular spot for watching the show, as were the grounds and upper floors of the courthouse.

The coal barges made the passage difficult. Some of the vessels traced circles in the current as they were trying to gather steam.[81] As they gained control, the boats maneuvered close to the Mississippi side and pounded the shore batteries, doing a great deal of damage to the lower batteries. The

ADMIRAL PORTER'S FLEET RUNNING THE REBEL BLOCKADE OF THE MISSISSIPPI AT VICKSBURG, APRIL 16TH 1863.

Currier and Ives lithograph of the Mississippi Squadron running the gauntlet at Vicksburg on April 16, 1863. U.S. Naval Historical Center image NH 76557 KN.

Confederates in turn were able to fire point-blank into some of the ironclads with every possible caliber of shell. The *Benton* fared well in the passage, but the boats behind it were less fortunate. The *Lafayette,* tied to the *General Sterling Price,* was greatly slowed by the added weight and the off-center propulsion of both vessels. The *Price* was hit and heavily damaged by friendly fire from the *Louisville,* forcing its captain, Lieutenant Commander Selim Woodworth, to cut the gunboat free from the ironclad.[82] The *Lafayette* and several of the other gunboats cut the coal barges free to allow the vessels to maneuver. The transport *Henry Clay* broke from the column and attempted to flee upstream to safety. The *Tuscumbia* turned to prevent this cowardly act. As the *Clay* attempted to resume its place within the column, a Confederate shell hit the boat and set it afire. The crew abandoned ship, and the captain followed after two additional rounds slammed into the transport. The shore gunners paid particular attention to the *Clay,* hoping that it might scatter the procession. The *Henry Clay* became an uncontrolled drifting inferno. The needless diversion of blasting the transport helped other vessels pass the gauntlet relatively unscathed. The *Tuscumbia* grounded, and as it tried to extricate itself, the vessel plowed into the *Forest Queen.* Both boats drifted downstream after taking multiple hits from the Rebel gunners.[83] The column ran the gauntlet as the *Henry Clay* trailed. Casualties were light, and Porter was somewhat disdainful of the Rebel batteries' prowess when he reported to Gideon Welles on April 19 that he suffered no dead, one or two badly wounded, and twelve total casualties, most of whom were walking wounded. As for the Rebel gunners, he wrote, "The shot the enemy fired was of the heaviest caliber, and some of excellent pattern; they came on board, but did no material damage beyond smashing the bulwarks."[84]

Grant was so enthusiastic about the successful run that he asked Porter to send more of the transports past the batteries. A few days later, on the night of April 22, an almost defenseless flotilla of five stern-wheelers, one side-wheeler, and twelve barges made a second successful attempt. Because of a lack of cotton bales, the boats used barrels of cured beef to protect the engines and boilers. The boats and barges carried 600,000 rations for the 13th Corps.[85] The only boat lost was the *Tigress*, Grant's flag boat at the Battle of Shiloh. The Confederates' overreliance on the use of batteries along and on the bluffs was evident in this second passage.

Porter's next task was to silence the batteries at Grand Gulf. He was very confident that his gunboats could do this since the bluffs were not nearly as high as those at Vicksburg, and he believed he had adequate resources to do this. Grant assembled his army in and around Hard Times Plantation, waiting for Porter to finish off the only obstacle in his way before he committed to the amphibious assault. Porter was ready on April 29, and his challenge to the batteries began at 8:15 A.M. Grand Gulf was actually two forts, Fort Cobun on the north and Fort Wade on the south. Covered ways and rifle pits connected these bastions.

The Mississippi Squadron in action at Grand Gulf, Mississippi, on April 29, 1863. From a drawing by Capt. Henry Walke. U.S. Naval Historical Center image NH 001852.

The flotilla worked in two groups. The *Pittsburg* led with the other Pook Turtles *Louisville, Carondelet*, and *Mound City*, following in that order, single file. They began firing, first pummeling Fort Cobun before leisurely steaming south to pound Fort Wade. After passing the southern fort, this group maintained battle order as they circled back to blast Wade again. Behind the first group was the second contingent led by the *Benton*, with the ironclads *Tuscumbia* and *Lafayette* following single file. This group trailed the wakes of the first and assaulted Cobun.[86] The forts and the ironclads exchanged heavy shelling with Fort Wade taking the most telling hits. The southern anchor was almost silenced. As the ironclads focused on Fort Wade, a gun from Cobun struck the *Benton* with Porter still aboard. The round entered the pilothouse, crashed through the deck, and exploded inside, destroying the ironclad's massive wheel. The *Benton* circled out of control and grounded where the Rebel gunners could not reach it.[87] As Fort Wade's firing withered and halted, the ironclads focused on Fort Cobun. The gunboats could not break the fort's large walls or silence its guns. Both sides maintained steady fire for five hours until Cobun's guns reduced their fire rate as their ammunition ran low; however, Porter was convinced that he could not reduce the works without a land assault, and Grant agreed. The flotilla moved upstream to Hard Times by 2:30 P.M.[88] It had been a long day with little to show for it. The *Benton* suffered twenty-four casualties. The *Tuscumbia* was seriously damaged. Much like its near sisters, the *Indianola* and *Chillicothe*, it was unable to deflect shells in an assault, proving it to have been poorly designed. It would spend most the remainder of the war on the ways, being repaired or patched. Porter described it as a "poor ship in a hot engagement."[89]

Grant and Porter decided that another tack must be taken. A runaway slave told the army commander that a place called Bruinsburg, six miles below Port Gibson, had a road that led inland. This was a good choice because the beachhead was still close to Hard Times. It was altered, and with the protection of the gunboats, the largest amphibious assault prior to Operation Torch in World War II was carried out in the spring of 1863.[90] Grant landed unopposed on April 30 and May 1, and although the Rebels did not yet know it, Vicksburg was doomed to fall.

Two operational feints kept the Confederates busy while the grand ferrying operation unfolded. In what has been called the greatest cavalry raid of the war, Colonel Benjamin Grierson led three regiments of horse soldiers starting with 1,700 troopers at the beginning of the operation. They ventured 600 miles deep into Rebel-held territory from La Grange, Tennessee, then down the eastern side of Mississippi and across the state, ending in Baton Rouge. This raid drew away cavalry and infantry units that could and should have warned the Confederate command of Grant's landing.[91]

Of more immediate concern to Vicksburg was another feint. Grant ordered Sherman to make a "demonstration" at Haynes' Bluff.[92] The naval force above Vicksburg was formidable. It consisted of the ironclads *Choctaw* and *Baron De Kalb*; the timberclad *Tyler*; Porter's flagship, the large tinclad *Black Hawk*; and the tinclads *Petrel*, *Romeo*, and *Signal*. The force included three mortar scows and ten of Sherman's transports with ten regiments of men. The gunboats fired enough rounds at the bluffs to make the Rebels believe that the attack was real, and Sherman's men disgorged and appeared to prepare for an assault before they withdrew. The Confederates believed this was the beginning of a major attack and held troops north of Vicksburg rather than sending them south to face Grant. This gave the Union commander the time and maneuvering room he needed.

Major General Henry Halleck, the army general-in-chief in Washington, wanted Grant to wait for reinforcements under Nathaniel Banks. Banks had been expected to take Port Hudson and join their forces. Grant had no intention of waiting for Banks, and this was the correct course. Although Banks outranked Grant and could have countermanded any order he received, the inept Banks did not know when to attack, moved tentatively, and did not want to play second fiddle to the audacious Grant. Grant secured Grand Gulf to protect his connection with Porter and then made a decision that spurred his career to true greatness. With some protection from Porter's fleet, he could have moved up the roads near the Mississippi River and attempted to destroy the Rebel works at Warrenton, Mississippi. From there, he could mount an attack on Vicksburg from the south. Instead, he moved his three corps northeast to Jackson, capturing the Confederate state capital. Grant knew there were two Rebel armies in the vicinity, Pemberton's army in Vicksburg and another army under General Joseph Johnston building somewhere north and east of Jackson.[93] Grant's decision to move away from the fortress on the bluffs baffled the Rebels. They immediately realized that the maneuver cut off all aid to the city from the interior of Mississippi. With the Mississippi Squadron dominating the river, Vicksburg was tightly squeezed. After Grant took Jackson, he turned due west and attempted to break the Vicksburg defenses, which he believed were only strong in that portion facing the river. He was wrong, and the Rebels met him outside their bulwarks. About halfway between Jackson and the Vicksburg defenses, the Confederates made a stand in open country, along a low ridge named Champion Hill, on May 16.[94] In what appeared to be a standoff, Grant was able to turn the Rebels' flank, and the southerners retreated back into the Vicksburg defenses. Grant and his corps commanders met and decided to attack in an attempt to implode the Confederate line. Two bloody attempts were made, the first on May 19 and the second on May 22, but both ended in repulses. The Confederates had almost a full year to strengthen their lines and had made them as strong as possible. Grant decided to settle in for a siege.

The Mississippi Squadron was not idle as Grant's army moved away from the river. After the squadron ferried Grant's force across, it then moved downstream and ferried Banks' men. The Squadron then steamed north and ran the batteries at Vicksburg. Porter then revisited Haynes' Bluff. He wanted to secure Grant's northern flank and reduce the threat posed to his vessels by any Confederate forces still operating in the Yazoo basin. He chose the ironclads *Baron De Kalb* and *Choctaw* and the tinclads *Forest Rose, Linden, Romeo,* and *Petrel* and prepared for a strike up the Yazoo into the heart of the basin. The flotilla found the Rebel works at Haynes' Bluff abandoned but intact.[95] He destroyed them on May 18 after hearing heavy firing near Vicksburg that indicated Grant was closing in from the east. Porter's force, under Lieutenant Commander John G. Walker aboard the *Baron DeKalb,* continued to Yazoo City, where it found three rams under construction at the naval base. Walker destroyed the *Mobile,* which was finished and ready to receive its iron plates, as well as the *Republic,* a ram with railroad rails for plating fitted to use a ram, and a third, unnamed vessel. Porter described this gunboat in his report to Gideon Welles as "a vessel on the stocks (a monster), 310 feet long and 70 feet beam. This vessel was to have been covered with 4½-inch iron plating, was to have had 6 engines, 4 side wheels, and two propellers; she would have given us much trouble."[96] Porter also reported on the naval yard that contained a sawmill, planing machines, a large machine shop, and carpenter and blacksmith shops.[97]

As Grant's hold on the Vicksburg defenses tightened, his engineers constructed extensive counterworks and extended his efforts to thwart the Rebels at every turn. He was concerned about a Rebel army to his rear, but he never lost focus on the objective at his front. Porter was able to resupply the army and conduct a constant bombardment with his mortar scows and some schooners. The admiral also assisted Grant and Sherman with missions when requested. One of these was cause for concern. On May 27, less than a week after the investment of the siege, Porter sent the *Cincinnati* down from the mouth of the Yazoo to conduct a fire mission to destroy a masked battery at the base of Fort Hill, the northern anchor of the bluff defenses. This battery prevented Sherman from executing a move against the hilltop fort. As the *Cincinnati* approached, the treacherous river currents caught the craft and spun it around. The captain attempted to use his two-gun stern battery against the shore guns, but accurate fire poured into the ironclad. One round pierced the magazine, slammed into the keel, and passed through the bottom of the hull. Water entered the stricken turtle like a geyser. Another round disintegrated the starboard tiller. The *Cincinnati* began to rotate, performing a macabre death spiral. Other plunging rounds cracked the casemates and heavily damaged the interior. The gunboat sank in nine feet of water as forty crewmen died, most of them drowning. Unlike the *Cairo*, the *Cincinnati* was raised to fight again. Porter was angry over the loss of the *Cincinnati* and worried that it had jeopardized his career. To demonstrate the support for the army, he and Thomas O. Selfridge, Jr., late commander of the *Cairo*, offered to set up an artillery battery of naval guns.[98]

While Grant pounded and starved Vicksburg into submission, Porter sent assistance to General Banks at Port Hudson, who could not crack the bastion's defenses. President Lincoln believed an invasion of Texas would help draw the war to an end, so Banks concocted a mission that might redeem his military career. Porter agreed to assist Banks with this awkwardly designed foray, called the Texas Overland Expedition, although it never reached that state. Porter's vessels steamed up the Red River as far as Alexandria and up the Ouachita to Fort Beauregard, between Trinity and Harrisonburg. Banks had no idea how to gain access to Texas with Port Hudson still not under his control, so the 1863 attempt to invade Texas ended with a whimper and not a bang.[99]

Grant's attempt to starve the Vicksburg garrison into submission succeeded. General Joe Johnston's relief force never arrived, and the city's defenders became desperate. On July 2, Confederate General John C. Pemberton held a council of war with his commanders to discuss his remaining options. He met Grant between the lines on July 3, and the particulars of surrender were hammered out. The southerners laid down their arms on Independence Day, July 4. Neither side realized that, as the two commanders met on July 3, the other great high-water mark of the war was ending with Pickett's Charge at the Battle of Gettysburg. Although historians of the eastern theater of the war—and much of the public as well—regard Gettysburg as *the* pivotal battle of the Civil War, it was the Vicksburg Campaign that split the Confederacy and ended any hope of succor from the Trans-Mississippi.

Port Hudson held out, surrendering only after receiving word that Vicksburg had fallen. Banks was deprived of his glorious battlefield victory once again. Grant moved to Tennessee and then Virginia and became the most famous Union general of the war. His solid friendship with Sherman and Porter continued. Porter and Banks would meet once more in the coming year, again in the Red River Valley.

One last tragedy was acted out as part of the Vicksburg Campaign. A little more than a week after the surrender of Vicksburg, Porter sent a flotilla comprised of the ironclad *Baron De Kalb*, the naval transport *New National*, the tinclads *Kenwood* and *Signal*, and army transports with 5,000 troops up the Yazoo again to clear any residual Rebel attempts at creating a surprise. Near Yazoo City, the *Baron De Kalb* stuck a Singer torpedo. This was a different design than the ones that sank the *Cairo*. The model was detonated using either a contact plunger or an electrical line strung from the shore to be remotely detonated. It was designed by the Singer Submarine Corporation, the same engineers who designed and built the Confederate submarine *Hunley*. The Singer torpedo was a much-improved version of the crude models that previously infested the Yazoo swamp.[100]

The crew felt a disturbance under the bow and water cascaded into the hull. The boat settled quickly by the bow. Adding insult to injury, the stern settled on another torpedo and blew a second hole in hull.[101] The *Baron De Kalb*, unlike its sister the *Cincinnati*, would be raised to fight again, but it would not be the last time that a Singer torpedo would sink a Union ironclad.

NOTES

1. Unquestionably, the finest examination of the role geography played in the Vicksburg Campaign is found in Warren E. Grabau, *Ninety-Eight Days: A Geographer's View of the Vicksburg Campaign* (Knoxville: University of Tennessee Press, 2000).

2. Paul H. Silverstone, *Warships of the Civil War Navies* (Annapolis, Md.: Naval Institute Press, 1989), 161.

3. *ORN* 24: 320.

4. *ORN* 24: 217–19.

5. *ORN* 24: 219–20.

6. *ORN* 24: 222.

7. *ORN* 24: 223–24; Maurice Melton, "From Vicksburg to Port Hudson: Porter's River Campaign," *Harper's Weekly* (February 28, 1983) 12, no. 10.

8. For a list of known Confederate vessels operating on the Red River between 1863 and 1865, see Gary D. Joiner, Marilyn S. Joiner, and Clifton D. Cardin, eds., *No Pardons to Ask nor Apologies to Make: The Journal of William Henry King, Gray's 28th Louisiana Infantry Regiment* (Knoxville: University of Tennessee Press, 2006), 251–52. By mid-1864, the fleet was augmented by the ironclad CSS *Missouri* and five *Hunley*-class submarines.

9. *ORN* 24: 224.

10. *ORN* 24: 224.

11. *ORN* 24: 225–26.

12. *ORN* 24: 384.

13. *ORN* 24: 376.

14. *ORN* 24: 376.

15. Jefferson Davis owned Brierfield, and his brother Joseph owned Hurricane Plantation. Both plantations were located south of Vicksburg.

16. *ORN* 24: 376–77.

17. *ORN* 24: 377.

18. The Black River is the lower portion of the Ouachita River.

19. *ORN* 24: 384.

20. For a thorough history of Fort DeRussy, see Steven Mayeux, *Earthen Walls, Iron Men: Fort DeRussy, Louisiana, and the Defense of Red River* (Knoxville: University of Tennessee Press, 2007).

21. *ORN* 24: 384–85.

22. *ORN* 24: 385.

23. *ORN* 24: 379–80.

24. The *Dr. Beatty*, also spelled *Dr. Batey* and *Dr. Beaty*, was a side-wheeler built in Louisville, Kentucky, in 1850. It was 171 feet long and carried one 6-pounder. See Silverstone, *Warships of the Civil War Navies*, 246.

25. *ORN* 24: 401–2. Confederate Major General Richard Taylor, commander of the District of Western Louisiana, conceived the mission. He ordered Major J. L. Brent of his staff to be in overall charge. *ORN* 24: 400–408.

26. *ORN* 24: 400–408. Lieutenant Commander Brown stated in his report of the incident that there was a fourth vessel, although he did not identify either of the cottonclad gunboats. *ORN* 24: 380–81.

27. Jack D. Coombe, *Thunder along the Mississippi: The River Battles That Split the Confederacy* (New York: Sarpedon, 1996), 196–97; *ORN* 24: 380–81, 400–408. Of the two official reports, it is likely that the Confederate version is more correct.

28. *ORN* 24: 400–408.

29. *ORN* 24: 380.

30. *ORN* 24: 380.

31. *ORN* 24: 380–81.

32. *ORN* 24: 393.

33. *ORN* 24: 395–96; Jerry Korn, *War on the Mississippi: Grant's Vicksburg Campaign* (Chicago: Time-Life Books, 1985), 78–79.

34. Korn, *War on the Mississippi*, 79.

35. *ORN* 24: 396.

36. *ORN* 24: 397.

37. *Vicksburg Whig*, March 5, 1863; *ORN* 24: 397.

38. For a thorough biography of Banks, see James G. Hollandsworth Jr., *Pretense of Glory: The Life of General Nathaniel P. Banks* (Baton Rouge: Louisiana State University Press, 1998).

39. The best accounts of Port Hudson siege operations and the naval operations against the Confederate fortifications are found in Lawrence Lee Hewitt, *Port Hudson: Confederate Bastion on the Mississippi* (Baton Rouge: Louisiana State University Press, 1986), and Edward Cunningham, *Port Hudson Campaign 1862–1863* (Baton Rouge: Louisiana State University Press, 1991).

40. George Dewey, *Autobiography of George Dewey: Admiral of the Navy* (New York: Charles Scribner's Sons, 1913), 88; Harrie Webster, *Some Personal Recollections and Reminiscences of the Battle of Port Hudson* (n.p., n.d.), 10, 13.

41. Frank Moore, ed., *The Rebellion Record: A Diary of American Events with Documents, Narratives, Illustrative Incidents, Poetry, etc.*, 12 vols. (New York: G. P. Putnam, 1861–1871), 7: 452.

42. Orton Clark, *The One Hundred and Sixteenth Regiment of New York Volunteers: Being a Complete History of Its Organization and of Its Nearly Three Years of Active Service in the Great Rebellion to Which Is Appended Memorial Sketches, and a Muster Roll of the Regiment. Containing the Name of Every Man Connected With It* (Buffalo, N.Y.: Matthews & Warren, 1868), 57.

43. Hewitt, *Port Hudson*, 81–82; *ORN* 19: 666, 671.

44. *ORN* 19: 666, 671, 707, 709, 711; *OR* 15: 277.

45. U.S. Senate, *Medal of Honor Recipients, 1862–1863* (Washington, D.C.: U.S. Government Printing Office, 1964), 465, 508–9, 558–59, 599; *ORN* 19: 673, 678.

46. *ORN* 19: 672, 677, 769; Dewey, *Autobiography of George Dewey*, 90.

47. *ORN* 19: 678–79.

48. *ORN* 19: 686–88.

49. Hewitt, *Port Hudson*, 75.

50. Dewey, *Autobiography of George Dewey*, 93–95.

51. Solid artillery rounds heated in ovens and fired with the intent of causing fires or explosions on a target.

52. Dewey, *Autobiography of George Dewey*, 98–100; *ORN* 19: 681.

53. Hewitt, *Port Hudson*, 91.

54. Clark, *The One Hundred and Sixteenth Regiment of New York Volunteers*, 57; *Memphis Daily Appeal*, March 16, 20, 1863; *ORN* 19: 676, 679, 682, 685, 688–89, 770.

55. Clark, *The One Hundred and Sixteenth Regiment of New York Volunteers*, 57; *OR* 15: 251, 262, 271, 275–76, 278; *OR* 26: 8.

56. Coombe, *Thunder along the Mississippi*, 202.

57. *ORN* 24: 515–16.

58. This was presumably either the *Arizona* or the *Estrella*, both of which operated near the mouth of the Red and occasionally made forays up to Fort DeRussy. See *ORN* 24: 645; see also a sketch by an unnamed Union artist of an action at Fort DeRussy in 1863, at the Spring Street Museum, Shreveport, Louisiana. The sketch shows the *Arizona* and the *Estrella*, both of which are labeled.

59. *ORN* 24: 522–26.

60. Edwin C. Bearss, *The Vicksburg Campaign*, 3 vols. (Dayton, Ohio: Morningside Bookshop, 1985–1986), 1: 482–83.

61. Michael B. Ballard, *Vicksburg: The Campaign That Opened the Mississippi* (Chapel Hill: University of North Carolina Press, 2004), 175.

62. Katherine Polk Gale, "Reminiscences of Life in the Southern Confederacy, 1861–1865," 10-11A, Gale and Polk Family Papers, Southern Historical Collection, Wilson Library, University of North Carolina at Chapel Hill, as quoted in Ballard, *Vicksburg*, 176.

63. Engineering troops used to clear paths and remove obstructions, among other duties.

64. Ballard, *Vicksburg*, 179.

65. *ORN* 24: 268, 272; *OR* 24: 412–13, 415–16.

66. Bearss, *The Vicksburg Campaign* 1: 521–23; *OR* 24: 412, 416; *ORN* 24: 247, 273–76.

67. Bearss, *The Vicksburg Campaign* 1: 524–26; *OR* 24: 380–83.

68. Grant and Prentiss certainly blamed the pace and conduct of the navy's actions squarely on Smith. Bearss, *The Vicksburg Campaign* 1: 524–26.

69. Ballard, *Vicksburg*, 184–85.

70. *ORN* 24: 474; *OR* 24: 474; *OR* 24 part 3: 112–13.

71. David Dixon Porter, *The Naval History of the Civil War* (New York: Appleton, 1886), 305.

72. Porter, *The Naval History of the Civil War*, 305.

73. Ballard, *Vicksburg*, 187.

74. Porter, *The Naval History of the Civil War*, 307.

75. The best manner to view the complex streams and point locations mentioned in this chapter is to examine topographic atlases for individual states. The author used the DeLorme *Louisiana Atlas and Gazetteer* and the DeLorme *Mississippi Atlas and Gazetteer*.

76. Ulysses S. Grant, *Personal Memoirs of U. S. Grant* (New York: Da Capo, 1982), 240.

77. Grant, *Personal Memoirs of U. S. Grant*, 241.

78. *ORN* 24: 553–54.

79. *ORN* 24: 553–54.

80. Grant, *Personal Memoirs of U. S. Grant*, 240.

81. Bearss, *The Vicksburg Campaign* 2: 266–68; *ORN* 24: 555–56.

82. *ORN* 24: 553, 556–58, 682.

83. *ORN* 24: 553. Porter's version was more heroic. He reported that the *Tuscumbia* stayed behind to assist the *Forest Queen* and then towed it to safety.

84. *ORN* 24: 554.

85. Ballard, *Vicksburg*, 202.

86. *ORN* 24: 607–8, 610–11, 613, 615–23, 625–26.

87. Bearss, *The Vicksburg Campaign* 2: 311.

88. *ORN* 24: 574–75; Grant, *Personal Memoirs of U. S. Grant*, 317.

89. *ORN* 24: 611.

90. Grant, *Personal Memoirs of U. S. Grant*, 251.

91. This raid was the basis for John Wayne's movie *The Horse Soldiers* in 1959. The best accounts of the raid are found in Bearss, *The Vicksburg Campaign* 2: 187–236, and Dee Alexander Brown, *Grierson's Raid* (Dayton, Ohio: Morningside Bookshop, 1981), reprinted from 1954.

92. W. T. Sherman, *Memoirs* (New York: The Library of America, 1990), 347; *OR* 24: 240–45.

93. For an excellent examination of Joseph E. Johnston during the Vicksburg Campaign, see Terrence J. Winschel, *Triumph and Defeat: The Vicksburg Campaign*, vol. 2 (New York: Savas Beatie, 2006), 115–28.

94. For the best analysis of the campaign prior to the siege of Vicksburg, see Bearss, *The Vicksburg Campaign*, and Ballard, *Vicksburg*. For the most in-depth treatment of the Battle of Champion Hill, see Timothy B. Smith, *Champion Hill: Decisive Battle for Vicksburg* (New York: Savas Beatie, 2004).

95. *ORN* 25: 5–6.

96. *ORN* 25: 8.

97. *ORN* 25: 8.

98. *ORN* 25: 56.

99. For an excellent account of this campaign, see Richard Lowe, *The Texas Overland Expedition of 1863* (Fort Worth, Tex.: Ryan Place Publishers, 1996).

100. Mark K. Ragan, *Union and Confederate Submarine Warfare in the Civil War* (Mason City, Iowa: Savas Publishing, 1999), 105, 179, 226, 233, 245.

101. Milton F. Perry, *Infernal Machines: The Story of Confederate Submarine and Mine Warfare* (Baton Rouge: Louisiana State University Press, 1965), 45.

8

✛

The Red River Campaign

I am clear of my troubles and my fleet is safe out in the broad Mississippi. I have had a hard and anxious time of it.

—Admiral David Dixon Porter

After the fall of Vicksburg, General Sherman lobbied for a campaign up the Red River, the only major tributary of the Mississippi River that the Mississippi Squadron did not patrol, toward the Confederate capital of Louisiana at Shreveport. A change in the political and military winds in the North looked promising, as General Grant was promoted to commanding general of the U.S. Army. With this assignment came the third star of a lieutenant general. General Halleck held the position of chief of staff of the army, and he and Grant worked well together in the East, although they had often disagreed while in the West.

Sherman lobbied Grant to put him in charge of the campaign, but his friend and superior was reluctant even to consider the operation. At that time, Grant was in the early process of planning the capture of Mobile, Alabama, and he believed that Sherman could not be spared. Halleck, however, pushed for it to begin, and President Lincoln desperately needed it.[1] The president insisted on electing members of Congress from Louisiana and Texas in the fall elections of 1864. Grant acquiesced to the plan and also to the use of a portion of Sherman's troops, although he would not send Sherman himself.[2]

By the end of January 1864, the Meridian Campaign occupied most of Sherman's time, giving him little chance to plan the Red River Campaign. Halleck wrote to Sherman and intimated that both he and Major General

143

Nathaniel Banks would lead the expedition once the Meridian Campaign had ended. He did not inform Grant of the planning and, therefore, did not tell him which troops would be used. Halleck knew that Grant would be angry if a large force were diverted from a campaign to take Mobile, thereby weakening Sherman's chances of taking Atlanta. The troops were needed to redirect Confederate forces from potentially attacking Sherman's flanks once the mission began. If the expedition were carried out, Admiral Porter offered his full support to Sherman. No doubt he thought that Sherman would lead the campaign and that it would be a great opportunity to work with his friend.[3] Sherman went to New Orleans on March 2 to meet with Banks, but the meeting did not go well. Banks pulled rank on Sherman, informing him that as senior officer, Banks would lead the campaign.[4] Sherman wrote to his wife, "I wanted to go up Red River, but as Banks was to command in person I thought it best not to go."[5]

Banks created an impossibly complex plan using four pincers of troops. Two would descend on Shreveport from Arkansas. A third staged near New Orleans, where the railroad and steamboats would transport the troops across the vast marshes of southern Louisiana. This group was then to march along the banks of Bayou Teche to near modern-day Opelousas and then up to Alexandria in the center of the state. There they would rendezvous with the fourth pincer, which consisted of 10,000 men loaned from Sherman. This force would travel on transports, in the company of Porter and the bulk of the Mississippi Squadron, from Vicksburg to the mouth of the Red River and then up the river to Alexandria. Porter boasted he would strip the inland force of available hulls and guns for the expedition, and the total of 210 large ordnance pieces loaded aboard Porter's flotilla proved his point. Porter promised Sherman that he would ascend the Red River "with every ironclad vessel in the fleet."[6]

The fleet included the ironclads *Benton, Carondelet, Chillicothe, Choctaw, Eastport, Essex, Lafayette, Louisville, Mound City*, and *Pittsburg*; the new Eads stern-wheeler large river monitors *Neosho* and *Osage*; the lesser river monitor *Ozark*; the large tinclads *Black Hawk* and *Ouachita*; the timberclad *Lexington*; and the tinclads *Covington, Cricket, Forest Rose, Fort Hindman, Gazelle, Juliet, Signal, St. Clair*, and *Tallahatchee*; the ram *General Sterling Price*; and support vessels that included dispatch boats, tenders, tugs, and supply vessels.[7] The Army Quartermaster Corps also had its own transport and supply vessels, and the Mississippi Marine Brigade supplied its rams, support vessels, and a hospital boat. In all, the fleet consisted of 104 vessels, one of the largest congregations of inland warfare craft in the Civil War.

The most impressive vessel was the *Eastport*, which with several other ironclads was sent on this expedition because Porter had been warned of the Confederate naval presence in Shreveport, particularly the existence of ironclads and submarines.[8] The memory of what the *Arkansas* had done to the fleet at Vicksburg remained vivid in his mind. Spies or informants had described the *Missouri*, which the Rebels built at Shreveport, as a smaller *Tennessee* or *Arkansas*. The spies told him two ironclads had been completed in Shreveport and that three others were under construction.[9] This was an exaggerated report from an intelligence operative, but it was perhaps the greatest influence on his thinking. Porter wanted to take no chances of getting caught with inadequate firepower in a narrow river; therefore, he would lead each leg of the journey with his largest and thus most cumbersome vessel, the *Eastport*. The two heaviest guns, 100-pounder rifles, were located in twin forward gun positions where they were able to be ironclad killers.

The campaign began on March 10 with the departure from Vicksburg of twenty-one Union steamboat troop transports packed as tightly as possible with Sherman's 10,000 men and equipment. The departure date was already three days delayed from the original timetable, creating tension.[10] Sherman's veterans proceeded down the Mississippi River to the mouth of the Red River, arriving on the evening of March 11. Porter, the Mississippi Squadron, and the Mississippi Marine Brigade met them there.[11] With the entire fleet gathered at the rendezvous point, Porter and Brigadier General Andrew Jackson Smith, who led Sherman's troops, confronted their first problem: how to enter the river and find the main channel.

The Red River did not look as it had when the *Queen of the West* forayed into it. The mouth of the Red, a jumble of ancient stream confluences, set the physical tableau for the beginning of the campaign.[12] Porter and Smith

USS Eastport. *Archives of Mansfield State Historic Site, Mansfield, Louisiana.*

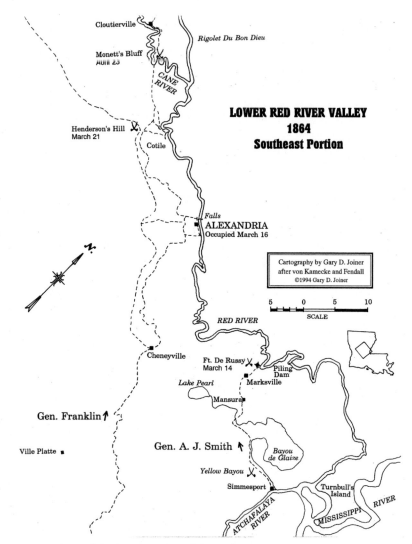

Cloutierville

Rigolet Du Bon Dieu

Monett's Bluff
April 23

CANE
RIVER

**LOWER RED RIVER VALLEY
1864
Southeast Portion**

Henderson's Hill
March 21

Cotile

Falls
■ ALEXANDRIA
Occupied March 16

Cartography by Gary D. Joiner
after von Kamecke and Fendall
©1994 Gary D. Joiner

5   0   5   10
SCALE

RED RIVER

Cheneyville

Ft. De Russy
March 14
Piling
Dam

Lake Pearl   Marksville

Mansura

Gen. Franklin

Yellow Bayou

Ville Platte ■

Gen. A. J. Smith

*Bayou
de Glaize*

Simmesport

Turnbull's
Island

ATCHAFALAYA
RIVER

MISSISSIPPI   RIVER

Map of the lower portion of the Red River in Louisiana.

decided to establish their toehold near the Red's mouth. Lieutenant Commander Seth Ledyard Phelps led the fleet with the *Eastport*, which grounded on a sandbar at the mouth of the river. After they wrestled it free, the venture continued with the other ironclads following for support in the event that Confederates awaited them. General Smith immediately brought his transports into Old River, an ancient arm of the Mississippi. Smith's men disembarked at Simmesport, the staging point for the attack on Fort DeRussy. Porter sent some of the ironclads up the Ouachita River to neutralize a Rebel fortification at Trinity.[13] The bulk of the fleet, however, proceeded up the Red to address the massive water battery guarding Fort DeRussy and "amuse the Fort until the army could land."[14] Their plan called for Smith's men to march on the fort from the rear, while Porter distracted them at the front.

Porter's vessels encountered a Confederate obstruction, or "raft," downstream at a sharp bend in the river the maps called the "bend of the Rappiones."[15] The admiral was challenged to devise a way to destroy it, as well as the "forest of trees" that the Confederates had driven into the channel.[16] Phelps ordered the *Fort Hindman* to remove the obstacles by alternately ramming and attaching the timbers to the boats' hawsers via ropes.[17] Although the obstruction delayed the vessels by several hours, the *Eastport* and her escorts eventually steamed upstream, and the naval crews watched the finale of the attack on the fort.

Sherman's men boarded the transports and accompanied the fleet to Alexandria.[18] Porter left the *Benton* and *Essex* at the fort for three days, as A. J. Smith's troops tried to destroy the works.[19] The *Benton* and *Essex* fired at point-blank range to destroy the water battery casemate but were unable to do so despite their powerful guns.[20] The two ironclads never ascended farther up the river to assist the fleet during the expedition. Instead, they performed picket duty, guarding the navy's rear from some undetermined Confederate threat. The delays at Fort DeRussy did not bother Porter. He wanted his arrival at Alexandria to coincide with Banks's, according to schedule.

Porter sent his heavy monitor *Osage* to accompany the army's transports as they prepared to take Alexandria. Lieutenant Commander Thomas O. Selfridge Jr. commanded the warship. The *Osage* arrived in Alexandria on the afternoon of Tuesday, March 15, and received the town's surrender without firing a shot.[21] Selfridge sent word back for Porter to hurry because he feared the citizens of Alexandria might realize that their population outnumbered his crew and might attempt to capture his boat. Sherman's troops landed only a few hours later. Porter had hoped to catch Confederate boats at the Alexandria wharves unawares, but he missed his opportunity by hours. The admiral brought the bulk of his fleet to Alexandria on March 15 and 16 and let his men enjoy the town while he waited for Banks to arrive.

With the city's surrender in hand and no sign of Banks and his legions, Porter struggled with the inactivity. To counter this, he decided to procure cotton, and with the Naval Prize Law on his side, he had the right to seize such war prizes from the property of a belligerent nation. On March 24, Porter wrote the U.S. district judge in Springfield, Illinois, requesting the adjudication of 2,129 bales of cotton, twenty-eight barrels of molasses, and eighteen bales of wool. He was very specific that this was all captured from the Confederate government. He listed twenty vessels that should share in "the prize," each theoretically contributing to the confiscation of cotton. These included all his ironclads and monitors as well as most of his tinclads. The list included both the *Benton* and the *Essex*, although they were at the mouth of the river, but excluded all vessels of the Mississippi Marine Brigade and the army's Quartermaster Corps.[22] The navy gathered more than 3,000 bales of cotton in and around Alexandria.[23] An exact number of bales may never be known, but neither will the total number of bales burned in retaliation by the Confederates.

In southern Louisiana, Banks had not endured the hazards and deprivations of the march with his infantry. He had floated into Alexandria the day before on a transport named *Black Hawk*.[24] Reporters and cotton speculators filled the vessel, and Porter was not amused. He considered Banks's choice of conveyance an insult. The admiral's flagship, the large tinclad also named *Black Hawk*, was his pride and joy, and the perceived insult was not lost on the admiral or his favored captains.[25]

Since Sherman had lived across the river from Alexandria during his years as superintendent of the Louisiana State Seminary of Learning and Military Institute, he explained to Porter that the Red River rose every

Photograph of a portion of the Mississippi Squadron at on the Red River above Alexandria shortly before the completion of Bailey's dam. The ironclad on the left of the image is the Louisville. *Its armor plating has been removed. The monitor is the* Neosho. *Note cotton on the deck. The vessel with the tall smokestacks is the* Lexington. *There are also three sisters of the* Louisville *in the photograph, one behind the* Neosho *and two to the left of the* Lexington. *Lord-Eltinge Papers, Rare Book, Manuscript, and Special Collections Library, Duke University, Durham, North Carolina.*

spring and that this was the only time the fleet, particularly the deep-draft gunboats, could get to Shreveport.[26] Porter had monitored the river levels since the day he arrived and watched for the anticipated rise; instead, he saw the river falling, sometimes an inch per day and sometimes an inch per hour.[27] While this concerned the admiral, he readily told any interested party who would listen that he could take his fleet, and he meant *his* fleet, "wherever the sand was damp."[28] Banks had a difficult time convincing the admiral that he needed his help, but he was finally successful. Then Porter, with his usual braggadocio, told the general that he would accompany him even if "I should lose all my boats."[29]

The admiral realized that he could wait no longer for the river to rise and prepared to move upstream. He sent light-draft vessels forward to check the channel depth at various places in and above Alexandria. He secured the services of a very experienced riverboat pilot, Wellington W. Withenbury, who advised him to take only his light-draft ironclads, monitors, tinclads, and army transports. Withenbury told Porter about the "falls," which were well known to steamboat men. The falls at Alexandria consisted of sandstone boulders, which were never seen in high water and thus were deep enough to cause no harm. In normal conditions in spring, the boulders could be navigated using care since swirls and eddies marked their positions. When water was particularly low, however, the boulders were visible, and this meant that the water levels were just a few feet above the channel floor.[30] Porter listened to Withenbury's counsel before telling him, against the latter's protests, to take the *Eastport* over the falls. Withenbury, serving as the pilot, objected and suggested taking the lighter-draft vessels over first. Porter again ordered him to lead with the *Eastport*.[31] Porter did not want to face a potential *Arkansas* with a tinclad on a narrow river.

Upstream, the Confederates prepared some unpleasant surprises for the Union fleet. Confederate Lieutenant General E. Kirby Smith, commanding the Trans-Mississippi Department in Shreveport, ordered several things to occur in sequence, as he and his staff anticipated the Union navy's ascent. He ordered the huge steamer *New Falls City* brought up from its hiding place in Coushatta Chute (Bayou Coushatta).[32] It steamed to the foot of Scopini Cut-off, one meander bend south of Tone's Bayou, about forty-five river miles below Shreveport.[33] Once there, the engineers wedged it crosswise in the channel, so tightly in fact that its bow and stern ran up fifteen feet on either side of the banks and a sandbar began to build upstream. The engineers then poured mud into the hold and cracked the keel, transforming the boat into an instant dam.[34]

After the placement of the *New Falls City*, other Confederate engineers used black powder to blow up the Hotchkiss dam, built the previous year at Tone's Bayou. The river water exited its channel into the old Tone's

Bayou channel and thence flowed directly into Bayou Pierre, just as the Confederates had planned. The bayou flowed back into the Red River a short distance above Grand Ecore, but just before this occurred, the bayou's floodplain opened into a nineteen-mile-diameter circular bowl, and this is where the bulk of the river water collected.[35] The admiral watched the river fall for several days before it rose briefly. This rise was the small portion of the flow exiting Bayou Pierre and coming back into the river. The rise gave him the encouragement to begin sending the fleet north.

Following Porter's refusal to keep the *Eastport* in deeper water, Withenbury piloted the huge ironclad toward the falls.[36] The experienced pilot's concern proved correct. The boat's draft was too deep, and it grounded in "the chute," the river's twisting course through the boulders. Despite the efforts of tugs and the lighter-draft gunboats pulling and tugging at the ironclad, it remained wedged on the boulders.[37] The great vessel acted like a dam, and eventually the water level rose enough to float the vessel, and it finally traversed the falls.[38]

Although Porter decided to leave some of his heavy ironclads at Alexandria, he still wanted to take the *Eastport*. He managed to move some of the light-draft gunboats past the grounded *Eastport* by sending them in relatively shallow water outside the chute. The *Eastport*'s bulk displaced enough water on either side to help facilitate the passage of the lighter boats. Among them were the ironclads *Carondelet, Chillicothe, Louisville, Mound City,* and *Pittsburg;* the monitors *Osage, Neosho,* and *Ozark;* the timberclad *Lexington;* and the tinclads *Cricket* and *Fort Hindman.*[39] After freeing the *Eastport,* Withenbury asked Porter's permission to go to Grand Ecore aboard the *Black Hawk,* Banks's headquarters boat, and the admiral agreed. They passed the *Eastport* on the way up the river, and Withenbury noted that it was grounded again. The fleet required four days to travel 100 river miles to Grand Ecore. The slow progress, as Withenbury pointed out, was due to the lighter-draft gunboats waiting for the heavier ones.[40] Porter's fears of a potential Confederate fleet waiting for him around each bend of the twisting river forced him to keep the vessels concentrated. He could not afford to have his light-draft vessels move too far forward of the heavy ironclads.

The Mississippi Marine Brigade's fast rams and support vessels moved past the falls, before the hospital boat, the *Woodford,* grounded. Its hull pierced, it sank and had to be burned.[41] Porter was pleased to receive orders that arrived aboard the naval tug *Alf Cutting*: Major General James McPherson, commanding at Vicksburg, needed the Marine Brigade and its vessels to patrol the Mississippi River since the Mississippi Squadron was not available for that duty.[42] Although Porter used the brigade for patrolling and nearshore interdiction missions, he still harbored a grudge against them for insubordination the prior year. The admiral believed they were not needed at this point in the campaign.

Withenbury was not a southern sympathizer or a patriot but rather a pragmatist. He claimed to be an informant for the Union army, and this placed him in position to be the Federal spy in Shreveport, passing information to the Federal authorities in New Orleans and possibly Confederate authorities in Shreveport.[43] He owned several hundred bales of cotton ready for shipment near Shreveport and did not want the navy to steal it or the Confederates to destroy it if the Union forces came close to capturing Shreveport.[44] To protect his holdings, Withenbury told Banks and Porter about the road system in the region, negating the roads that ran beside the

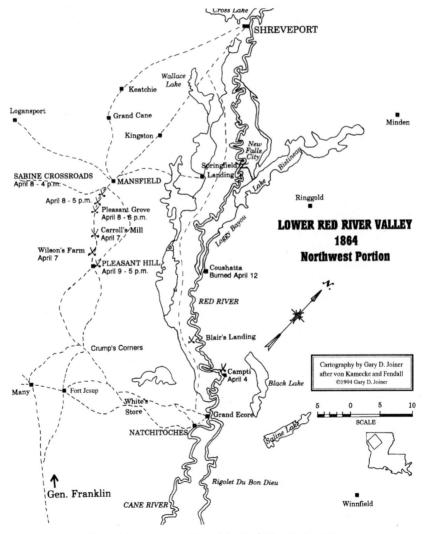

Map of the upper portion of the Red River in Louisiana.

river and emphasizing in particular the road that led away from the river at Grand Ecore, ran west for several miles, then branched off to the north, passing through the village of Pleasant Hill and the town of Mansfield, before entering Shreveport from the southwest. He did not lie about the inland roads to Shreveport, but he convinced Banks to move away from the river.

Withenbury changed the course of the campaign in a single night. Banks, eager to take Shreveport and claim his glory, trusted the river pilot. The pilot denied the Union army the support of the great guns on the naval warships and gave it a false sense of security. If there were no roads for Banks to ascend to Shreveport beside the river, the Confederates could not flank him through the piney wilderness that he saw from the heights of Grand Ecore. Withenbury saved his cotton and, except perhaps in Porter's eyes, was still a good Union man.

Once Porter began his move toward Shreveport, he wrote his friend Sherman that he saw the road and the fields filled with corn and herds of cattle grazing near the west bank of the river. Porter wrote, "It struck me very forcibly that this would have been the route for the army, where they could have travelled without all that immense train, the country supporting them as they proceeded along. The roads are good, wide fields on all sides, a river protecting the right flank of the army, and gun-boats in company."[45] Porter was very confused that Banks had chosen an alternate route.

Banks and Porter agreed to meet at a point opposite Springfield Landing in northern DeSoto Parish on April 10.[46] Springfield Landing was located just four miles from the Red River on Bayou Pierre on a narrow channel connecting Bayou Pierre Lake and Lake Cannisnia.[47] The landing was about sixty miles by road and over 100 miles by river from Grand Ecore.[48] According to the plan, Banks was to leave Grand Ecore on April 6, and Porter was to leave on April 7.[49] At Springfield Landing or near it, Porter's fleet and the army transport vessels would replenish Banks's supply trains, and the two groups would make the final approach to Shreveport. Withenbury did not accompany Porter upriver, and the admiral had been only as far upstream as Alexandria in 1863; therefore, Grand Ecore was Porter's deepest penetration into the Red River Valley at the time. Porter did not completely trust his maps or the local riverboat pilots, so the admiral would not know where he was when he reached Springfield Landing.

He also had to consider which vessels were best suited for the river above his base of operations in Natchitoches Parish. The *Eastport* was now such a liability that Porter decided to leave it at Grand Ecore. All the maps showed the river between Grand Ecore and Shreveport to be winding and contorted. In fact, river pilots referred to this stretch as "The Narrows." Porter correctly assumed that if the *Eastport* grounded in a tight bend, he might not be able to free it. He decided to compose his final assault force with the lightest-draft gunboats. He chose six vessels: the monitors *Osage*

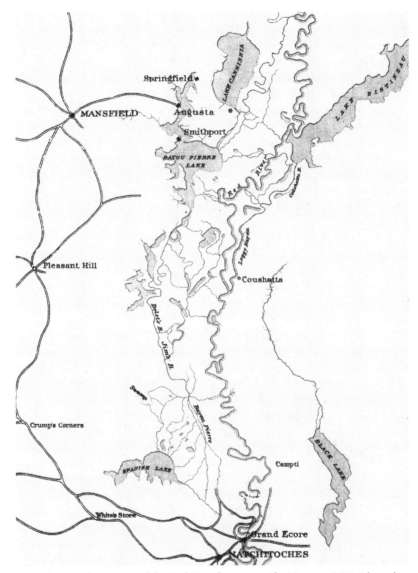

Map showing the portion of the Red River known as "the Narrows." OR Atlas, plate LII. Additional cartography by Gary D. Joiner.

and *Neosho*, the timberclad *Lexington*, and the tinclads *Cricket*, *Fort Hindman*, and *Chillicothe*.[50] The admiral made the *Cricket* his flagship. The gunboats accompanied twenty army transports loaded with supplies and Brigadier General T. Kilby Smith's small division of about 2,300 men from the 17th Corps for protection.[51] Porter had his portion of the force defined and hoped that the army was using as much forethought.

Porter selected one ironclad, two monitors, three tinclads, and a timberclad to lead this segment of the mission. The monitors were the *Osage* and *Neosho*. Each was equipped with two 11-inch naval smoothbore guns in a single turret mounted at the bow. The monitors were sister boats, built by James Buchanan Eads. They were the only stern-wheel monitors built during the war. In spite of their great weight, they needed only four-and-one-half feet of water beneath their decks to float. With huge turrets in the bow and massive armored engine houses in the stern, the vessels tended to be unwieldy and difficult to steer in tight places. The ironclad was the *Chillicothe*, and the timberclad was the *Lexington*. The three tinclads were the *Fort Hindman*, the *Juliet*, and the *Cricket*. The *Fort Hindman* required only two feet four inches of water to float.[52] The *Cricket* was a sternwheeler and had a draft of four feet.[53] Porter picked the *Cricket* as his flagship.

The remainder of the U.S. Navy's contingent consisted of the tugs *Dahlia* and *William H. Brown* and the supply transport *Benefit*. Of the three, the *William H. Brown* was the only one armed. It was large for a tug and was often used as a dispatch boat.[54] These vessels guarded and herded the army's transports. The quartermaster's boats held supplies for the main column and Kilby Smith's men. Smith had armed most if not all of these boats with army field cannon mounted on the decks. He had also placed bales of cotton and sacks of oats on the decks for barricades from which his men could fire in relative safety.[55]

The fleet headed north and reached Campti at 5:00 that afternoon.[56] The next morning as the force got underway, the transport *Iberville* ran aground almost immediately and was wedged so tightly against a sandbar that it took several hours to get it afloat. The *Iberville* was pulled off the bar, and as Porter passed north of the Grand Ecore hill complex and the mouth of Bayou Pierre, he had no way of knowing that the river was starved for water because of the Confederates' destruction of the Tone's Bayou dam on March 18. The water level continued to drop at a steady rate. The fleet slowly ascended the river as the crews called out the locations of snags in the channel bottom. Travel was slowed to just above steerage in the now gentle current. The fleet reached the town of Coushatta and the mouth of Bayou Coushatta or Coushatta Chute at 6:00 P.M. T. K. Smith sent a brigade ashore to guard the fleet from attack, and they took two prisoners.[57]

At 9:00 A.M. on April 8, the fleet headed north again, moving in single file because of the narrow, winding river. Porter saw the river road that Banks could have used, and other than the small band of Confederates seen at Coushatta, there was no opposition. The day passed uneventfully, as did April 9. At 2:00 P.M. on April 10, the fleet reached the mouth of what Porter believed to be Loggy Bayou.[58] This body of water was not the same stream shown on his map.[59] It may never be known just how far north he came. If the water level was sufficiently deep for his convoy to stay afloat, he must have traveled another four river miles and anchored opposite a small stream one mile south of the foot of Scopini's Cut-off. It is possible that the admiral was as close as two miles south of Tone's Bayou or as much as four to five miles below the bayou.[60]

While anchored opposite the stream, T. K. Smith sent a landing party to scatter some Confederates, who were watching them. Then, after traveling another mile, Porter and Smith saw a sight that halted any further progress. Porter described it in a letter to General Sherman:

> FLAG-SHIP CRICKET, *OFF ALEXANDRIA, LA.,*
> April 16, 1864.
>
> Maj. Gen. W. T. SHERMAN,
> *Comdg. Mil. Div. of the Miss., Nashville, Tenn.:*
>
> When I arrived at Springfield Landing I found a sight that made me laugh; it was the smartest thing I ever knew the rebels to do. They had gotten that huge steamer, New Falls City, across Red River, 1 mile above Leggy [*sic*] Bayou, 15 feet of her on shore on each side, the boat broken down in the middle, and a sand-bar making below her. An invitation in large letters to attend a ball in Shreveport was kindly left stuck up by the rebels, which invitation we were never able to accept.
>
> DAVID D. PORTER,
> *Rear-Admiral.*[61]

Porter began working on the problem of moving the *New Falls City*, and T. Kilby Smith landed troops to secure the position. Shortly after this, Captain William Andres of the 14th New York Cavalry rode up with fifty of his troops and told them of Banks's defeat on April 8 at the Battle of Mansfield. He carried with him several dispatches and specific verbal orders for T. K. Smith to return to Grand Ecore.[62] No mention was made of Porter's fleet.

Smith and Porter decided that they must return to Grand Ecore before the Confederates could bring their artillery to the banks of the river and effectively blockade them. That could easily lead to either the capture or the destruction of the fleet. Porter and Smith ordered additional artillery placed on the upper decks of the transports, and barricades of any materials available were made for firing positions for the infantrymen.[63] Now the fleet began the arduous downstream passage from the Federal forces' deepest penetration into the Red River Valley.

The fleet was in a difficult position. From the time they entered "The Narrows," the vessels had to contend with the winding river and shallow channel bottoms. They were wedged bow to stern with the *New Falls City* blocking them, and the channel was so narrow that they could not turn around. This forced the largest vessels to back down the river sternfirst for several miles.[64] The physical strains of this type of movement over an extended course caused severe problems with steerage assemblies and major mechanical malfunctions.

Snags in the channel and along the shore made the backward passage even more difficult. Almost immediately, the *Chillicothe* impaled itself on a submerged tree. The tree pieced the hull, and patching it halted the fleet for more than two hours. The *Chillicothe* was not able to move until the *Black Hawk*, using the *Chillicothe*'s hawser, was able to free it from the snag; the repair was then made.[65] Other vessels suffered damage as rudders became unshipped and paddles splintered. Additionally, the *Emerald* ran hard aground.[66] To make matters worse, the Confederates had hastily sent men and as much artillery as they could muster to high points along the banks north of Grand Ecore to harass the fleet. The sound of the Confederates' minié balls careening off the hulls, casemates, and superstructures of the *Benefit*, *Black Hawk*, and *Osage* was ear shattering.[67] These vessels responded to the ineffective long-arm fire with the *Osage*'s 11-inch naval guns, and this "must have been like hunting partridges with a howitzer."[68] In addition, on the morning of April 12 when the fleet reached Coushatta Chute, the *Lexington* collided with the transport *Rob Roy*, spearing the latter's wheelhouse and launch as well as damaging the smokestacks.[69]

The fleet approached Blair's Landing, located due east of Pleasant Hill and approximately forty-five miles north of Grand Ecore. Confederate Brigadier General Tom Green's cavalry had moved there to harass and possibly halt the progress of the Union navy. Porter's fleet, transports, and armed vessels alike passed the landing under cannon and small-arms fire.[70] Some naval personnel were wounded, and the vessels received damage from the Confederate artillery, which was well placed and concealed. Bringing up the rear of the flotilla were the timberclad *Lexington* and the monitor *Osage*. Strapped to the *Osage* was the transport *Black Hawk*. In making the tight turn above the landing, the *Osage* slewed and ran aground. Green and his 2,500 men were near the bank at this time. They dismounted, tied their horses, formed into three ranks, and began pouring fire into the three boats. Banks's *Black Hawk* took such devastating fire that forty soldiers on the decks had to be evacuated into the safe confines of the cramped metal hull of the *Osage*. All hands aboard followed.[71] The crews aboard the *Osage* and *Black Hawk* struggled to free the monitor from the sandbar as the *Lexington* carried on the fight with the Confederate artillery. After an intense engagement of over an hour, the Confederates showed no signs of lessening the strength of their attack. The *Lexington* finally silenced Green's four-gun artillery battery with its 8-inch guns.[72]

Once the *Osage* was freed, its commander, Thomas O. Selfridge Jr., cut the lines to the *Black Hawk*, and without running the engines, he let the current move the boat close to the Confederates. Selfridge brought one of the vessel's 11-inch guns to bear on the troops. The crews aboard the *Osage* aimed the naval gun with the first periscope used in battle.[73] At a distance of only twenty yards, the vessel fired a load of canister directly at the officer on horseback, General Green. The blast partially decapitated him, and the Confederates subsequently broke ranks, moving away from the riverbank. This ended what Selfridge would later recount as "one of the most curious fights of the war, 2,500 infantry against a gunboat aground."[74]

Porter kept the vessels moving past sunset and into the night. With only torches and perhaps moonlight to light the way, this was a very perilous journey. Normally, the admiral did not take such risks; however, the prospects of rejoining the vessels at Grand Ecore and of regaining the support of the army to keep the Confederate army at bay were powerful incentives. The flotilla finally anchored at 1:00 A.M. on the morning of April 13. Several transports had run aground during the night, and after dawn the next morning, the Quartermaster's boat *John Warner* went aground, further delaying the progress of the fleet. Porter made several attempts to extricate the *John Warner* throughout the day. The Confederates, who had placed field pieces on a high bank, fired at the vessels before *Osage* scattered them. The *Rob Roy* then lost its rudder and had to be placed under tow by the transport *Clara Bell*.[75]

USS Osage. *Library of Congress image LCB816-3126.*

*Lieutenant Commander Thomas O. Selfridge Jr.
U.S. Naval Historical Center image NH 2858.*

The *John Warner* resisted all attempts to remove the vessel from the sandy river bottom to which it was firmly affixed. Fearing that the Confederates were preparing a trap, at daylight on the morning of April 14, T. Kilby Smith ordered his transports and their protecting gunboats ahead to Campti. He left the tinclad *Fort Hindman* to stay with the *John Warner* for protection. The next day, the *Fort Hindman* managed to pull the vessel off the bar, and they returned to the fleet at Grand Ecore on April 15, where the naval forces were safely under the army's guns.[76] The navy was finally in contact with the army, largely because of the skills and composure of Porter and Smith.[77]

Arriving at Grand Ecore, Porter visited Banks in his headquarters tent. The admiral found Banks's accommodations well appointed, even opulent, for field conditions. Banks was dressed in a fine dressing gown, velvet cap and comfortable slippers. He was reading *Scott's Tactics*, his usual nightly ritual.[78] Banks made it plain that he considered the Battle of Mansfield, known to the Federals as the Battle of Sabine Crossroads, to be a victory and that the subsequent battle of Pleasant Hill was simply a withdrawing action. Banks claimed that he withdrew only for lack of water. The admiral informed him that if that were the case, the army had been only six miles from water at Mansfield. Totally disgusted with Banks and his excuses for retreat, the admiral later wrote "that he should have read it [*Scott's Tactics*] before he went to Sabine Cross Roads."[79] Porter told Banks that under no circumstance would the navy go back upstream.[80]

With the river falling rapidly at Grand Ecore, the fleet and the army were forced to withdraw from this region, which had held so much promise for them. The army began marching along the river road to Alexandria. On April 16, after some navigation problems and further mechanical failures, the fleet proceeded downstream three miles with *Eastport* in the lead. In mid-March, the Confederates had placed six Singer torpedoes below the ferry at Grand Ecore, knowing that the fleet could only return on the same route it took north.[81] The *Eastport* struck one of these Confederate torpedoes, but only a few people aboard felt the shock. The ironclad took on water rapidly and came to rest on the bottom. Fortunately, the bottom was only a few feet at most below the keel, and the vessel settled in the soft sand.[82]

The *Eastport* became a potential obstacle as threatening as the *New Falls City* but perhaps more deadly. It was wedged at the forefront of the flotilla and blocked the fleet's passage. The pump boat *Champion No. 5* was used to bilge out the water. The guns were removed and placed on flat rafts that the *Cricket* towed. The *Eastport*'s captain, Lieutenant Commander Phelps, and his crew worked day and night to save the vessel.[83] It was finally refloated on April 21, and despite some groundings as it still took on water, the *Eastport* proceeded downstream another forty miles. Near the town of Montgomery, it ran into submerged snags and became firmly stuck on April 26. The *Champion No. 3* and the *Fort Hindman* joined the pump boat *Champion No. 5* in attempts to wrest the vessel free. The captain of the *Fort Hindman*, Acting Volunteer Lieutenant John Pearce, and Lieutenant Commander Phelps made several attempts to rock the *Eastport* free, but they were unsuccessful. Porter received news that the water level downstream was falling. Knowing that the fleet was in danger of being bottled up behind the great ironclad, Porter ordered a ton of powder placed throughout the *Eastport*. Combustible materials available at the time were packed into the boat, and at 1:45 P.M. on April 26, the *Eastport* was destroyed.[84]

Fort Hindman, *Cricket*, *Juliet*, *Champion No. 3*, and *Champion No. 5* made their way downstream and approached the mouth of the Cane River, where they were met by four Confederate artillery pieces and 200 riflemen.[85] The Rebels heaped accurate fire on the vessels, and the *Champion No. 3* was sunk. Below the decks, more than 100 slaves being carried to freedom were scalded to death. The *Champion No. 5* was also heavily damaged, grounded, and finally abandoned by its crew. The *Fort Hindman*, *Cricket*, and *Juliet* were severely damaged but passed through the gauntlet.[86] A tribute to the ferocity of this attack is that in five minutes, the *Fort Hindman* suffered three killed and four or five wounded, and half the *Juliet*'s crew were lost, as fifteen men were killed or wounded. The *Cricket*, with Porter aboard, was hit some thirty-eight times and lost fully half its crew, suffering twenty-five dead and wounded.[87]

Porter displayed great personal bravery in keeping the tinclad in the fight. A shell hit the aft gun and killed the entire gun crew. Another eliminated the forward gun and its crew. A third shell hit the fire room, where the stokers kept steam pressure up in the boilers, and all but one man were killed. Porter gathered some refugee slaves that the *Cricket* had taken aboard, showed them how to fire a gun, and turned them into a gun crew to try to keep the Confederates' heads down long enough for the vessel to escape. He then went to the engine room and, finding the chief

Photo # NH 61569   USS Fort Hindman, during the Civil War

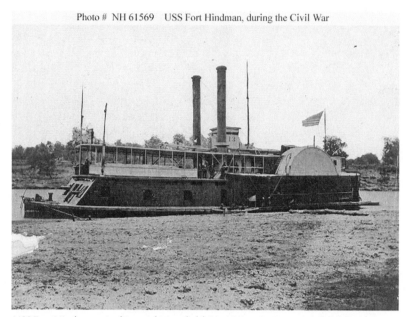

USS Fort Hindman. *Archives of Mansfield State Historic Site, Mansfield, Louisiana.*

engineer dead, put the assistant engineer in charge and told him to build up the steam pressure. Porter discovered that another shell had wounded one of the pilots in the pilothouse and that the remaining crew on the bridge were hiding. With his customary aplomb, Porter took charge of the *Cricket* and moved the vessel past the battery that had nearly sent it to the bottom.[88]

Porter's fleet limped into the northern approaches to Alexandria as the Red River fell rapidly. He had lost the most powerful ironclad in the fleet. Two of his tugs/pump boats had also been sunk, and three of his tinclads had been severely damaged. Most of the army transport vessels had received either mechanical or battle damage. To make matters worse, the river had fallen a full six feet since the flotilla's ascent, and most of his fleet was now trapped above the falls.[89] While Porter tended to his wounded fleet, his transports and smaller gunboats ventured down the Red River, having crossed the falls several days before when the water level was higher. The vessels were about thirty miles below Alexandria when Confederate Captain John A. West's Grosse Tete (Louisiana) Flying Artillery Battery, under Lieutenant W. H. Lyne, engaged the vessels and burned the transport *Emma*.[90]

Three days later on May 4, they attacked and captured the *City Belle* on its way to Alexandria with reinforcements. On board were 700 men of the

Union army Quartermaster Corps transports at the wharves at Alexandria, Louisiana, in April or May 1864. Library of Congress image LCB816-3120.

120th Ohio Infantry. About half these men were captured, and the remainder were killed or wounded.[91] Subsequent reports stated that the *City Belle* was destroyed in the attack but later salvaged by the Rebels.[92]

On that same day, the *John Warner* and *Covington* left Alexandria, and the *Signal* soon joined them. The *John Warner* carried the men of the 56th Ohio Infantry, who were leaving on veterans' furloughs.[93] The vessels had received small-arms fire throughout the day. At night, the small convoy tied up on the river bank about twenty miles south of Alexandria. Confederates fired at them as they ate their evening meal.[94] At 4:45 A.M. the next morning, as the gunboats reached Dunn's Bayou, artillery and musketry fell on the *Warner*. The *Covington* and *Signal* fired back on the attackers. The Confederate artillery disabled the *Warner*'s rudders, and the vessel drifted to the bank below the attack. The Rebel artillery continued to fire at it, and the Confederate cavalry joined in the attack until the *Warner* was pounded into a floating pile of debris.[95] The 56th Ohio, still aboard, was torn to shreds. The *Covington* tried to torch the boat to sink it rather than allow its capture after the captain of the *Warner* raised the white flag. The colonel of the 56th Ohio begged the party from the *Covington* not to burn the vessel because 125 of his men lay dead or dying on the decks.[96]

The artillery from Dunn's Bayou then arrived to pour more fire on the warships. The *Covington* and *Signal* tried to retire upstream, but the *Signal* lost its steering assembly and port engine. The *Covington* threw a towline to the *Signal* and began pulling it against the current. An artillery shell

USS Covington. *Lord-Eltinge Papers, Rare Book, Manuscript, and Special Collections Library, Duke University, Durham, North Carolina.*

then hit one of the *Signal's* steam pipes, and the crew believed the boilers were going to explode. The *Covington* then cut the vessel loose and tried to escape, but its rudder had been hit as well. The captain tied the gunboat to the opposite bank, and his crew returned fire for a short time until they ran out of ammunition. The captain ordered the guns spiked and set fire to the tinclad. The *Signal* was forced to surrender under the combined battery fire after the *Covington* began to burn. The Confederates also reported that they drove off another gunboat that tried to offer assistance.[97] The navy suffered more losses in vessels and men than it had on April 22 below Grand Ecore.[98] They were not alone in their adversity. Inside the defensive perimeter at Alexandria, Porter was dealing with other problems.

Normally confident, Porter's resolve was shaken, as he considered destroying his fleet to keep it from falling into enemy hands. During the previous year, he had faced the green hell of Deer Creek. Now it was low water and rocks that confounded him. The water level had fallen until the sand and rocks of the falls were showing as only damp indications of their usual underwater treachery. The *Louisville* and sister vessels needed seven feet to float, but the river level at the chute or navigable channel was only three feet four inches deep.[99] While Porter had sent his transports and smaller gunboats over the falls while the river was deeper, the potential disaster lay ahead in the fact that the majority of the most powerful vessels were trapped above the rocks. These included the *Lexington, Osage, Neosho, Mound City, Louisville, Pittsburg, Carondelet, Chillicothe, Choctaw, Ozark,* and *Fort Hindman*.[100] If the navy retreated, these vessels would have to be destroyed. It was unthinkable to lose these very expensive, powerful boats, and their loss would seriously harm or destroy Porter's career. Porter reported his plight to Gideon Welles, and this resulted in Grant's decision to keep A. J. Smith's men with Porter to protect the fleet.

Porter had to make a decision about the fate of the fleet, and the number of possible actions was limited if the fleet was to be saved. A huge number of men would be tied down at Alexandria waiting for the autumn rains to raise the river level, and that appealed to no one. The only other possibility was to force the water level to rise at Alexandria. Lieutenant Colonel Joseph Bailey of Wisconsin, one of Franklin's engineers, advanced this option, which was to make him famous during the war and give him the highest awards his country bestowed. Bailey had worked in the logging industry in Wisconsin and was familiar with the practice of building temporary dams to increase water levels to float logs downstream to sawmills in dry weather. During the previous year at Port Hudson, he had used the

USS Ozark, Choctaw, *and* Fort Hindman *trapped above Bailey's Dam on the Red River in May 1864. Marshall Dunham Photographic Album (Mss. 3241), Louisiana and Lower Mississippi Valley Collections, LSU Libraries, Baton Rouge, Louisiana.*

technique to salvage two steamers. Bailey had watched the water levels drop for three weeks, and he suggested that dams might be needed to float the fleet.[101]

On April 29, Bailey attended a meeting with Banks, and that same day construction began. Bailey's task of dam building was more difficult than he expected. The site he chose for the main dam was 758 feet wide. The water level varied from four to six feet, and as the dam was formed, the level rose and the current increased to ten miles per hour.[102] In addition, building materials for the dam were not uniform. Bailey began to disassemble buildings in Alexandria and across the river in Pineville. Bricks, stones, wall segments, and even pieces of furniture were used. Ironically, some of the dam's structure included portions of Sherman's beloved Louisiana Seminary for Learning and Military Institute, located in Pineville.

After a week of work, a dam made of trees that had been cut, bound, and stacked together extended 300 feet from the western bank to make segments for a crib dam. Four coal barges loaded with brick and stone were lashed together and sunk to extend it farther. From the other side, the crib dam was extended to meet the barges on May 8.[103] The lightest-draft vessels, the *Osage*, *Neosho*, and *Fort Hindman*, floated to the area

USS Forest Rose assisting in the Construction of Bailey's Dam at Alexandria, Louisiana, in May 1864. Library of Congress image LC-USZ262-62499.

above the dam. The others did not follow, although the water was deep enough for them to do so. The ironclads were still filled with cotton. Its removal would have lightened them sufficiently to pass through the dam on May 8, but the Federals were not willing to lose the white gold. The water level was rising significantly and exerting pressure on the cribs and barges. Finally, at 5:00 A.M. on May 9, the river pushed the center barges aside. Porter ordered the *Lexington* through the gap before the water level fell, and it managed to pull through with a full head of steam. The *Osage*, *Neosho*, and *Fort Hindman* followed with only the *Neosho* suffering minor hull damage from the rocks.[104]

The other vessels had not been moved up to the pool above the dam, so they were unable to get through when the water level decreased.[105] Bailey immediately began repairs on the dam and decided that other structures, called wing dams, must be built to channel the water above the main dam. This delay affected Banks's plan for evacuation. By May 9, McClernand had arrived from Texas, and Banks now had to deal with more troops.[106] By May 11, Banks sent word to Porter that the navy must be ready to move its boats as soon as the wing dams were built.[107]

Banks wrote Grant that forage supplies were running very low for the animals on which the train and artillery depended.[108] He then expressed his concern to Porter that it would be perilous to remain in Alexandria more than one more day.[109] Porter believed that Banks was ready to bolt and leave the fleet behind. Whether there was actual cause for Porter's suspicions is uncertain, but the admiral attempted to halt any plans of abandoning the navy.[110] A. J. Smith assured the admiral that he and his men would remain with Porter regardless of Banks's actions.[111] Porter promised Banks that once the river rose another foot, the boats could move and Banks would be free to leave. The admiral was very condescending to Banks and treated him as he would a small child, even going so far as to say, "Now general, I really see nothing that should make us despond. You have a fine army, and I shall have a strong fleet of gunboats to drive away an inferior force in our front."[112] Banks replied that he never intended to abandon the fleet but that he had received complaints that the army was doing all the work on the dams and that the navy was doing nothing to rescue its own boats.[113]

Porter began removing guns and iron plating from the ironclads to lighten their weight. The guns, ammunition, and needed supplies were placed on wagons and carried below the falls. Iron plating was removed from some of the ironclads and dumped in the river. Tar was then smeared on the exposed wood to fool anyone who saw the vessels without their armor.[114] Porter chose not to carry eleven 32-pounder smoothbore cannon and had them spiked and dumped into the river.[115] By May 11, the wing dams were complete, but water was not rising sufficiently to float the vessels over the dam. A bracket dam was hastily built upstream about one-half mile above the crib dams. Two days later, the water was high enough for the ironclads to shoot through a gap in the dam.[116]

The dam system was a daring, innovative undertaking.[117] For his efforts and ingenuity, Joseph Bailey was awarded the Medal of Honor and the "Thanks of Congress." By May 15, Porter pushed his fleet out of the Red River and into the wide waters of the Mississippi. He wrote to his mother, "I am clear of my troubles and my fleet is safe out in the broad Mississippi. I have had a hard and anxious time of it."[118]

NOTES

1. *OR* 34, part 2: 224–25.
2. *OR* 34, part 2: 224–25.
3. *ORN* 26: 747–78.
4. *ORN* 26: 747–78.
5. M. A. DeWolfe Howe, ed., *Home Letters of General Sherman* (New York, 1909), 286–87.
6. *ORN* 26: 747–48.
7. Thomas O. Selfridge Jr. "The Navy in the Red River," in Johnson and Buel, eds., *Battles and Leaders*, 4: 366; David Dixon Porter, *The Naval History of the Civil War* (New York: Appleton, 1886), 494–533, 548–53.
8. *ORN* 26: 36.
9. Jonathan H. Carter, *Carter Correspondence Book*, Manuscript in the National Archives, Carter to Mallory, February 1, 1863; Katherine Brash Jeter, *A Man and His Boat: The Civil War Career and Correspondence of Lieutenant Jonathan H. Carter, CSN* (Lafayette, La.: Center for Louisiana Studies, 1996), x; Certificate of Death of James O'Leary, RG 68, February 14, 1863, Louisiana State Museum, New Orleans. The reverse side of this document contains a spy map presented to Porter on or shortly after February 14 and certainly influenced his decision as to which vessels to bring up the Red River. See Gary D. Joiner, *Through the Howling Wilderness: The 1864 Red River Campaign and Union Failure in the West* (Knoxville: University of Tennessee Press, 2006), 21–26.
10. John Scott, *Story of the Thirty Second Iowa Infantry Volunteers* (Nevada, Iowa: Author, 1896), 130; Edmund Newsome, *Experience in the War of the Rebellion* (Carbondale, Ill.: Author, 1880), 111; Walter G. Smith, ed., *Life and Letters of T. Kilby Smith* (New York: G. P. Putnam's Sons, 1898), 356.
11. *OR* 34: 304.
12. *OR* 34: 304.
13. *ORN* 25: 787–88.
14. *OR* 34: 312; Ezra J. Warner, *Generals in Blue: Lives of the Union Commanders* (Baton Rouge: Louisiana State University Press, 1964), 338–39.
15. Porter, *The Naval History of the Civil War*, 496.
16. Porter, *The Naval History of the Civil War*, 496.
17. Porter, *The Naval History of the Civil War*, 496.
18. *OR* 34: 306.

19. *ORN* 26: 28, 30–31.

20. *ORN* 26: 32.

21. Johnson and Buel, *Battles and Leaders* 4: 362.

22. Dispatch in the personal collection of Mr. Richard Self, Shreveport, Louisiana.

23. John D. Winters, *The Civil War in Louisiana* (Baton Rouge: Louisiana State University Press, 1963), 331.

24. Ludwell H. Johnson, *Red River Campaign: Politics and Cotton in the Civil War* (Kent, Ohio: Kent State University Press, 1993), 99; Joiner and Vetter, "Union Naval Expedition," 47.

25. Johnson and Buel, *Battles and Leaders* 4: 366; Porter, *The Naval History of the Civil War*, 494–533.

26. U.S. Congress, *Report on the Joint Committee on the Conduct of the War, 1863–1866*, vol. 2, *Red River Expedition* (Millwood, N.Y.: Krauss Reprint, 1977), 281–83 (hereinafter cited as *JCCW*).

27. Porter, *The Naval History of the Civil War*, 500.

28. *JCCW*, 8–9.

29. *JCCW*, 275; *ORN* 26: 50.

30. *JCCW*, 282.

31. *JCCW*, 282–83.

32. *OR* 34, part 2: 1056–57.

33. Lavender Soil Map (1906), Archives and Special Collections, Noel Memorial Library, Louisiana State University in Shreveport.

34. *OR* 34, part 3: 172.

35. *OR Atlas*, plate 52.

36. *JCCW*, 282.

37. *JCCW*, 282–83.

38. *JCCW*, 282–83.

39. *JCCW*, 282–83; *ORN* 26: 50.

40. *JCCW*, 282–83.

41. *JCCW*, 7, 322.

42. *OR* 34, part 2: 735; William D. Crandall and Isaac D. Newell, *History of the Ram Fleet and the Mississippi Marine Brigade in the War for the Union on the Mississippi and Its Tributaries: The Story of the Ellets and Their Men* (St. Louis, Mo.: Society of Survivors, 1907), 378.

43. *JCCW*, 285.

44. *JCCW*, 285. After the campaign, Withenbury was listed as a claimant to some of the cotton that the Union navy confiscated.

45. *ORN* 26: 60.

46. James K. Ewer, *The Third Massachusetts Cavalry in the War for the Union* (Maplewood, Mass.: Historical Committee of the Regimental Association, 1903), 201, 276, 323.

47. *JCCW*, 201, 276, 323.

48. *OR Atlas*, plate 52.

49. *OR* 34: 284; *JCCW*, 323; *ORN* 26: 51.

50. Johnson and Buel, *Battles and Leaders*, 4: 363.

51. *ORN* 26: 51; *JCCW*, 201, 323; Newsome, *Experience in the War of the Rebellion*, 124.

52. Paul H. Silverstone, *Warships of the Civil War Navies* (Annapolis, Md.: Naval Institute Press, 1989), 168.

53. Silverstone, *Warships of the Civil War Navies*, 170.

54. Silverstone, *Warships of the Civil War Navies*, 183.

55. *OR* 34: 168, 179–80.

56. *OR* 34: 168, 179–80.

57. *OR* 34: 380.

58. *OR* 34: 380.

59. *OR Atlas*, plate LII; Lavender Soil Map (1906), Archives and Special Collections, Noel Memorial Library, Louisiana State University in Shreveport.

60. Lavender Soil Map.

61. *OR* 34, part 3: 172.

62. *OR* 34: 98–99; *ORN* 26: 51, 60, 789; *JCCW*, 203.

63. *OR* 34: 168, 179–80.

64. Newsome, *Experience in the War of the Rebellion*, 126.

65. Robert L. Kerby, *Kirby Smith's Confederacy: The Trans-Mississippi South, 1863–1865* (Tuscaloosa: University of Alabama Press, 1972), 309; Abstract log of *USS Chillicothe*, March 7–June 8, 1864, National Archives and Records Administration, Washington, D.C.; *ORN* 26: 777–78.

66. *OR* 34: 381.

67. *ORN* 26: 778, 781, 789; *OR* 34: 633.

68. *ORN* 26: 26, 778, 781, 789; *OR* 34: 34, 633.

69. Abstract log of *USS Lexington*, March 1–June 28, 1864, National Archives and Records Administration, Washington, D.C.; *ORN* 26: 789.

70. Richard Taylor, Letter to General John George Walker, April 9, 1864, John George Walker Papers #910Z, Southern Historical Collection, University of North Carolina at Chapel Hill; *OR* 34: 570–71; Anne J. Bailey, "Chasing Banks Out of Louisiana: Parsons' Texas Cavalry in the Red River Campaign," *Civil War Regiments* 2, no. 3: 219.

71. Porter, *The Naval History of the Civil War*, 512. On examination of the *Black Hawk*, Porter stated "that there was not a place six inches square not perforated by a bullet."

72. Porter, *The Naval History of the Civil War*, 512–13.

73. Thomas O. Selfridge Jr., *What Finer Tradition: The Memoirs of Thomas O. Selfridge, Jr., Rear Admiral U.S.N.* (Columbia: University of South Carolina Press, 1987), 102.

74. Selfridge, *What Finer Tradition*, 102; *ORN* 26: 49.

75. *OR* 34: 382.

76. *OR* 34: 382.

77. Elias P. Pellet, *History of the 114th Regiment, New York State Volunteers . . .* (Norwich, N.Y.: Telegraph and Chronicle Press Print, 1866), 222.

78. David Dixon Porter, *Incidents and Anecdotes* (New York: Appleton, 1885), 235–36.

79. Porter, *Incidents and Anecdotes*, 235–36; Porter, *The Naval History of the Civil War*, 517.

80. *OR* 34: 190.

81. *OR* 34: 505; *ORN* 26: 62.

82. *ORN* 26: 62.

83. *ORN* 26: 78.

84. *ORN* 26: 72–77.

85. *ORN* 26: 74–75, 167, 169, 781–82, 786.

86. *ORN* 26: 75, 81, 83.

87. *ORN* 26: 26, 76; Richard Taylor, *Destruction and Reconstruction: Personal Experiences in the Civil War* (New York: Da Capo, 1995), 218.

88. Porter, *The Naval History of the Civil War*, 523–24. Although prone to epic bouts of self-aggrandizement, Admiral Porter's actions were noted by fellow officers.

89. Porter, *The Naval History of the Civil War*, 524.

90. Porter, *The Naval History of the Civil War*; *ORN* 26: 102.

91. *OR* 34: 475; Taylor, *Destruction and Reconstruction*, 186.

92. Charles Dana Gibson and E. Kay Gibson, *Dictionary of Transports and Combatant Vessels, Steam and Sail, Employed by the U.S. Army, 1861–1868* (Camden, Maine: Ensign Press, 1995), 60.

93. Thomas J. Williams, *An Historical Sketch of the 56th Ohio Volunteer Infantry . . .* (Columbus, Ohio: The Lawrence Press, 1899), 73.

94. Williams, *An Historical Sketch*, 73.

95. *ORN* 26: 113, 117–18; Williams, *An Historical Sketch*, 74–78.

96. *ORN* 26: 113, 117–18; Williams, *An Historical Sketch*, 74–78.

97. Williams, *An Historical Sketch of the 56th Ohio Volunteer Infantry . . .* , 74–78; *ORN* 26: 114, 118–19, 134.

98. *ORN* 26: 114, 119, 123, 134; Taylor, *Destruction and Reconstruction*, 185–86; *OR* 34: 442, 475, 621, 623.

99. *ORN* 26: 94; *OR* 34, part 3: 316; Silverstone, *Warships of the Civil War Navies*, 151–53. The actual depth of the keel was six feet on *Cairo-* or City-class ironclads.

100. *ORN* 26: 94; *OR* 34, part 3: 316.

101. Johnson and Buel, *Battles and Leaders*, 4: 358.

102. *OR* 34: 403, Johnson and Buel, *Battles and Leaders*, 4: 358.

103. *OR* 34: 209, 254; *ORN* 26: 131.

104. *OR* 34: 209, 254; *ORN* 26: 131.

105. Porter, *The Naval History of the Civil War*, 526.

106. *OR* 34: 68, 443; part 3: 294, 296.

107. *ORN* 26: 136.

108. Nathaniel P. Banks to U. S. Grant, May 4, 1864, Banks Papers, Essex Institute, Salem, Massachusetts, Microfilm copy at University of Texas, Austin, Texas; *ORN* 26: 147.

109. *ORN* 26: 136.

110. Johnson, *Red River Campaign*, 264–65.

111. Johnson, *Red River Campaign*, 140; Scott, *Story of the Thirty Second Iowa Infantry Volunteers*, 250–51.

112. *ORN* 26: 140–41.

113. *ORN* 26: 141.

114. *ORN* 26: 132, 149; *OR* 34: 255; *JCCW*, 84; E. Cort Williams, "Recollections of the Red River Expedition," in *Sketches of War History 1861–1865, Papers Read before the Ohio Commandery of the Military Order of the Loyal Legion of the United States 1886–1888* (Cincinnati: Robert Clarke and Company, 1888), 115.

115. *ORN* 26: 132, 149; *OR* 34: 255; *JCCW*, 84; Williams, "Recollections of the Red River Expedition," 115.

116. *ORN* 26: 132, 149; *OR* 34: 255; Brigadier General C. J. Polignac, "The Defense of the Red River," in Johnson and Buel, *Battles and Leaders*, 4: 373.

117. For a thorough treatment of the dam, see Michael C. Robinson, *Gunboats, Low Water, and Yankee Ingenuity: A History of Bailey's Dam* (Baton Rouge: Louisiana State University Press, 1991).

118. David Dixon Porter, letter to his mother dated May 18, 1864, David D. Porter Papers, Division of Manuscripts, Library of Congress; *ORN* 26: 130–35.

Epilogue

✝

To the End of the War and After

May God save us from any such war in the future!

—Admiral David Dixon Porter

The Red River Campaign was considered a Confederate victory by both sides. It perhaps lengthened the war by weeks but had no other effects on land fighting, especially in the East, where Grant and the Army of the Potomac relentlessly ground Confederate forces to near nonexistence. The navy learned some valuable lessons in this campaign. The Anaconda Plan, as practiced by the navy, could afford to leave the Red River alone, treating the region like the tail of the snake and not its head. Cut off the head, and the body would eventually die. There would never be another time during the war that so many inland vessels were concentrated in such a confined area. Every engagement that followed would pale in comparison in scope and violence. The Mississippi Squadron would never again act in concert.

Following the Red River Campaign, the main threat to the Mississippi Squadron was from guerrillas who operated sporadically near the banks of the Mississippi; in the lower portions of the Red, Ouachita, and Black rivers; and in the upper reaches of the Tennessee and Cumberland rivers. With fewer dangers visible ahead, Porter ordered the Mississippi Squadron to engage in patrol duties throughout the length of the Mississippi Valley, with the exception of the navigable portion of the Red River and its tributaries beyond a few miles upstream from their mouths. The Red was left to the Rebels above David's Ferry and Egg Bend. The Squadron was dispersed into strictly defined operations areas.

Admiral Porter relied on a plan he had created after the fall of Vicksburg in order to establish naval districts within the great river valley.[1] To meet the new operational environment, he altered the structure of the command with General Order No. 195 on May 20, 1864, and then adjusted it a week later with General Order No. 199. These orders were given shortly after Porter's gunboats left the Red River and General Nathaniel Banks retreated across the Atchafalaya.[2] Under Porter's hand, the Mississippi River Valley was divided into ten operational districts. The new jurisdictions and the vessels that patrolled them were the First District, from New Orleans to Donaldsonville, with the *Essex, Argosy, General Price, St. Clair*, and *Alexandria*; the Second District, from Donaldsonville to Morganza,[3] with the *Lafayette, Juliet, Kenwood, Ouachita, Avenger, Nymph*, and *Chickasaw*; the Third District, from Morganza to Fort Adams,[4] with the *Choctaw, Gazelle, Neosho, Ozark, Winnebago, General Bragg, Little Rebel, Fort Hindman, Cricket*, and *Naiad*; the Fourth District, from Fort Adams to Natchez, with the *Siren, Champion*,[5] *Chillicothe, Cincinnati, Lexington*, and *Peri (Petrel)*; the Fifth District, from Natchez to Vicksburg, with the *Benton, Pittsburg, Curlew, Mound City, Rattler, Judge Torrence*, and *Forest Rose*; the Sixth District, from Vicksburg to Arkansas River, with the *Romeo, Louisville, Marmora, Prairie Bird*, and two other light drafts; the Seventh District, from Arkansas River to Memphis, with the *Hastings, Fearn, Naumkeag, Tyler, Queen City, Exchange, Silver Cloud*, and *Linden*; the Eighth District, from Memphis to Columbus, with the *Osage, Carondelet, Huntress*, and *New Era*; the Ninth District, from Cairo to the head of Tennessee River, with the *Tawah, Elfin, Tuscumbia, Key West, Undine, Paw Paw, Robb*, and *Peosta*; and the Tenth District, the Cumberland River and Upper Ohio, with the *Brilliant, Moose, Victory, Fair Play, Springfield, Reindeer*, and *Silver Lake*. Additionally, the *Fairy* and *Sibyl* patrolled at station at Cairo and were to be ready at all times for the admiral's service.[6]

Porter ordered that no commander could give vessels from one district to another unless it could be shown that a great emergency existed. He added that commanders of districts must cooperate with each other. Furthermore, when occasion required additional resources, adjacent districts should render all the aid and assistance in their power.[7] Porter gave the commands of the districts to the vessel captains who were ultimately loyal to him. At times, a single officer might command two adjoining districts. Among the officers leading the naval districts were Lieutenant Commander James P. Foster, 2nd and 3rd Districts; Lieutenant Commander James A. Greer, 4th and 5th Districts; Lieutenant Commander Frank M. Ramsay, 3rd and 4th Districts; Lieutenant Commander Seth Ledyard Phelps, 5th, 6th, and 7th Districts; Lieutenant Commander Thomas O. Selfridge Jr., 5th District; Lieutenant Commander E. K. Owen, 5th District;

Lieutenant Commander John G. Mitchell, 8th District; and Lieutenant Commander Le Roy Fitch, 10th District.[8]

The district system worked as planned. The rivers were never without a well-armed patrol, and the gunboats appeared along the same stretch of river often but at irregular intervals. The greatest burdens went to the tinclads because they were more numerous and were able to navigate narrower streams with shallower depths than the ironclads. The Yazoo River basin, particularly the area around Yazoo City, continued to cause Porter trouble. During and following the Red River Campaign, the *Petrel* and the *Marmora* were engaged in several duels with shore batteries and guerrillas there and on the Arkansas shore as well.[9]

The lower Red River, with its complex structure intertwined with the Black and Atchafalaya rivers, also received the squadron's attention. On June 8, 1864, Lieutenant Commander Frank M. Ramsey forayed the *Chillicothe*, *Neosho*, and *Fort Hindman* down the Atchafalaya. Less than two miles south of Simmesport, an artillery battery of two 30-pounder Parrott rifles met them. The gunboats returned fire and scattered the Rebel gun crews. When Ramsey landed, he discovered that the guns had a short time before belonged to General Banks.[10]

Porter learned of the existence of Rebel submarines on the Red River in June, if not before, and prepared a solution. On June 25, he ordered Lieutenant Commander Ramsey to prepare a chain extending across the mouth of the Red with segments anchored on floats so that vessels could pass through if necessary. He also reminded Ramsey that Old River was occasionally navigable and that it must also be monitored.[11]

The Squadron sent flotillas up the Arkansas, Cumberland, and Tennessee rivers to quell threats from guerrillas during the summer and into autumn of 1864. All of them, as Porter later wrote, were "well managed."[12] The most convenient method of moving troops on resupply or interdiction missions remained by steamboat. Guerrilla activity in several areas remained high, so convoys were mandated, and each convoy received gunboat escorts.

Following the Red River Campaign, Porter requested a change of command. He was rewarded on September 22, 1864, when he assumed command of the North Atlantic Blockading Squadron, replacing his ailing foster brother, David Glascow Farragut.[13] Porter took many (but not all) of his favorite captains with him. One of those left behind was Seth Ledyard Phelps, who saw little prospect in remaining in what he considered to be a dead-end job. Porter could not forgive the loss of the *Eastport*, and he unjustly blamed Phelps for the loss of the giant ironclad. Phelps resigned on October 27, 1864, taking a job as a coaling station manager in Acapulco, Mexico.[14]

Secretary of the Navy Gideon Welles replaced Porter with Acting Rear Admiral Samuel Phillips Lee, who served as the commander of the Mississippi Squadron through the end of hostilities in April 1865.[15] Lee did not have an easy transition into his new command. Action on the Tennessee River increased in November when the Confederates ambushed an armed river patrol, and the gunboats fared the worse. The Mississippi Squadron lost the *Undine, Towah,* and *Key West,* and the Army Quartermaster Corps lost eight transports.[16] The battle cost the Squadron three of its eight gunboats in the 9th District. The Squadron immediately reasserted its presence, not willing to relinquish control.

The Cumberland River was again the scene of action in December as the Squadron supported Major General George Thomas at Nashville, Tennessee, against the forces of Confederate Lieutenant General John Bell Hood. The Confederates had captured three army transports, the *Magnet, Prairie State,* and *Prima Donna.* On December 4, Admiral Lee dispatched the ironclad *Carondelet,* the monitor *Neosho,* and the tinclads *Fair Play, Moose, Reindeer,* and *Silver Lake* to destroy shore batteries that the Rebels had recently constructed near Nashville.[17] The *Reindeer* and *Moose* saw the most action, fighting while lashed together in a smoke-filled river bottom. The tinclads eventually forced the Rebels to abandon their guns, and the flotilla recaptured all three transports.[18] Fighting resumed on December 9 with the *Neosho,* and some of the tinclads escorted a convoy of supplies to General Thomas. The convoy was ambushed, and the *Neosho* bore the brunt of the shore batteries' fire. Although the monitor was very well protected, all the wooden structures erected on the deck, particularly the fair-weather pilothouse, were subject to destruction. The Rebels fired rapidly and accurately at the *Neosho* until the wooden pilothouse was weakened to the extent that the vessel's captain, Lieutenant Commander Le Roy Fitch, believed it might fall and obstruct the view from the armored "fighting pilothouse." After two-and-one-half hours of fighting, Fitch withdrew to clear the debris from the low-slung deck. Fitch then returned with the *Carondelet.* He ordered that vessel to be tied up to the bank and not to fire until the *Neosho* was engaged. Fitch then ran the batteries and set up crossfire with the two ironclads destroying the shore guns.[19] These actions were among the last on the Tennessee or the Cumberland as warfare in that region diminished.

The final engagement of the Squadron occurred just before the war ended. The hated ram *William H. Webb,* unknown to Porter or Lee, was at Shreveport, Louisiana, undergoing repair. The Mississippi Squadron patrolled the lower reaches of the Red and Black rivers but did not venture far upstream. Its captain, Charles Read, took the *Webb* down the Red and Mississippi beginning on April 22, 1865. Much of the Squadron chased it as far as Algiers, Louisiana. The Webb outpaced every vessel in the

Squadron but could not contend with West Gulf Blockading Squadron sloops anchored below New Orleans. The naval vessels of both squadrons received faulty intelligence that both Jefferson Davis and John Wilkes Booth were aboard, and they had no intention of allowing the speedy ram to break out into the open sea. The *Webb* was trapped when it became apparent that it could not pass the *Richmond*. Read grounded the ram and set it afire.[20] Robert E. Lee had surrendered to U. S. Grant at Appomattox Courthouse in Virginia thirteen days before.

One day shy of two months after Lee's surrender in Virginia, the final episode in the Mississippi Valley occurred. Confederate Navy Lieutenant Jonathan Carter surrendered the Confederacy's final warship on inland waters. He brought the *Missouri*, the ironclad that Porter had greatly feared, out from its base at Shreveport and surrendered it on June 3.[21] It became the USS *Missouri* at that point. Once Shreveport surrendered to naval forces on June 8, 1865, the Squadron's work was complete.

The Mississippi Squadron patrolled the inland waters until it was certain that hostilities would not continue or renew. The U.S. government then decided that it did not require the vast array of warships. The guns and armor were stripped from most of the vessels, and they were sold to either foreign governments or to private citizens as steam packets or for scrap. Most of the gunboats were decommissioned on July 20, 1865, and sold at auction between November 19 and 29, 1865.[22]

The Mississippi Squadron and its predecessor, the Western Gunboat Flotilla, rendered invaluable service to the Union cause during the Civil War. The command did not single-handedly turn the tide of fighting, but it is fair to say that the war in the West could not have succeeded without the brown water fleet. Perhaps Admiral Porter summed up the importance of the Mississippi Squadron best when he wrote, "It was a link in the great chain that helped to bind the Briarean arms of the demon of rebellion. The services of the Navy in the West had as much effect in reducing the South to submission as the greater battles fought in the East."[23]

NOTES

1. *ORN* 25: 377. This was General Order No. 80, dated August 20, 1863.
2. *ORN* 26: 317–18; 329–30.
3. Morganza was located a few miles below the mouth of the Red River.
4. Fort Adams was in the extreme southwest portion of Mississippi, a short distance above the Louisiana state boundary.
5. The *Champion* was a tinclad, not to be confused with the two pump boats.
6. *ORN* 26: 329–30.
7. *ORN* 26: 318, 330.
8. *ORN* 26: 268, 278, 296, 297, 309, 316, 322, 327, 328, 336, 370, 535.

9. David Dixon Porter, *The Naval History of the Civil War* (New York: Appleton, 1886), 559–61.

10. Porter, *The Naval History of the Civil War*, 561; *ORN* 26: 369–70.

11. *ORN* 26: 538–39.

12. Porter, *The Naval History of the Civil War*, 562–63.

13. Jay Slagle, *Ironclad Captain: Seth Ledyard Phelps and the U.S. Navy, 1841–1864* (Kent, Ohio: Kent State University Press, 1996), 389.

14. Slagle, *Ironclad Captain*, 390.

15. William B. Cogar, *Dictionary of Admirals of the U.S. Navy, Volume I: 1862–1900* (Annapolis, Md.: Naval Institute Press, 1989), 96–97.

16. Porter, *The Naval History of the Civil War*, 803.

17. *ORN* 256: 641-42.

18. *ORN* 256: 641–42.

19. Porter, *The Naval History of the Civil War*, 803–4.

20. Bob Weems, *Charles Read: Confederate Buccaneer* (Jackson, Miss.: Heritage Books, 1982), 163–73.

21. Paul H. Silverstone, *Warships of the Civil War Navies* (Annapolis, Md.: Naval Institute Press, 1989), 207.

22. Silverstone, *Warships of the Civil War Navies*, 147–84.

23. Porter, *The Naval History of the Civil War*, 564.

Bibliography

PRIMARY SOURCES

Banks, Nathaniel P. Papers. Essex Institute. Salem, Massachusetts; Microfilm copy at University of Texas, Austin, Texas.

Bearss, Margie. "Identification Colors for Chimney Bands," from a list by a Mr. Shepard, engineer on the *Carondelet*. USS *Cairo* Museum, Vicksburg National Military Park, Vicksburg, Mississippi, n.p., n.d.

Bissell, J. W. "Sawing Out the Channel Above Island Number Ten." In *Battles and Leaders of the Civil War*, vol. 1: *Opening Battles*, edited by Robert Underwood Johnson, 460–61. Edison, N.J.: Castle/Book Sales, 1990; orig. pub. Century Company, 1883.

Carter, Jonathan H. *Correspondence Book*, manuscript in the National Archives and Records Administration, Washington, D.C.

Clark, Orton. *The One Hundred and Sixteenth Regiment of New York Volunteers: Being a Complete History of Its Organization and of Its Nearly Three Years of Active Service in the Great Rebellion to Which Is Appended Memorial Sketches, and a Muster Roll of the Regiment. Containing the Name of Every Man Connected with It.* Buffalo, N.Y.: Matthews & Warren, 1868.

Crandall, William D., and Isaac D. Newell. *History of the Ram Fleet and the Mississippi Marine Brigade in the War for the Union on the Mississippi and Its Tributaries, The Story of the Ellets and their Men.* St. Louis, Mo.: Society of Survivors, 1907.

Currie, George E. *Warfare along the Mississippi; The Letters of Lt. George E. Currie.* Letterbook. Edited by Norman E. Clark. Mount Pleasant: Central Michigan University, 1961.

Dewey, George. *Autobiography of George Dewey: Admiral of the Navy.* New York: Charles Scribner's Sons, 1913.

Eads, James Buchanan. Papers. Missouri Historical Society, St. Louis, Missouri.

Ewer, James K. *The Third Massachusetts Cavalry in the War for the Union*. Maplewood, Mass.: Historical Committee of the Regimental Association, 1903.

Fox, Gustavus. *Confidential Correspondence of Gustavus Vasa Fox, Assistant Secretary of the Navy, 1861–1865*. New York: Naval Historical Society, 1918.

Gale, Katherine Polk. "Reminiscences of Life in the Southern Confederacy, 1861–1865," 10-11A. Gale and Polk Family Papers. Southern Historical Collection, Wilson Library, University of North Carolina at Chapel Hill, North Carolina.

Grant, Ulysses S. *Personal Memoirs of U. S. Grant*. New York: Da Capo, 1982.

Hedley, F. Y. *Marching through Georgia: Pen-Pictures of Every-Day Life in General Sherman's Army, from the Beginning of the Atlanta Campaign until the Closing of the War*. Chicago: Donohue, Henneberry & Co., 1890.

Howe, M. A. DeWolfe, ed. *Home Letters of General Sherman*. New York: 1909.

Johnson, Robert Underwood, ed. *Battles and Leaders of the Civil War*, vol. 1: *Opening Battles*. Edison, N.J.: Castle/Book Sales, 1990; orig. pub. Century Company, 1883.

Johnson, Robert Underwood, and Clarence Buel, eds. *Battles and Leaders of the Civil War, Being for the Most Part Contributions By Union and Confederate Officers*. 4 vols. Edison, N.J.: Thomas Yoseloff, 1956.

Moore, Frank, ed. *The Rebellion Record, A Diary of American Events with Documents, Narratives, Illustrative Incidents, Poetry, etc.* 12 vols. New York: G. P. Putnam, 1861–1871.

Morse, John T., ed. *The Diary of Gideon Welles*. 3 vols. Boston: Athenaeum, 1909–1911.

National Archives and Records Administration. Abstract Log of the *USS Chillicothe*, March 7–June 8, 1864. Washington, D.C.

Naval Historical Division. *Civil War Naval Chronology 1861–1865*. Washington, D.C.: U.S. Government Printing Office, 1971.

Newsome, Edmund. *Experience in the War of the Rebellion*. Carbondale, Ill.: Author, 1880.

Pellet, Elias P. *History of the 114th Regiment, New York State Volunteers* . . . Norwich, N.Y.: Telegraph and Chronicle Press Print, 1866.

Porter, David Dixon. *Incidents and Anecdotes*. New York: Appleton, 1885.

———. *The Naval History of the Civil War*. New York: Appleton, 1886.

———. Dispatch in the collection of Richard Self, Shreveport, Louisiana.

———. Papers. Division of Manuscripts, Library of Congress, Washington, D.C.

Scott, John. *Story of the Thirty Second Iowa Infantry Volunteers*. Nevada, Iowa: Author, 1896.

Selfridge, Thomas O., Jr. *What Finer Tradition: The Memoirs of Thomas O. Selfridge, Jr., Rear Admiral U.S.N.* Columbia: University of South Carolina Press, 1987.

Sherman, William T. *Home Letters of General Sherman*. Edited by Mark Anthony DeWolfe Howe. New York: Charles Scribner's Sons, 1909.

———. *Memoirs*. 2 vols. Reprint. New York: The Library of America, 1990.

Smith, Walter G., ed. *Life and Letters of T. Kilby Smith* . . . New York: G. P. Putnam's Sons, 1898.

Taylor, Richard. *Destruction and Reconstruction: Personal Experiences in the Civil War*. New York: Da Capo, 1995.

———. Letter to General John George Walker. April 9, 1864, John George Walker Papers #910Z. Southern Historical Collection, University of North Carolina at Chapel Hill, North Carolina.

Thomas, B. F. "Soldier Life: A Narrative of the Civil War." Privately printed, unpaginated. Archives and collections of Shiloh National Military Park Library, Shiloh, Tennessee.

U.S. Congress. *Report on the Joint Committee on the Conduct of the War, 1863–1866.* Vol. 2, *Red River Expedition.* Millwood, N.Y.: Krauss Reprint, 1977.

U.S. Department of Commerce. Untabulated returns from the Eighth Decennial Census (1860) for Memphis, Tennessee. Western Tennessee Historical Society Library, University of Memphis; McWherter Library Special Collections, Memphis, Tennessee.

U.S. Senate. *Medal of Honor Recipients, 1862–1863.* Washington, D.C.: U.S. Government Printing Office, 1964.

U.S. War Department. *Atlas to Accompany the Official Records of the Union and Confederate Armies.* Washington, D.C.: U.S. Government Printing Office, 1891–1895.

———. *Official Records of the Union and Confederate Navies in the War of the Rebellion.* 31 vols. Washington, D.C.: U.S. Government Printing Office, 1895–1929.

———. *War of the Rebellion: The Official Records of the Union and Confederate Armies.* 128 vols. Washington, D.C.: U.S. Government Printing Office, 1890–1901.

Walke, Henry. "The Gun-Boats at Belmont and Fort Henry." In *Battles and Leaders of the Civil War*, vol. 1: *Opening Battles*, edited by Robert Underwood Johnson, 358–67. Edison, N.J.: Castle/Book Sales, 1990; orig. pub. Century Company, 1883.

———. "The Western Flotilla at Fort Donelson, Island Number Ten, Fort Pillow, and Memphis." In *Battles and Leaders of the Civil War*, vol. 1: *Opening Battles*, new edited by Robert Underwood Johnson, 430–52. Edison, N.J.: Castle/Book Sales, 1990; orig. pub. Century Company, 1883.

Webster, Harrie. *Some Personal Recollections and Reminiscences of the Battle of Port Hudson.* N.p., n.d.

Williams, E. Cort. "Recollections of the Red River Expedition." In *Sketches of War History 1861–1865, Papers Read before the Ohio Commandery of the Military Order of the Loyal Legion of the United States 1886–1888.* Cincinnati: Robert Clarke and Company, 1888.

Williams, Thomas J. *An Historical Sketch of the 56th Ohio Volunteer Infantry . . .* Columbus, Ohio: The Lawrence Press, 1899.

Welles, Gideon. Papers. Huntington Library, Malibu, California.

Zook, Christian. Letter to Father, March 24, 1862, 46th Ohio Infantry File, Shiloh National Military Park, Shiloh, Tennessee.

Secondary Sources

Ambrose, Stephen A. *Halleck, Lincoln's Chief of Staff.* Baton Rouge: Louisiana State University Press, 1962.

Anderson, Bern. *By Sea and by River: The Naval History of the Civil War.* New York: Knopf, 1962.

Anonymous. *John C. Frémont: Pathfinder of the West*. Boston: John Hancock Mutual Life Insurance Company, 1927.

Bailey, Anne J. "Chasing Banks Out of Louisiana: Parsons' Texas Cavalry in the Red River Campaign." *Civil War Regiments*, 3, no. 1 (1993), 212–35.

Ballard, Michael B. *Vicksburg: The Campaign That Opened the Mississippi*. Chapel Hill: University of North Carolina Press, 2004.

Barry, John M. *Rising Tide: The Great Mississippi Flood of 1927 and How It Changed America*. New York: Simon & Schuster, 1997.

Bearss, Edwin C. *Hardluck Ironclad: The Sinking and Salvage of the "Cairo."* Baton Rouge: Louisiana State University Press, 1966.

——. *The Vicksburg Campaign*. 3 vols. Dayton, Ohio: Morningside Bookshop, 1985–1986.

Bennett, Michael J. *Union Jacks: Yankee Sailors in the Civil War*. Chapel Hill: University of North Carolina Press, 2004.

Brown, Dee Alexander. *Grierson's Raid*. Dayton, Ohio: Morningside Bookshop, 1981. Reprinted from 1954.

Buttgenbach, Walter J. "Coast Defense in the Civil War." *Journal of the United States Artillery* 39 (March–April 1913).

Canney, Donald L. *Lincoln's Navy: The Ships, Men and Organizations, 1861–65*. Annapolis, Md.: Naval Institute Press, 1998.

——. *The Old Steam Navy Volume Two: The Ironclads, 1842–1885*. Annapolis, Md.: Naval Institute Press, 1993.

Catton, Bruce. *This Hallowed Ground*. New York: Pocket Books, 1982.

Cogar, William B. *Dictionary of Admirals of the U.S. Navy, Volume I: 1862–1900*. Annapolis, Md.: Naval Institute Press, 1989.

Cooling, Benjamin Franklin. *Forts Henry and Donelson: The Key to the Confederate Heartland*. Knoxville: University of Tennessee Press, 1987.

Coombe, Jack D. *Thunder along the Mississippi: The River Battles That Split the Confederacy*. New York: Sarpedon, 1996.

Cunningham, Edward. *The Port Hudson Campaign 1862–1863*. Baton Rouge: Louisiana State University Press, 1986.

Daniel, Larry J., and Lynn N. Bock. *Island No. 10: Struggle for the Mississippi Valley*. Tuscaloosa: University of Alabama Press, 1996.

Dufour, Charles L. *The Night the War Was Lost*. Garden City, N.Y.: Doubleday, 1960.

Fowler, William M., Jr. *Under Two Flags: The American Navy in the Civil War*. Annapolis, Md.: Naval Institute Press, 2001.

Freeman, Douglas Southall. *Lee's Lieutenants: A Study in Command*. 3 vols. New York: Scribner, 1942–1944.

Gibson, Charles Dana, and E. Kay Gibson. *Assault and Logistics: Union Army Coastal and River Operations, 1861–1866*. Camden, Maine: Ensign Press, 1995.

——. *Dictionary of Transports and Combatant Vessels Steam and Sail, Employed by the Union Army, 1861–1868*. Camden, Maine: Ensign Press, 1995.

Gosnell, H. Allen. *Guns on the Western Waters: The Story of the River Gunboats in the Civil War*. Baton Rouge: Louisiana State University Press, 1949.

Gott, Kendall. *Where the South Lost the War: An Analysis of the Fort Henry-Fort Donelson Campaign, February 1862*. Mechanicsburg, Pa.: Stackpole, 2003.

Grabau, Warren E. *Ninety-Eight Days: A Geographer's View of the Vicksburg Campaign.* Knoxville: University of Tennessee Press, 2000.

Harris, NiNi. *History of Carondelet.* St. Louis, Mo.: Southern Commercial Bank, 1991.

Hearn, Chester G. *Admiral David Dixon Porter: The Civil War Years.* Annapolis, Md.: Naval Institute Press, 1996.

———. *Ellet's Brigade: The Strangest Outfit of All.* Baton Rouge: Louisiana State University Press, 2000.

Henry, R. S. *"First with the Most" Forrest.* Indianapolis: Bobbs-Merrill Company, 1944.

Hewitt, Lawrence Lee. *Port Hudson: Confederate Bastion On the Mississippi.* Baton Rouge: Louisiana State University Press, 1986.

Hollandsworth, James P., Jr. *Pretense of Glory: The Life of General Nathaniel P. Banks.* Baton Rouge: Louisiana State University Press, 1998.

Jeter, Katherine Brash. *A Man and His Boat: The Civil War Career and Correspondence of Lieutenant Jonathan H. Carter, CSN.* Lafayette, La.: Center for Louisiana Studies, 1996.

Johnson, Ludwell H. *Red River Campaign: Politics and Cotton in the Civil War.* Kent, Ohio: Kent State University Press, 1993.

Joiner, Gary D. *Through the Howling Wilderness: The 1864 Red River Campaign and Union Defeat in the West.* Knoxville: University of Tennessee Press, 2006.

Joiner, Gary D., Marilyn S. Joiner, and Clifton D. Cardin, eds. *No Pardons to Ask nor Apologies to Make: The Journal of William Henry King, Gray's 28th Louisiana Infantry Regiment.* Knoxville: University of Tennessee Press, 2006.

Joyner, Elizabeth Hoxie. *The USS Cairo: History and Artifacts of a Civil War Ironclad.* Jefferson, N.C.: McFarland & Company, 2006.

Kerby, Robert L. *Kirby Smith's Confederacy: The Trans-Mississippi South, 1863–1865.* Tuscaloosa: University of Alabama Press, 1972.

Korn, Jerry. *War on the Mississippi: Grant's Vicksburg Campaign.* Chicago: Time-Life Books, 1985.

Lowe, Richard. *The Texas Overland Expedition of 1863.* Fort Worth, Tex.: Ryan Place Publishers, 1996.

Marshall-Cornwall, James. *Grant as Military Commander.* New York: Van Nostrand Reinhold Company, 1970.

Marzalek, John F. *Commander of All Lincoln's Armies: A Life of General Henry W. Halleck.* Cambridge, Mass.: Harvard University Press, 2004.

Mayeux, Steven M. *Earthen Walls, Iron Men: Fort DeRussy, Louisiana, and the Defense of Red River.* Knoxville: University of Tennessee Press, 2007.

Melia, Tamara Moser. *"Damn the Torpedoes": A Short History of U.S. Naval Mine Countermeasures, 1777–1991.* Contributions to Naval History, no. 4. Washington, D.C.: Naval Historical Center, 1991.

Musicant, Ivan. *Divided Waters: The Naval History of the Civil War.* New York: HarperCollins, 1995.

Nash, Howard P., Jr. *A Naval History of the Civil War.* New York: A. S. Barnes and Company, 1972.

Nevins, Allan. *The War for the Union, Vol. I: The Improvised War 1861–1862.* New York: Charles Scribner's Sons, 1959.

Niven, John. *Gideon Welles: Lincoln's Secretary of the Navy*. Baton Rouge: Louisiana State University Press, 1994.

Perry, Milton F. *Infernal Machines: The Story of Confederate Submarine and Mine Warfare*. Baton Rouge: Louisiana State University Press, 1965.

Ragan, Mark K. *Union and Confederate Submarine Warfare in the Civil War*. Mason City, Iowa: Savas Publishing, 1999.

Reilly, John C., Jr. *The Iron Guns of Willard Park: Washington Navy Yard*. Washington, D.C.: Naval Historical Center, 1991.

Ringle, Dennis J. *Life in Mr. Lincoln's Navy*. Annapolis, Md.: Naval Institute Press, 1998.

Robinson, Michael. *Gunboats, Low Water, and Yankee Ingenuity: A History of Bailey's Dam*. Baton Rouge, La.: F.P.H.C., 1991.

Roman, Alfred. *The Military Operations of General Beauregard in the War between the States*. 2 vols. New York: Harper, 1884.

Ropp, Theodore. "Anaconda Anyone?" *Military Affairs* 27 (summer 1963).

Shea, William L., and Terrence J. Winshel. *Vicksburg Is the Key: The Struggle for the Mississippi River*. Omaha: University of Nebraska Press, 2003.

Silverstone, Paul H. *Civil War Navies: 1855–1883*. Annapolis, Md.: Naval Institute Press, 2001.

———. *Warships of the Civil War Navies*. Annapolis, Md.: Naval Institute Press, 1989.

Simson, Jay W. *Naval Strategies of the Civil War: Confederate Innovations and Federal Opportunism*. Nashville, Tenn.: Cumberland House, 2001.

Slagle, Jay. *Ironclad Captain: Seth Ledyard Phelps and the U.S. Navy, 1841–1864*. Kent, Ohio: Kent State University Press, 1996.

Smith, Timothy B. *Champion Hill: Decisive Battle For Vicksburg*. New York: Savas Beatie, 2004.

———. *The Untold Story of Shiloh: The Battle and the Battlefield*. Knoxville: University of Tennessee Press, 2006.

Tap, Bruce. *Over Lincoln's Shoulder: The Committee on the Conduct of the War*. Lawrence: University Press of Kansas, 1998.

Throne, Mildred, ed. *The Civil War Diary of Cyrus F. Boyd: Fifteenth Iowa Infantry, 1861–1863*. Baton Rouge: Louisiana State University Press, 1953.

Tucker, Spencer C. *Andrew Foote: Civil War Admiral on Western Waters*. Annapolis, Md.: Naval Institute Press, 2000.

Vetter, Charles Edmund. *Sherman: Merchant of Terror, Advocate of Peace*. Gretna, La.: Pelican Publishing Company, 1992.

Warner, Ezra J. *Generals in Blue: Lives of the Union Commanders*. Baton Rouge: Louisiana State University, 1964.

———. *Generals in Gray: Lives of the Confederate Commanders*. Baton Rouge: Louisiana State University Press, 1959.

Weems, Bob. *Charles Read: Confederate Buccaneer*. Jackson, Miss.: Heritage Books, 1982.

West, Richard S., Jr. *The Second Admiral: A Life of David Dixon Porter*. New York: Coward-McCann, 1937.

Wideman, John C. *The Sinking of the USS* Cairo. Jackson: University Press of Mississippi, 1993.

Winschel, Terrence J. *Chickasaw Bayou: A Battlefield Guide*. Brochure, n.p., n.d.
——. "Fighting Politician: John A. McClernand." In *Grant's Lieutenants From Cairo to Vicksburg*, edited by Steven E. Woodworth. Lawrence: University of Kansas Press, 2001, 129–50.
——. *Triumph and Defeat: The Vicksburg Campaign*. Vol. 2. New York: Savas Beatie, 2006.
Winters, John D. *The Civil War in Louisiana*. Baton Rouge: Louisiana State University Press, 1963.
Wyeth, John. *That Devil Forrest: Life of General Nathan Bedford Forrest*. New York: Harper and Brothers, 1959.

NEWSPAPERS

Memphis Daily Appeal, March 16, 1863.
Memphis Daily Appeal, March 20, 1863.
Mobile Daily Tribune, July 2, 1862.
Vicksburg Whig, March 5, 1863.

MAPS

Arkansas Atlas and Gazetteer. Yarmouth, Maine: Delorme, 2nd ed., 2004.
LaTourette Map (ca. 1850), National Archives and Records Administration, Washington, D.C. Record Group 77, folio M72.
Lavender Soil Map (1906). Archives and Special Collections, Noel Memorial Library, Louisiana State University in Shreveport.
Louisiana Atlas and Gazetteer. Yarmouth, Maine: Delorme, 2nd ed., 2004.
Mississippi Atlas and Gazetteer. Yarmouth, Maine: Delorme, 2nd ed., 2004.
Missouri Atlas and Gazetteer. Yarmouth, Maine: Delorme, 2nd ed., 2004.
Tennessee Atlas and Gazetteer. Yarmouth, Maine: Delorme, 2nd ed., 2004.
TOPO! Arkansas. National Geographic Society digital 3-dimensional data.
TOPO! Louisiana. National Geographic Society digital 3-dimensional data.
TOPO! Mississippi. National Geographic Society digital 3-dimensional data.
TOPO! Tennessee. National Geographic Society digital 3-dimensional data.
U.S.G.S. 7.5 minute Topographic Quadrangle Map, Pittsburg Landing.

PHOTOGRAPHIC ARCHIVES

Naval Historical Center, Washington Navy Yard, Washington, D.C.
Noel Memorial Library, Louisiana State University in Shreveport, Louisiana.
Rare Book, Manuscript, and Special Collection Library, Duke University, Durham, North Carolina.

DISSERTATION

Otis Edward Cunningham, unpublished doctoral dissertation, Hill Memorial Library, Louisiana State University, Baton Rouge, Louisiana.

INTERNET SITE

www.amphilsoc.org/library/guides/stanton/3644.htm.

Index

About the Author

Gary D. Joiner is a historian and award-winning author who teaches history and geography at Louisiana State University in Shreveport, where he is an assistant professor of history and also director of the Red River Regional Studies Center. He earned his bachelor's degree from Louisiana Tech with a double major in history and geography and a master's degree in history from the same institution. He received a doctorate of history from St. Martin's College, Lancaster University, in Lancaster, England. Dr. Joiner's interest in the U.S. Civil War has led him to mapping activities for Civil War battlefields and parks. He is consulting cartographer for the Civil War Preservation Trust and has been involved in mapping several battlefields, including Vicksburg, Petersburg, Gettysburg, Mansfield, Pleasant Hill, and Jenkins Ferry. His books include *Red River Steamboats*, author with Eric Brock; *Historic Shreveport-Bossier*, author with Dr. Marguerite Plummer; *One Damn Blunder from Beginning to End: The Red River Campaign in 1864*, Scholarly Resources, now Rowman & Littlefield, winner of two national awards, the Albert Castel Award and the A. M. Pate Jr. Award; *The Red River Campaign: Studies in Union and Confederate Leadership in Louisiana*, editor with Theodore Savas and David Woodbury; *No Pardons to Ask, nor Apologies to Make*, editor with Marilyn S. Joiner and Clifton D. Cardin; *Through the Howling Wilderness: The Red River Campaign of 1864 and Union Defeat in the West*; *Shiloh and Western Campaign of 1862*, Savas Beatie, editor with Timothy Smith; and *Little to Eat and Thin to Drink: Letters, Diaries, and Memoirs from the Red River Campaigns, 1863–1864*, editor.